THE YPRES SALIENT

This book is dedicated to all those
who, in dying for others,
lie buried within the area of
the former ill-famed 'Ypres Salient'
including the many thousands
who have no known grave.

The Ypres Salient

JOHN GILES

LEO COOPER · LONDON

First published in 1970 by
LEO COOPER LTD.
196 Shaftesbury Avenue
London WC2

ISBN 0 85052 025 5

Set by Gavin Martin Ltd, London
Printed in Great Britain at Slough by
Hollen Street Press Ltd

CONTENTS

From the 'Britannica':

'Flanders, county of, a powerful medieval principality in the south-west of the Low Countries, which occupied territories that are now divided between the French *departement* of Nord, the Belgian provinces of East Flanders and West Flanders, and the Dutch province of Zeeland. The name appears in the 8th century and is believed to mean "flooded land" . . .'

There was fighting there during World War I.

A total of over 200,000 men of the British Commonwealth (eighty per cent of whom came from the United Kingdom) lie buried within the boundaries of the old Salient. With the presence there of over 150 military cemeteries, it is no exaggeration to say that this corner of Flanders is probably the largest graveyard in history.

PREFACE

Over fifty years have passed since the guns of the First World War fell silent. Half a century, and in the Ypres Salient the scars of war have healed; save in a few instances there is little to show that the gentle countryside of Flanders once resembled the pitted wastes of the moon.

Today, in summertime, ripening corn bends with the wind and trees sway gently in lush woods that were once a splintered and broken wilderness. Swifts wheel through the air and cattle browse contentedly in attractive pastures near the tiny streams known as 'beeks' which were once flooded swamps of mud and filth. Villages that were heaps of rubble have been solidly rebuilt and church steeples are again prominent in the flat Flanders landscape.

There are not many men alive today who fought with the armies of the former British Empire in the Great War and few of those would recognise the Salient as it now is. Life rushes on and as the years proceed the few will become fewer and eventually none at all. Someday, that 'war to end wars' will be forgotten and the name of Ypres will fade into the mists of history. Only the memorials and the cemeteries will remain to recall the suffering and tragedy of those far off days. Weathered by rain, eroded by time, they will stand forever as stone sentinels marking the honour, courage, and sacrifice of men.

J.G.

ACKNOWLEDGEMENTS

This work has necessitated the collation of a large number of photographs, of which over 100 came from the Imperial War Museum. In this connection sincere thanks are expressed to Dr A. N. Frankland, DFC, MA (Director General) Dr C. H. Roads (Deputy Director) and Mr D. G. Lance (Keeper of Libraries and Archives), together with various members of their staffs including Mr J. F. Goldman, Miss R. Coombs (Librarian), Mr M. J. Willis, and others, all of whom have been so helpful and co-operative in various ways.

A word of thanks is also due to the Commonwealth War Graves Commission, that has done so much to care for the graves of our war dead throughout the world and whose invaluable work is apparent in the quiet fields of Flanders today. Beyond this, thanks are expressed to the CWGC for several photographs included in this book and to Mr M. J. Lawless in particular for his assistance in that connection.

In Flanders itself are people to whom I am more than grateful, for through their kind support and friendship I have been able to glean much information about the area. Firstly I must mention Monsieur and Madame Deleu-Van Uxem, former proprietor and proprietress of the Hotel Britannique in the Grand Place, Ypres. To this kindly Belgian couple who, every year since 1960, welcomed me and took care of my needs, I am especially indebted. Sad to relate, however, Madame has not lived to see the publication of the book to which her kindness and encouragement contributed so much.

Another friend is Dr A. Caenepeel who, apart from owning a wonderful collection of books and maps of the Great War, retains a profound knowledge of the old Salient in his mind. On a number of occasions we have sat in his study discussing the strategy and outcome of former battles and it has always been difficult to tear oneself away late at night after a long session of animated conversation combined with the hospitality of himself and his family.

Just outside Ypres, at Hooge, I have enjoyed the company and hospitality of Baron Yves de Vinck, owner of Hooge Chateau. Those occasions when I have talked to the Baron and have walked with him around his lovely estate (and have even collected scraps of 'iron' and shrapnel balls from his fields) have not only been delightful but also most useful in completing a picture of what went on in those grim days when only mud and thousands of shell-holes surrounded the remnants of the old chateau.

Other pleasant and rewarding contacts have been made, such as with Monsieur Daniel, photographer in Ypres who has made contributions to this book; Mr J. Picanol, owner of the lovely house standing on the site of the building once known as 'Stirling Castle' near the shell-swept Menin Road; and, after hours of searching in Ostend, Miss Gabrielle Antony and her sister, daughters of the eminent (now deceased) photographer, Antony of Ypres. Also one should mention Mr and Mrs Moon, former caretakers of Hill 60, and Marcel, taxi driver and World War 1 veteran, who first introduced me to the towns and villages of the Old Salient.

This list of acknowledgements would not be complete (one way or another) without a sincere thank you to the ladies who gave such invaluable assistance with the typing — Mrs J. Hiley, Mrs P. Dixon, Miss V. Hughes, Miss S. Woodham, and Miss C. Berry. Also, a special thank you is extended to Jim and Jeremy Byron for their help in identifying old vehicles and equipment.

Then there is my close friend, Mr Christopher Short, author of a number of books, who was always readily available with sound advice. To him, too, I owe much.

Lastly goes a special word of thanks to my dear wife Margery who, with patience and tolerance, has for so long accepted the consequences of the concentrated effort needed for the preparation of a work of this nature. Her unstinted support and encouragement made it possible for me to continue in spite of the pressure of all the other things involved in the process of living.

I am extremely grateful to the following for allowing me to utilise material in the form of written experiences, sketch maps, or documents connected directly or indirectly with the old Salient.

Hutchinson Publishing Group : Extracts from *Stand To: A Diary of the Trenches*, by Captain F.C. Hitchcock. Originally published by Hurst & Blackett Ltd in 1936 and reprinted by Cedric Chivers Ltd of Bath, 1965. These extracts appear in this book against the initials 'FCH'.

Hutchinson Publishing Group : Extracts from *Warrior* by Lt-Col. G.S. Hutchison and used in this book under that same pseudonym.

Thomas Nelson & Sons, Ltd : Sketch maps from *Nelson's History of the War*, by John Buchan. Also for permission to draw on John Buchan's work for factual information.

Alexander Barrie, Esq., Author of *War Underground* : Sketch map, chart, and other details of the Mines of Messines.

Associated Book Publishers, Ltd : Extracts from *Passchendaele and the Somme* by Hugh Quigley. 'HQ' in this book.

Sidgwick & Jackson Ltd : Poems of Rupert Brook.

Curtis Brown Ltd : Extracts from *The Realities of War* by Sir Philip Gibbs.

Beaverbrook Newspapers Ltd : Sketch map from *War Memoirs of David Lloyd George*.

Regimental Association of the Middlesex Regt (DCO). : Sketch map of Second Ypres from *The Die-Hards in the Great War*.

The British Legion : Poem, 'In Flanders Fields'.

H.A. Bigel, Esq. : Poem, 'The Road to Hooge'.

Mrs D.C. Costelloe and Lt-Cmdr. F.A. Costelloe RN (Ret'd) : Papers relating to Private A. Carter.

S.T.H. Ross, Esq. : Article, 'Messines, the early days in retrospect', and other items.

W.F. Chapman, Esq. : Personal documents and reminiscences.

Lorne Manchester, Esq., Managing Editor of *Legion*. : Copies of articles from the national magazine of the Royal Canadian Legion.

John Swettenham, Esq., Historian, Canadian War Museum. : Author of above-mentioned articles.

A.E. Slack, Esq. : Sketches and other items

Unless otherwise credited, all photographs are by the author.

FLANDERS

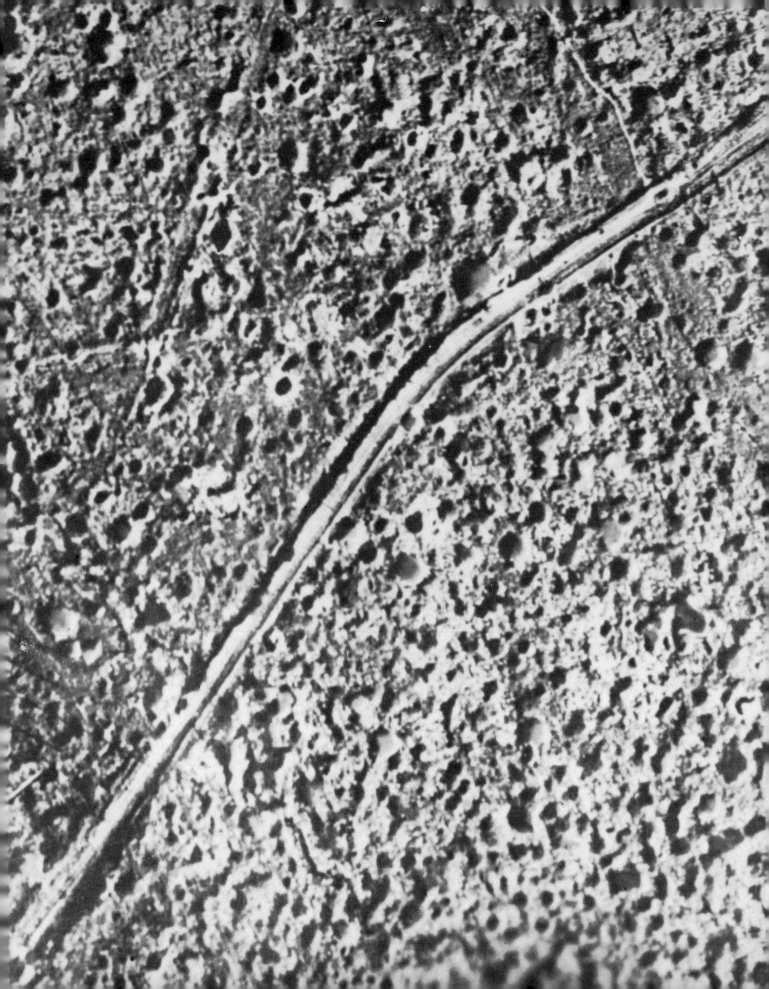

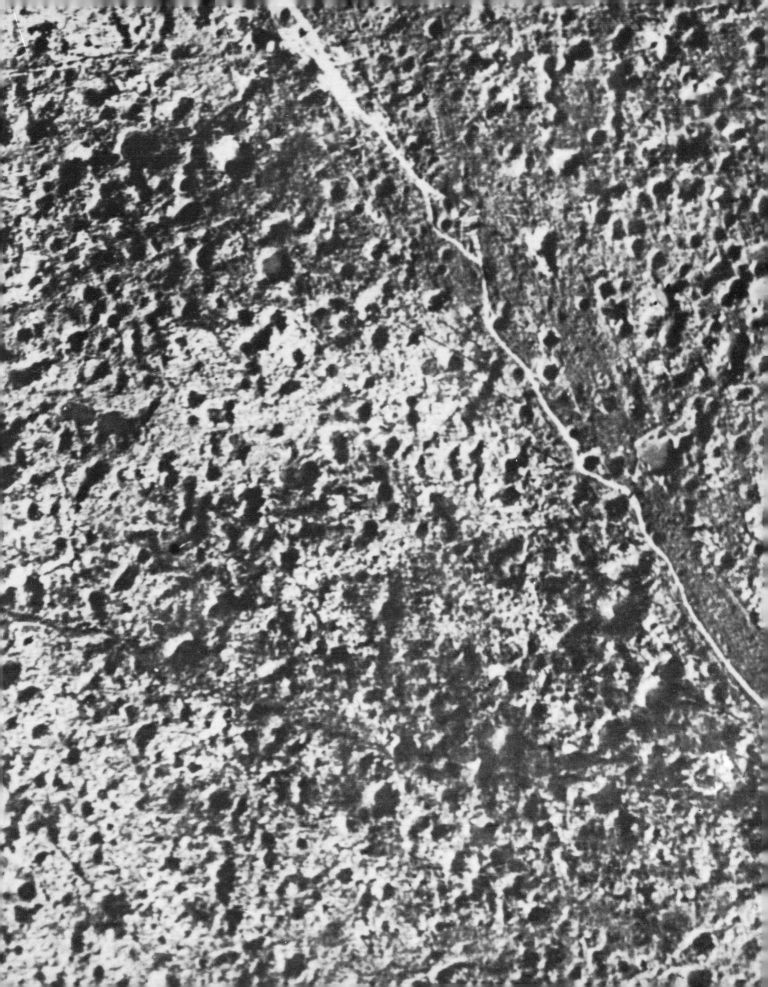

Page 1. Lonely are the dead. A soldier fallen somewhere in the wasteland near Zonnebeke. [IWM]

Pages 2 & 3. The Salient. An aerial photograph of the Ypres Salient taken west of Zouave Wood (south of the Menin Road at Hooge and close to Sanctuary Wood). [IWM]

Pages 4 & 5. Tyne Cot Cemetery just after the War; thousands upon thousands of British crosses. [CWGC]

Page 7. German dead. German trench on the Messines Ridge, smashed by the British bombardment, 7 June 1917. [IWM]

FROM A PRIVATE MEMORIAL NEAR ARMENTIERES

He whom this memorial commemorates
was numbered among those who,
at the call of King and Country,
left all that was dear to them,
endured hardness, faced danger,
and finally passed out of the sight of men
by the path of duty and self-sacrifice,
giving up their own lives
that others might live in freedom.
Let those who come after see to it,
that his name not be forgotten.

October 1914

Age 36

Age 18

I think of him in silence
No one may see me weep   My only son
But deep within my heart
His memory I will keep

February 1915

Killed in action and buried by the
enemy ... but whose grave is now
lost.

November 1914

His country called
He answered.

May 1915

Age 24

Killed in action

March 1915

Age 20

In loving memory of our
dear and only son

They have a curious way of finding direction in Belgium. The landscape has no salient features of its own; everything blasted to mud — railway embankments, woods, roads confused in shell-holes and mine-craters. Trees are only skeletons, and masses of obscene ruins mark farms or houses. You look in vain for a wood where such is marked on the map. The only way at night is to bend down close to the ground and gaze at the skyline for black shadows of pill-boxes; by those shadows you find your way. Or, to remember a road once shown, the oddest details must be noted — a solitary length of rail or wire, a 'dud' shell, three stakes together, a fragmentary hedge, a deserted water-logged trench, dead men lying at various angles, and the position of pill-boxes in relation to the track followed.

[HQ; *Photo:* IWM]

10

An uneventful day. Our supports, Daly's Company, got badly crumped with 5.9s and had casualties. I went out on patrol with Sergt Sweeney. It was a dark night, and we lay for a long time in the muddy, shell-pitted No-Man's-Land. We heard nothing. Everything was as silent as the grave, with the exception of the rats, which were squeaking and capering around us. Now and then a star-shell winged its way aloft, showing up the enemy's barbed wire, taut, shiny grey, and forbidding-looking, immediately in our front, and beyond it their sand-bagged parapet. We remained lying out for some time; the pitch darkness made patrolling impossible. The Hun was very quiet.

After the spout of a star-shell had died away, we withdrew to our front line. In returning across the 150 yards of No-Man's-Land we must have been heard by an enemy listening post, as Very lights were put up in quick succession, which pinned us to the chewed-up ground. A machine-gun traversed right over us as we sprawled across shell craters. We made more ground as its fire swung round and again flattened ourselves as it traversed back. The bullets were going low, just whistling 'softly like', as Sweeney afterwards said, past our ears, and cutting our barbed wire, as we saw the sparks flying from the strands as they were cut.

We had difficulty in finding the gap in our own barbed wire to get back to the trench as it had been made in a zigzag way, so as not to be apparent to the enemy. Eventually we found it, and stumbled into our front line.

[FCH]

12

'You will have read of Belgium in every newspaper dispatch and every book writter on war. The best I can do is simply to tell you what I experienced — and suffered more or less patiently. The country resembles a sewage-heap more than anything else, pitted with shell-holes of every conceivable size, and filled to the brim with green, slimy water, above which a blackened arm or leg might project. It becomes a matter of great skill picking a way across such a network of death-traps, for drowning is almost certain in one of them.'

[HQ; photo: IWM]

Mutilated machinery. A British Mark IV tank (27 tons, 4 mph, and a crew of 8) after taking a direct hit on the gun turret.

A dead soldier and a British helmet are in the foreground. The white-topped stake (for visibility at night) in the middle of the photograph marks a path through the glutinous countryside; just behind it may be seen a screw picket which was used to string barbed wire. [IWM]

SARAJEVO TO GHELUVELT

The murderous battles fought in Flanders stemmed originally from the assassination of Archduke Francis Ferdinand, heir to the Austrian throne, on 28th June 1914 in Sarajevo. From that incident arose the confrontation of giants and the ultimate slaughter of some 10,000,000 human beings. Cities and villages were razed to the ground; there was burning, pillaging, hunger and, eventually, revolution. The placid world of Edwardian Europe was irretrievably shattered and the crowned heads tumbled from their thrones as defeated and demoralised countries became republics. New ideologies replaced old ones (and in consequence were sown the seeds of future wars). Sarajevo was the match that lit the gunpowder trail which led to the explosion of World War I, for Sarajevo was the excuse used by the Austrians in an attempt to enforce their will on the Serbians' and by Germany to embark upon the course for which she had so long prepared.

Russia supported Serbia and Germany declared war on Russia; France as an ally of Russia quickly declared war on Germany. Britain, with the world's most powerful navy and a small but highly trained army, was at that time uncommitted — as she had no alliance with France, and Germany presumed that she would remain neutral. Consequently, the Germans attacked France following the Schlieffen Plan which called for a gigantic flanking movement by their armies. This, however, could be effected only by a march through Belgium whose neutrality had been guaranteed by the Great Powers — including Britain.

On Sunday, 2nd August, Belgium was invaded and on the evening of the 3rd Britain sent Germany an ultimatum to withdraw. The ultimatum was ignored and on 4th August the United Kingdom declared war. Young men rushed to join the colours as the vanguard of the 1½ million Britishers who would be under arms by Christmas 1914. In the Dominions and Colonies of what was then the greatest Empire in the world, contingents of troops were quickly prepared for service side by side with the mother country.

The British Expeditionary Force, amounting to about 100,000 men and large numbers of horses, guns, and the other paraphernalia of war, began to cross the Channel on 12th August. Within a few days the whole force had been smoothly transferred to French soil where they received a rapturous welcome from the civilian population. Enthusiastically they marched forward to take up their planned positions on the left of the French armies; every step brought them closer to a powerful enemy already flushed with the early fruits of victory.

On Sunday, 23rd August 1914, less than three weeks after the declaration of war, occurred the first major clash between the forces of Great Britain and Germany. The place was Mons, a small Belgian mining town which was soon to gain a niche of its own in history.

In the wake of the massive German right hook towards the capital of France, the city of Louvain was burning, the forts of Liège had

FORMATION OF THE SALIENT AND FIRST YPRES

been battered to pieces by huge siege guns, and Brussels had fallen to General von Kluck's legions. The Germans had swept across Belgium from the north-east pushing aside the vastly outnumbered Belgian Army. The main part of Britain's small professional army lay waiting for them in shallow trenches at Mons. The twenty-mile front of the British Expeditionary Force was comprised of two Corps under Generals Sir Douglas Haig and Sir Horace Smith-Dorrien, and supported by General Allenby's Cavalry Division (a total of about 86,000 men).

Early in the morning of the 23rd the first shells began to fall and the angry chorus quickly increased as more and more guns on each side went into action. Then swarms of German soldiers advanced across the open fields in massed formation disdaining the hail of bullets from British rifles and machine-guns. The attackers withered away before the storm of lead, reformed, and were again beaten back. Time after time the enemy bravely advanced in the face of heavy and rapid small arms fire; time after time they faltered and retired leaving still, grey-clad, figures on the field behind them. One of the most famous German regiments, the Brandenburg Fusiliers, incurred severe losses at Mons; from that time the Germans had much more respect for the 'contemptible little army' which they had previously so arrogantly dismissed.

The British casualties were also heavy considering the time and numbers involved and such famous regiments as the 4th Royal Fusiliers, 1st West Kents, 4th Middlesex, 2nd Royal Scots, 2nd Yorkshire Light Infantry, 1st Northumberland Fusiliers, 1st East

Map from *Nelson's History of the War* (John Buchan) by permission of Thomas Nelson & Sons Ltd.

Position of the line at Ypres on 21st October.

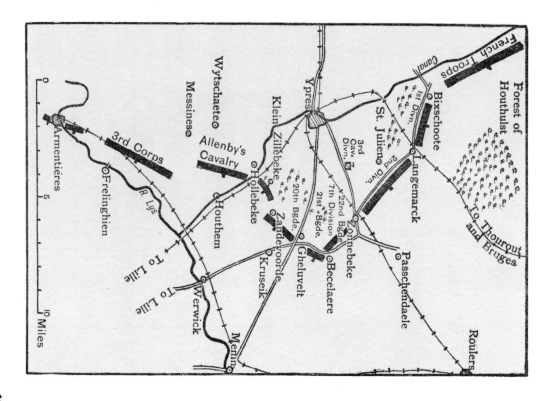

15

Surreys, and 1st Gordons, paid the price of determined defence under fierce and prolonged bombardment. Despite their courage it soon became clear that the position at Mons was untenable; both flanks had become exposed, bridges had been lost, and the French had retired on the right from the line of the River Sambre. Sir John French could make only one decision. He must retire to a new line in order to avoid having his forces cut off, surrounded, and destroyed. Thus began the famous 'Retreat from Mons' which was to continue almost to the gates of Paris save for a brief stand made by the footsore and desperately tired British troops at Le Cateau. There they fought a splendid defensive action which gave the withdrawing troops a short breathing space. German pressure intensified again and the long weary march continued all the way to the line of the River Marne, where General Joffre, French Commander-in-Chief, turned and fought back. So began, in the early part of September, the battle which was to alter the course of the war.

Due to various manoeuvres in the confused fighting a thirty-mile gap inadvertently opened up between two of the invading German armies under von Below and von Kluck. Allied troops were poured into that gap. The tables were abruptly turned and now the Germans were forced to fall back to new, strong positions on the line of the River Aisne – positions that hardly changed for the whole of the war. The Allies soon found that they could not shift the enemy from his hold on the heights of the Aisne and there then followed a period of rapid lateral movement known as the 'Race for the Sea' in which each side attempted to outflank the other.

Large numbers of first class German troops were moved north but attempts made to break through at Arras and elsewhere proved fruitless. In the far northern sector, though, Antwerp fell on the 7th October and Ghent and Ostend followed in quick succession.

On the 19th October, Sir Douglas Haig's I Corps detrained at St Omer after experiencing hard fighting on the Aisne and were promptly ordered to advance towards Bruges and Ghent via Ypres.

Beyond Ypres, however, Haig found himself confronted by the enemy in strength and the I Corps was formed up as the left wing of the British forces destined for the approaching struggle. Meantime, Sir Henry Rawlinson's troops (including the famous 7th Division) had travelled from Antwerp, and been ordered to seize Menin, a task made almost impossible by the lack of supports. The initial move was executed as ordered, but the covering cavalry on the left flank soon encountered large enemy forces coming from the direction of Roulers. Other enemy masses were met advancing from the railhead of Courtrai and the progress of the British was halted about three miles from Menin. Shortly afterwards it was necessary to fall back to a line just east of the Gheluvelt cross-roads. The first great struggle for Ypres was about to begin.

FIRST YPRES

By the 19th October, after ten weeks of almost constant action, the utterly exhausted Belgians had fallen back on the extreme left to the line of the Yser. On their right a French army and DeMitry's cavalry (which also acted as a reinforcement to the British left – i.e. Haig's I Corps) were temporarily located. Below them was Rawlinson's IV Corps, including the 7th Division, holding the ground between Zonnebeke and Zandvoorde, followed by Allenby's Cavalry Corps. To their right, covering Armentieres, was III Corps, with the Indian Corps and the French again on their right.

So the stage was set for the grim bloody fighting that began on 21st October. The main attack was made by the bulk of four new German Corps against the front of the 7th Division. Other less weighty attacks were directed at many other points. On the 22nd and 23rd there was heavy action all along the line and one or two gaps opened which the Germans failed to exploit. Severe fighting took place including bayonet attacks and the enemy incurred crushing losses around Langemarck with about 1,500 German dead being counted on the battlefield. French reinforcements then arrived on the left which enabled the British to support the beleaguered 7th Division, still warding off strong frontal attacks (the Wiltshires formed the point of the Salient and had the most difficult part of the fight).

On the 24th the position became desperate when the gallant Wiltshires were forced to give way at last. Repeatedly the Germans pierced our line, but failed to follow up their successes.

Backwards and forwards the battle raged with serious threats constantly forcing readjustments in the siting of our forces. The 7th Division suffered terrible losses and the extent of its front had to be shortened. The 1st Division took over from Gheluvelt cross-roads to Reutal on the left. For a month the 7th had been engaged in continuous marching and fighting, and for almost two days had held a front of eight miles against forces four times their number.

On the 29th began the sternest test of 'First Ypres'. Waves of enemy troops broke against the Gheluvelt cross-roads and drove back the 1st Division but a massive counter attack forced the enemy to release his gains. German artillery fire then shattered our trenches and created a dreadful din as the battle continued on the 30th where, on the right a retirement had to be effected, and the situation became desperately critical. The German Emperor was near the scene urging his troops to take Ypres at all costs; indeed the thin line of British troops was finding it almost impossible to hold off the masses assailing them.

It seemed that the end had come on the 31st October, when after a furious bombardment, a heavy attack developed against Gheluvelt. The 1st and 3rd Brigades of the 1st Division were drawn back, the line gave way, and our men then retreated into woods at the rear. Hooge Chateau, which at that time was the headquarters of the 1st and 2nd Divisions, was shelled — the two divisional commanders were wounded and six of their staff were killed. Whole battalions in the line were virtually annihilated and our losses grew heavier hourly as the Germans poured through the Gheluvelt gap. On the right, the French struggled to lend support to the British and further south Allenby's cavalry were desperately holding the advance of two nearly fresh German Corps pending the arrival of French reinforcements. The most critical point in the whole of 'First Ypres' was estimated to be in the afternoon of the 31st, for at that time it seemed that nothing could stem the tide and

that inevitably the Allies must withdraw west of Ypres. Then, a near miracle happened. Not a heavenly miracle but one of discipline and valour. The 2nd Worcesters, a regiment with a fine history, saved the day with a bayonet charge which retook Gheluvelt and allowed our line to be reformed. Brigadier General FitzClarence, VC, Commanding the 1st Guards Brigade, had come upon the Worcesters in support at Polygon Wood. Under his leadership they dashed forward, opened heavy flank fire on the Germans, and broke their attack. It was the turning point of the battle. The gap was closed and the crisis past.

Even so the fighting continued on 1st November, with heavy shelling of our line and two further attacks. French reinforcements now lightened the burden of Allenby's cavalry but before they came up the Germans seized Hollebeke and Messines. Wytschaete was also taken after heavy fighting and it was in this area that the London Scottish Territorials acquitted themselves like veterans after only just coming into the line for the first time. On the 2nd November Wytschaete was retaken, but subsequently passed into German hands and stayed there until the great Battle of Messines in 1917.

First Ypres then slackened into an artillery duel for several days, but on the 6th November a fresh attack developed at Klein Zillebeke. It was here that the dismounted Household Cavalry in company with their French allies saved the British position with a hard, savage charge that belied the pomp and glamour surrounding these fine units in peacetime.

On 11th November, after a period of comparative quiet, the Prussian Guards were ordered to take Ypres. With incredible discipline they advanced along the Menin Road against Gheluvelt and, in spite of dreadful losses, pierced our front in three places. After taking our first line of trenches, however, they faltered and were eventually driven back from practically all of their gains. It was during this action that the gallant FitzClarence fell and joined so many of his comrades who had died to save Ypres. Spasmodic fighting continued until 17th November when the battle finally faded away with the onset of bad weather.

So ended First Ypres, a bitter, bloody confrontation where during the worst part of the fighting three British Divisions and cavalry were opposed by five Army Corps. Only 30,000 troops kept the German army at bay until other British forces could be brought up from the Aisne. The cost was heavy. About 50,000 casualties were incurred by the British and to this must be added the losses of the French and the Belgians; the Germans were estimated to have lost about 150,000. First Ypres was a victory won with blood. It was mainly a British victory — but would not have been possible without the vital assistance of our Allies. Ypres was held, nonetheless, and the German dream of an easy conquest and capture of the channel ports was dashed. Tragically, it also saw the virtual destruction of the old British regular army, the discipline and courage of which has never been exceeded.

NIEUPORT AND DIXMUDE

In October of 1914 the Belgian Centre between Nieuport and Dixmude gave way under terrific enemy pressure which had caused the Belgian reserves to be used up. A stand was then made on the railway embankment between Dixmude and Nieuport and King Albert ordered the lock gates at Nieuport to be opened thus allowing the sea to flood the surrounding countryisde. This created a major water barrier and the Germans were forced to retire across the Yser Canal to avoid being either drowned or cut off.

Through this gallant action the line was held on the left flank and the enemy failed to obtain a break through to Dunkirk and Calais.

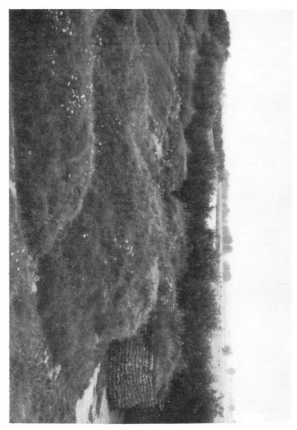

Area on the Yser Canal near Dixmude known as the 'Trench of Death'. This old Belgian trench system has been preserved with cement filled sandbags and was the scene of bitter fighting where at one time the main trenches were shared by both German and Belgian troops.

Nieuport: The Belgian War Memorial on the extreme left of the original Allied line, by the Yser Canal.

In the centre can be seen the statue of King Albert 1, Commander-in-Chief of the Belgian Army, who in the final advance of 1918 was in supreme command of the combined British, French, and Belgian forces in Flanders. These forces consisted at the time of the Belgian Army, a French division, and General Plumer's Second Army.

It was near the site of this memorial that the British suffered a severe reverse in 1917, prior to the commencement of Third Ypres, which thwarted plans for a seaborne landing behind the German lines.

Dixmude: The Square, with the towers of the Town Hall and Church on the right. In the Town Hall, which is also a museum, are various items relating to 1914-1918 including a famous picture depicting this whole area in flames. Another shows the square covered with the bodies of German and Belgian soldiers during the fierce fighting which took place before the town was finally captured by the enemy in 1914.

First Battle of Ypres, 1914. The first casualty of the 2nd Scots Guards in the Great War, 1914-1918. Drummer Steer, who received a direct hit from a shell during a reconnaissance in force towards Gheluvelt, 20th October 1914.

The artist Fortunino Matania's impression of a scene at Kruiseecke Cross-roads about a mile from Gheluvelt on the Menin side, and centre of the bitter battles fought in October/November 1914. A group of soldiers can be seen proceeding along the road which leads to the hamlet of Kruiseecke and that other area of fierce fighting, Zandvoorde.

A framed print of the event hangs in a room at the rear of the building in the right centre.

On the picture is the legend:
'Presented to the Family Vanden Broucke
by
The Green Howards (Alexandra, Princess
of Wales' Own Yorkshire Regiment) in
memory of October 1914'.

A brass plaque affixed to the picture is inscribed with the following names:
'R.S.M.F. Hatton, Col. C.A. King, Capt. C.G. Forsythe, Sgt. H. Lucas, Pte. Hali, Lieut. F.C. Ledgard, Lieut. R.H. Phayre. Carrying wounded, Pte. H. Tandy VC, DCM, MM Officer on stretcher, Capt. C.G. Jeffery.'

This area is known by the Germans as 'Deinlingseecke' (i.e. Deinling Corner) after General Deinling, Commander of XV Corps, who called a conference here on 31st October 1914 during which British shells fell on the cross-roads killing and wounding several senior officers. The General was himself slightly wounded.

These same Cross-roads were once more the scene of a hectic action in September 1918 during the early stages of the Allied advance to victory. Shortly after that fight, the Salient abruptly ceased to exist after four terrible years of destruction, bloodshed, and suffering.

GHELUVELT

Although only a small village, the capture of Gheluvelt was considered by the Germans to be of prime importance as it lay astride the Menin Road, their main axis of advance towards Ypres and the Channel coast. It also had a height advantage over the surrounding countryside and thus dominated the eastern approaches to the Flemish town that was soon to become famous in history.

Urged on by the Kaiser who was waiting nearby for a triumphal entry into Ypres, the cry of the German leaders became: 'Take Ypres or die.' First though, they had to take Gheluvelt. With much gallantry the men in field grey hurled themselves forward in response to their Emperor's bidding. Masses of enemy soldiers burst upon the thinly held defences of Gheluvelt preceeded by artillery bombardments of terrible intensity. Even more gallantly the British defenders fought back inflicting heavy casualties on the attackers but suffering appalling losses themselves.

Eventually, by sheer weight of numbers the Germans took Gheluvelt, were thrown back by the famous counter-attack of the 2nd Worcesters but subsequently regained the destroyed village which then stayed in enemy hands – except for a brief spell during Third Ypres – until the final victorious advance of the Allies in 1918.

Nevertheless the bitter fighting at Gheluvelt, in which many fine British units all but disappeared as effective formations, changed the course of the war and Ypres itself (and in consequence the Channel ports) remained as an unobtainable goal to a brave but disillusioned enemy who had previously envisaged an easy conquest of that corner of Belgium.

Photograph of a framed picture of the 2nd Worcesters attacking across the grounds of Gheluvelt Chateau during their famous charge of 31st October 1914 which routed the enemy after he had smashed through our lines and created a dangerous gap. By this valiant action Gheluvelt was retaken and the gap closed.

The original painting of this action by Fortunino Matania now hangs in the Officers Mess of the Worcester Regiment at Norton Barracks, Worcester.

Right: *The village of Gheluvelt* showing the ground across which the Worcesters, in company with survivors of the South Wales Borderers who lined the side of the ditch on the right, poured a heavy flanking fire at the Germans.

On 31st October 1914 this area, including the village, constituted an enemy salient in our lines and was a mass of flame and explosives, rifle and machine gun fire.

Bodies littered the slope and fierce fighting was taking place amongst the broken houses topping the rise.

Far Right: *The rebuilt Gheluvelt Chateau*, at peace and shuttered for the summer holiday period, where once the grass was littered with bodies and which was later a heap of broken bricks in a wasteland of mud and desolation.

The war has given birth to that weird courage which inspires a man to great bravery even when he knows no reward will or can possibly accrue: the daring is reasoned, like the clarity of a man meeting death open-eyed and never wavering, even an eye-lid. I can see it in the men around me — men who have been wounded and gone home, who possess no illusions about its horror, yet go willingly enough without cowardly shrinking or backward appeal. I have always that fear beside me, the fear of showing myself unworthy, cowardly — if I had that mastered, or even shelved, I could be as resigned as the others; but the future haunts one so much.

[HQ]

Grave of Lord Worsley, killed in the heavy fighting at the end of October 1914.

The body was originally found by the Germans who buried it at Zandvoorde from where it was eventually transferred to its present resting place in Ypres Cemetery.

At the place where Lord Worsley's body was originally found now stands the memorial to the Household Cavalry.

24

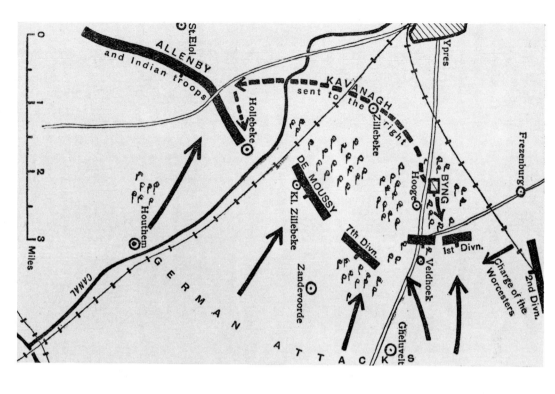

Fighting at Gheluvelt on October 31. The critical moment. Map from *Nelson's History of the War* (John Buchan) by permission of Thomas Nelson & Sons Ltd.

'Nonne Boschen' Wood (*The Nun's Wood*) close to Polygon Wood, which was reached by some of the Prussian Guards before their attack was stopped and beaten back after a desperate struggle. The enemy got within seventy yards of the guns of the 41st Brigade RFA hidden in the Wood, but were halted by fire of an improvised defence consisting of spare gunners, Engineers, cooks, officers' servants, and other odd hands.

In 1917 'Nonne Boschen' bristled with many concrete emplacements housing machine guns which caused heavy casualties to our troops.

THE EARLY DAYS AND MESSINES IN RETROSPECT

Sunday, 3rd August 1914 and London was agog! No wireless in those days and very, very, few telephones.

Rumour and counter-rumour caused excited crowds at Buckingham Palace and at key points everywhere. I happened to be at Waterloo Station where the movement and excitement affected me considerably for with war imminent there was a tremendous atmosphere which was enhanced by many hundreds of reservists hurrying to catch trains to their planned destinations.

After an hour or so of observation I made for home — a much subdued and impressed nineteen-year-old.

On Monday 4th August at 8 a.m. I was at my normal job. As a morse telegraphist my office usually disposed of some 300 telegrams a day but today the output was fantastic. Every message was vibrant and fatalistic and I helped to clear perhaps around 1000 telegrams before eventually taking my leave.

With war declared I realised in a bemused kind of way that I was very quickly to be involved as a member of the Territorial Army and that from now on I would not be paid to be either subdued or impressed.

The first duty on the morning of Tuesday, 5th August was to present myself to my regiment and by doing so I became part of the huge war machine that was slowly beginning to grind into action.

Discipline took over and one immediately found that sense of cameradie and a spirit of orderly tolerance which helped to shape us into healthy and capable second-line troops. The terms of my four-year engagement enlisted me for Home Service but on the 20th August, whilst enjoying (and I say that in the fullness of youth) very intensive training in the St. Albans area, we were individually given an option of volunteering for Active Service.

Ninety per cent of the Battalion, including myself, immediately said 'yes' and on the 14th September, six weeks after we had mobilised, left for Southampton and Le Havre.

Within six weeks of that date 380 of those healthy and lively volunteers were either dead, wounded, POWs or on the sick list.

From the 15th September until late October we were employed on prisoner escort duties, at Dressing Stations with hundreds of dirty, unshaven, wounded or at Railheads working twenty hours out of twenty-four. Meantime our Regular soldiers had shown on the retirement from Mons, on the Marne and the Aisne that, despite decimation and fatigue they were still not permitting the enemy the break-through he was fighting for.

At 5.00 pm on 29th October we were served out with fifty rounds of ball ammunition and left our base at St Omer about 800 strong and transported in buses which had solid tyres and open tops. After skidding continuously over the uneven pave roads which were completely unknown to the drivers we eventually arrived at Ypres, Belgium, at 3.00 am with those on top being thoroughly wet through. After standing and sitting around for some time in the Square we eventually filed in to the magnificent Cloth Hall where we slept fitfully from about 5.00 am until 8.00 am. Following reveille we enjoyed a brew-up of tea together with some biscuits and Ticklers Jam prior to falling in and marching over the Ramparts and on to the Menin Road where, after being spaced out into companies and sections, we marched off towards Hooge. The close proximity of bursting shells and accompanying noise caused a number of comments but was accepted without too much concern at this early stage due perhaps to the fact that we were all still excited at the fact that we were now well and truly in it and that the prospects of real battle loomed ahead.

However it was not to be quite yet for we suddenly reversed our direction of march as it was understood that our men further up were holding their own.

Back we went to Ypres and once again we boarded the buses with our new destination being St Eloi, a small village about six kilo-

[Contributed by S.T.H. Ross formerly 1st Bn London Scottish TA]

metres away. We arrived there at about 9.00 pm and although the village was bereft of civilians there were many troops about including some French 'Cuirassiers' in addition to our own Scots Greys and men from a variety of other regiments.

We waited for a while then smashed in doors and windows for the purpose of billeting ourselves in the rather forlorn looking evacuated cottages in which we rested until 4.00 am 31st October, (Halloween!). Heavy gun fire was heard all through the night and in the early morning light we fell in and commenced marching towards Messines. We learned that a spy was supposed to be signalling to the enemy by moving windmill sails and whether this was true or not was not known, but we certainly lost men *en route* besides seeing marked evidence of smashed vehicles and dead horses.

After effecting preliminary dispositions across hop fields and woodlands we advanced in earnest towards the Germans, using the short, sharp rushes and the signals of our Section Sergeant — as per the Wimbledon Common Drill Book exercises which we had been trained on. We 'entrenched' by stages and as well as we could with small entrenching tools for no-one in those days ever saw a spade or shovel. We had casualties of course and Jerry's 'Jack Johnsons', as we called them, were more than frightening, especially to this boy of nineteen tender years.

At night under a full moon, we advanced again and once more dug shallow trenches. The Germans were then just a short distance away and we could actually hear a band they were making use of. This we learned subsequently was because they really thought they were about to break through and completely over-run the remnant of the BEF facing them.

Bullets were flying around but when Jerry attacked fiercely our BG and H Companies met them headlong with the bayonet. I was told to go forward for wounded and I managed to assist a Sergeant of G Company who had been hit. By using improvised stretchers (e.g. doors, for we had no proper stretchers) some other chaps and I managed to get about twelve wounded back to a hayrick. Fires were blazing in the vicinity but for a short while anyway we were able to rest.

After various adventures, with some of our wounded having died as we carried them, we eventually got to Kemmel at around 6.00 am on Sunday, 1st November where the Battalion subsequently mustered some 300 strong, although more of our chaps turned up later.

I had, incidentally, lost my pack, practically all of my useful equipment, and my rifle and bayonet which were left in the 'trenches' from where I had originally gone forward. Rumour had it that we were going up again but instead we fell in and moved back to Bailleul tired, footsore and saddened.

On Wednesday, 4th November we were inspected by General Smith-Dorrien and also told by General Allenby and others how useful we had proved to be at a time of crisis.

Saturday, 7th November, arrived and we paraded once more and set off again marching towards Ypres which was then in flames with the beautiful Cloth Hall being well alight. We avoided going through the centre of the town and upon reaching the Menin Road continued marching until this time we actually reached Hooge Chateau, the point we had moved towards originally. Here we had some kind of cover and shelter and the cooks rustled up some very welcome tea. I slept somewhat fitfully in what I remember to be a cow or horse shed until we were fallen in to go a short way into some woodland that was fast being knocked about.

For the next seven or eight days we were subject to all kinds of 'strafing' but no attack developed. However the weather and lack of sleep did not help matters and with the absence of any cooking facilities we were left to engineer our own salvation. We scrounged wood from some cottages a little behind our trenches but in the main used some '4 x 4' material plus cut up candles, thrusting our jack-knives into the wall of the trench whilst frizzling up some 'bully' and making water hot enough for some tea.

Meanwhile Jerry was opposite at distances varying from 60 to 150 yards, probably doing something similar although every so often we fired at each other just to prove our presence.

Around mid-November we were relieved, having lost some 150 men and as part of the First Brigade of the 1st Division we extracted ourselves from a morass of mud and discomfort for a two-day march which was terribly hard going.

We got back to Pradelles or Strazeele and shortly afterwards I had to go sick with dysentry, suspected frostbite, and hernia.

By mid-December I had been brought back to England and after a spell in hospital and convalescent leave I was eventually able to rejoin our Second Battalion for further service.

This, then, was my experience of the early days and Messines and my introduction to war. It was not to end there though because I again saw service in the Salient between December 1916 and January 1918. That however is another story!

PEACE

Now, God be thanked Who has matched us with His hour,
And caught our youth, and wakened us from sleeping,
With hand made sure, clear eye, and sharpened power,
To turn, as swimmers into cleanness leaping,
Glad from a world grown old and cold and weary,
Leave the sick hearts that honour could not move,
And half-men, and their dirty songs and dreary,
And all the little emptiness of love!

Oh! we, who have known shame, we have have found release there,
Where there's no ill, no grief, but sleep has mending.
Naught broken save this body, lost but breath;
Nothing to shake the laughing heart's long peace there
But only agony, and that has ending;
And the worst friend and enemy is but Death.

Rupert Brooke

[By courtesy of Sidgwick & Jackson Ltd]

Messines Church. This unusually shaped church is a landmark for miles around due to its location on the Messines Ridge, where fierce fighting took place in 1914, 1917, and 1918. The Square in front of the church was littered with the bodies of Germans in 1914.

Messines Ridge The London Scottish Memorial at the scene of the desperate fighting in 1914. It was here that the London Territorial unit won its spurs against overwhelming odds after being rushed to this crumbling front in old London buses. This was a terrible introduction to the horrors of war for men who but a short while before were civilians and had not had time to become acquainted with shellfire or the vicious bayonet battles of those fatal days. Although beaten back after ferocious struggles, the London Scottish came out with honour and earned the respect of the regular troops.

The original shell-damaged wooden Calvary Cross in Ypres Town Cemetery. This photograph clearly shows the bullet holes and shrapnel scars of battle as well as a medium-weight German field-gun shell embedded just behind the figure on the Cross. This (and the shell), which had together survived bombardment and the ravages of time for over fifty years were dismantled in 1969 to make room for a new memorial.

YPRES

Ypres, known to so many old soldiers as 'Wipers', is situated in the western corner of Belgium, fairly close to the French border. North and north-west lies the flat plain of the Yser valley, extending to the sea; to the north-east and south-east are a series of low ridges which slope gently down to the hollow in which the town stands. About twenty-five miles to the north-west and across the French border is another town of immortal fame — Dunkirk — and due north at approximately the same distance is Ostend — the Belgian gateway to the Continent. This corner of Belgium has long been known as the 'Cockpit of Europe': persistently over the centuries men have fought bloody battles there.

Ypres itself has often suffered siege, bombardment, fire, and plunder, as the French, the Dutch, and the Spanish took their turns in conquering the town and surrounding countryside. Even the English, under the Bishop of Norwich, laid siege to Ypres for two months in 1383 until the approach of a large French army caused a hasty withdrawal (this relief of the city from the English is still commemorated at an annual festival in Ypres during August). But the paths of history are strange, and over five hundred years later, in another bitter siege, England gallantly defended the beleaguered city and the graves of thousands upon thousands of her sons lie beside Scots, Welsh, Irish and Commonwealth dead as a silent reminder of a debt re-paid with honour.

We first hear of Ypres in AD 960 when it was just a cluster of huts in swampy ground. From this small beginning it grew to become, during the fourteenth century, the greatest city in Flanders with a population said to have been over 200,000. Its prosperity stemmed mainly from the weaving of cloth which was marketed in the famous Cloth Hall.

The Cloth Hall dates back to the twelfth century and stood, solid and magnificent in the main square of Ypres, until it was pounded to rubble by German guns. After four years of bombardment only a small portion of the Cloth Hall tower and a fragment of wall remained; the rest of the town was a stark ruin of jumbled brickwork, a few feet high.

Long before that wholesale destruction, however, Ypres had been reduced in importance to a minor town and in 1914 the population amounted only to about seventeen-and-a-half thousand. Wars and revolt had taken a heavy toll, and the celebrated cloth trade had declined drastically. Some of the weavers actually migrated to England where they successfully established their craft much to England's benefit. Just before the first battle of 1914, Ypres was a quiet town populated chiefly by tradesmen and artisans, and some of the old burgher families and property owners.

In the surrounding countryside prosperous farms produced the basic necessities of life and hereditary mansions and fine chateaux housed members of the old nobility with famous names. Some of these lovely chateaux — Hooge, for example — were to become the

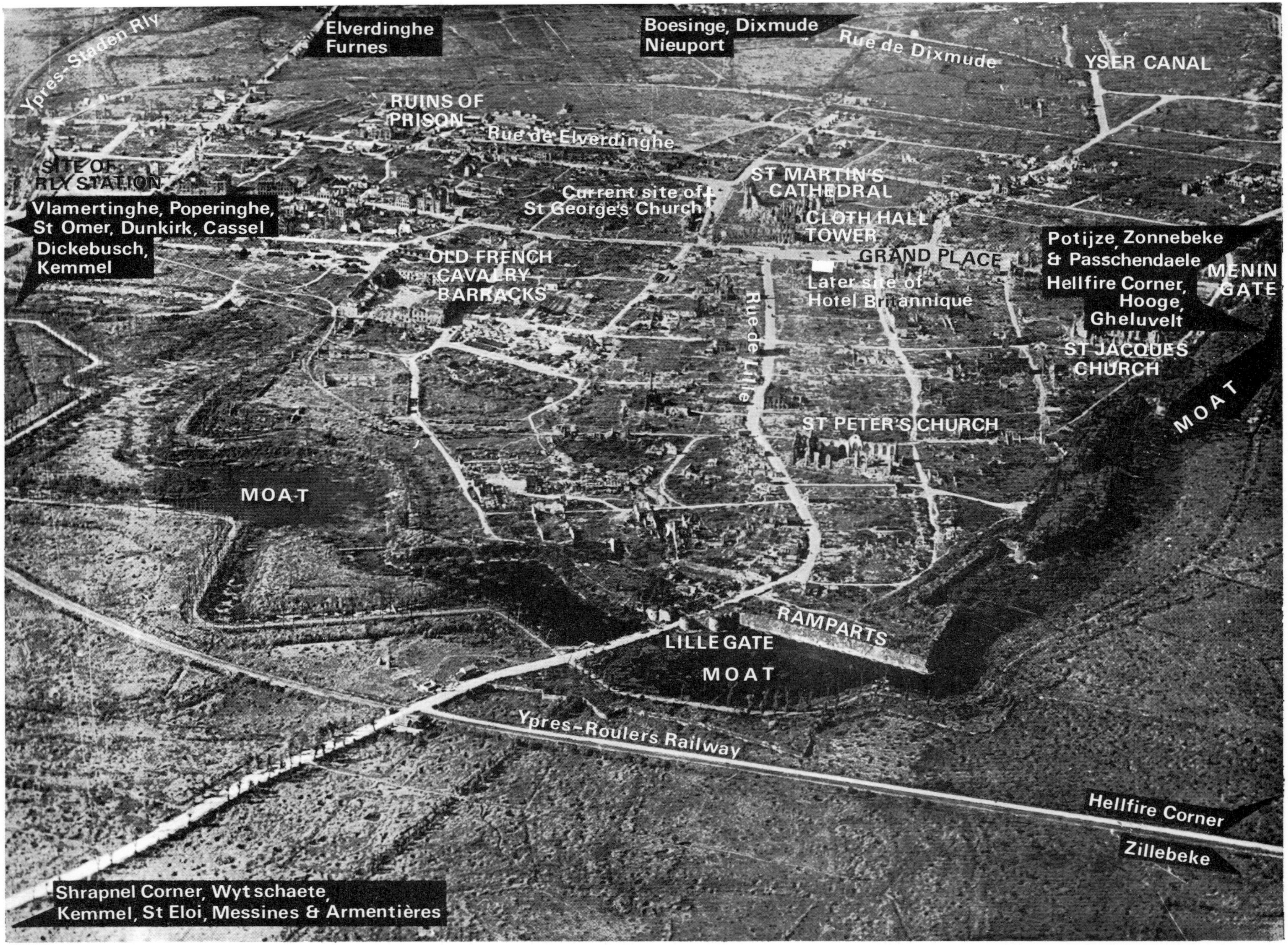

YSER CANAL

MOAT

Hellfire Corner

Zillebeke

Potijze, Zonnebeke
& Passchendaele

MENIN
GATE

Hellfire Corner,
Hooge,
Gheluvelt

ST JACQUES
CHURCH

Rue de Dixmude

Boesinge, Dixmude
Nieuport

Rue de Elverdinghe

ST MARTIN'S
CATHEDRAL

CLOTH HALL
TOWER

GRAND PLACE

Later site of
Hotel Britannique

ST PETER'S CHURCH

RAMPARTS

Rue de Lille

LILLE GATE
MOAT

Current site of
St George's Church

Elverdinghe
Furnes

RUINS OF
PRISON

OLD FRENCH
CAVALRY
BARRACKS

Ypres–Roulers Railway

Ypres–Staden Riv

SITE OF
RLY STATION

Vlamertinghe, Poperinghe,
St Omer, Dunkirk, Cassel
Dickebusch,
Kemmel

MOAT

Shrapnel Corner, Wytschaete
Kemmel, St Eloi, Messines & Armentières

32

focus of horror and violent death over the next four years. During November 1914 the town received its first limited baptism of fire from heavy German guns and in April 1915, during the Second Battle of Ypres, endured a concentrated bombardment of startling ferocity.

Those members of the civilian population who had so far decided to risk enemy shellfire (and there were quite a number) fled from the town although many were killed by the shells or were buried beneath crashing houses. When the enemy failed to break through, Ypres and its vital road net work came under prolonged fire from the German artillery. Day after day, week after week, month after month, high explosive shells including mighty seventeen-inchers crashed into the city until by the end of the war they had smashed everything to brickdust and rubble — all, that is, except the fantastically strong Ramparts, which were said to have been built during Napoleonic times and which held firm. These same Ramparts were put to good use by the few men who were forced to remain in Ypres and cellars and shelters are still to be seen where our soldiers were protected by their thick walls and roofs.

In due course Ypres became a city of the dead. It was populated only by limited numbers of troops, a few stray animals, and legions of rats. Reinforcements going towards the front or those returning from the battlefield passed through the broken city as quickly as possible. No-one loitered in the Grand Place with its all-pervading smells of decay, cordite, gas, mortar dust, and chloride of lime.

The desolation of Ypres was emphasised at night when the loneliness and emptiness of the ruins were silhouetted in the glare of flares and bursting shells.

Ypres indeed became a martyred city upon which was hurled the full fury of a relentless enemy who had treated it as a major objective but had been frustrated in his attempts to take it. This must have been particularly galling to the enemy for a strong German cavalry reconnoitering force passed through the town early in October 1914 before being forced to fall back, but from that time until the end of the war no German set foot in the town unless as a prisoner of war.

Today Ypres, including the Cloth Hall and St Martin's Cathedral, stands completely rebuilt (mostly in its pre-1914 aspect) and the Cathedral boast a beautiful spire as an addition to the original building, the cost being borne by German reparations.

The Grand Place, still fully cobbled until 1964, has been changed in order to cope with the steadily growing volume of traffic; the numerous bars around the square enjoy a steady trade from numerous tourists in the summer months. There are shops and bright lights in Ypres now and on Saturdays a weekly market is held in the Grand Place. Almost everything can be purchased from the multitude of stalls and at times from within the precincts of the Cloth Hall itself. Ypres has risen from its ashes and is once more a busy thriving township of some 18,000 souls to whom the future is gradually becoming more important than the past.

There were many weird pronunciations of the name Ypres. I always noted that men belonging to our 1st Battalion invariably alluded to the place as 'E-prey', but the 2nd Battalion were satisfied with its more familiar name of 'Wipers'. Quite recently the writer was shown a letter written by one of Marlborough's officers from Flanders: 'The men speak of the town as Wypirs', wrote this eighteenth-century soldier.

[FCH]

Photo on the preceding page:
Aerial view of Ypres at the end of 1918. The whole area is covered with shell holes and hardly a wall remains standing. [IWM]

The Cloth Hall on fire, 22 November 1914. The wooden scaffolding had been erected for earlier repair work. (Photo by Antony of Ypres, courtesy of Miss Gabrielle Antony (Ostend)

NOTHING is to be written on this side except the date and signature of the sender. Sentences not required may be erased. If anything else is added the post card will be destroyed.

I am quite well.

I have been admitted into hospital
 { sick } and am going on well.
 { wounded } and hope to be discharged soon.

I am being sent down to the base.

I have received your { letter dated
 { telegram „
 { parcel „

Letters follows at first opportunity.

I have received no letter from you
 { lately.
 { for a long time.

Signature only. } Arthur.

Date 10 – 2 – 15.

[Postage must be prepaid on any letter or post card addressed to the sender of this card.]

(6461) Wt. W3497-293 1,000m. 11/14 F. T. & Co., Ltd.

An Army Field Service Postcard. This is dated 10th February 1915 and was sent by 'Private A. Carter' of the 5th Royal Irish Lancers. The list of messages has been crossed out except for 'I am quite well.'

An old photograph of 'Private Carter'. The real name of this soldier was Coady but he changed it to Carter in order to join up whilst being under age.

[Contributed by Lt-Commander F.A. Costelloe, RN (Ret'd) by permission of Mrs. D.C. Costelloe, Dublin, (Sister of 'Private Carter']

36

A famous name outside the Cloth Hall before the first bombardment, 1914. Waring and Gillow are a famous London furniture store existing to this day. Their lorry, an old Manchester, was borrowed or commandeered for transport duties by the Expeditionary Force. Note the solid tyres and the blackout headlamps. Under the vehicle on the left we can pick out the white disc used to guide the following vehicle when blacked out convoys bumped forward over the roads of the Salient. [IWM]

The vehicle on the right cannot be identified, but its un-blacked headlamps, pneumatic tyres, and general aura of luxury suggest that it was probably a staff car. [IWM]

Above, left: The grave of HRH Prince Maurice Victor Donald of Battenberg, KCVO. The copper cross over his grave in the cemetery at Ypres on 10th January 1915. The cross disappeared during the war and was never found. Prince Maurice was a lieutenant serving with the 1st Battalion of the King's Royal Rifle Corps. On 27th October 1914, the 1/KRRC attacked towards Keiberg. Prince Maurice was leading his men across an open space when a shell fell and burst beside him. He knew that his injuries were mortal and wished his men goodbye. He was carried to a field dressing room but died before it could be reached.

Prince Maurice was a grandson of Queen Victoria. His uncle, Ludovic von Battenberg, resigned as First Sea Lord in 1914 and changed his name to Mountbatten. Ludovic was the father of the present Earl Mountbatten of Burma.

A cousin of Prince Maurice's, Prince Christian Victor of Schlesswig-Holstein, served in the German army. Prince Maurice's sister Ena, who died in 1969, was the widow of Alphonse XIII, King of Spain; she often visited her brother's grave. [IWM; Research: Dr A. Caenepeel]

Below, left: The grave of Prince Maurice today.

37

17TH JUNE 1915

Macartney, the Padre, and I went down in the evening to see Ypres. The city was deserted and desolate. The atmosphere was heavy with the smell of decaying bodies, for the first shells had surprised the inhabitants, and had caught many in their beds. A number of the houses had been knocked down by direct hits, and others had one of the walls blown down, showing the furniture of the stories above, like scenery in a theatre.

Few houses had been left unscathed. The square in front of the Cloth Hall was in a dreadful state, strewn all over with parts of British GS waggons, bones of dead horses, broken rifles, and web equipment. The streets throughout Ypres were pitted with shell craters, beside the Cloth Hall there was the crater of a 16-inch shell. I measured it, and found it was fifty-two paces around, 30 feet deep and 48 feet across from lip to lip.

[FCH]

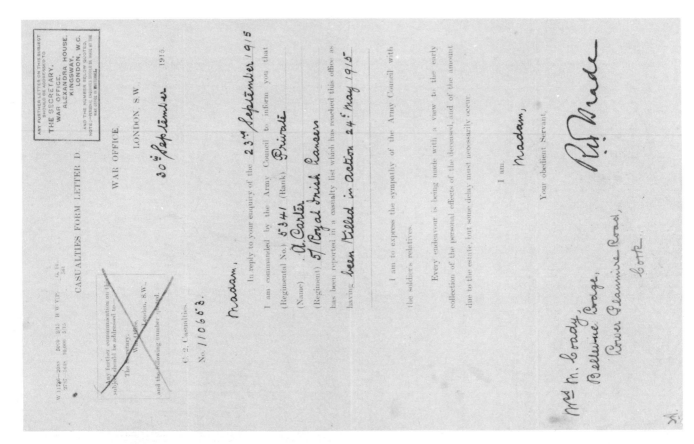

[Contributed by Lt-Comdr F.A. Costelloe RN (Ret'd) by permission of Mrs D.C. Costelloe]

Our battalion had entrained almost as far as Ypres, and we rested beside the railway for some time, with the engine standing stationary sending a high pillar of smoke into the air. I expect the German observation balloons had seen it, for the enemy began to place shells on each side of the railway at regular intervals for about two hundred yards. Then we began to cross the railway: our two companies had just got over when I heard a scream of a shell. Instantly we got on our noses: I looked up cautiously, just in time to see it explode in a thick mass of the other companies on the railway. The scream of despair and agony was dreadful to hear, men shell-shocked out of reason and others dying of frightful wounds. That shell caused sixty casualties and shook the whole battalion for several days. Even when going through the market-square of Ypres, beneath the yellow flash of great howitzers and the roar of naval guns, we thought shells were bursting among us and looked fearfully at every corner, nerve-shaken and absolutely afraid. The sudden roar of a gun made us start guiltily, half-ashamed, and yet unable to control our agitation. That cry of dying men will ring in my ears for a long time after everything else will be forgotten.

[HQ]

Above: Ypres Railway Station, 1916. [IWM]. Below, the station today with a trim, modern outline.

D

One always marched in an attitude of tension, with ears cocked, going through Ypres — awaiting the ever-expected roar of an approaching shell. The men were silent, nothing was to be heard but the clank of hobnailed boots against the uneven cobbles, and the jingle of the mess-tins and accoutrements against the web equipment.

[FCH]

Left:

The Grand Place, 1915. A gendarme and two citizens of Ypres examine dead horses in front of the battered Cloth Hall just after the April bombardments of Second **Ypres**. Note how quickly bloating has affected the carcasses. The semi-circular building to the right is actually the apse of St Martin's Cathedral whose square tower can be seen a little further to the left. [Photograph by Antony of Ypres. By courtesy of Miss Gabrielle Antony (Ostend)].

Above right:

The Grand Place, October 1917. A photograph from the same perspective shows Australian troops going up to relieve the front line with the ruins of the Cloth Hall and St Martin's in the background. A transport column can be seen forming up in the mid-background. The vehicles with weather-proof hoods over the cabs are probably early steam-driven Renaults. The other vehicles are Crosley Tenders. At the extreme rear of the transport column can be seen an early Model T pickup truck with artillery wheels. [IWM]

Below right:

The Grand Place, fifty years later. A Renault of more recent design in front of the reconstructed Cloth Hall and the spire of St Martin's. Electric lighting has replaced the gas lamps of the past and French Citroens and Renaults, British Cortinas and Standards, mix freely with German Opels and Mercedes in the macadamised Grand Place. The car in the right foreground would be on approximately the same spot as the dead horses in the earlier photograph.

The Square, Ypres, September 1917. It is difficult to estimate the size of artillery from photographs, but this is almost certainly the burst of a German 5.9 howitzer — perhaps the most successful artillery piece in the war. In the right background is a farm cart with an astonishingly unconcerned driver. [IWM].

The Square, Ypres, over fifty years later. On a bright summer's day bicyclists, bus passengers, and motor vehicles disperse unconcernedly through an area which once echoed to the crash of shells and the rumble of falling masonry.

The bus marks the approximate site of the shell burst in the photograph above. A Belgian Army jeep can be seen in the right foreground.

Working on our parapets all night; the enemy sent some colossal shells into Ypres. More 'Roscrea mails', as the men called them ironically. They certainly did sound like trains going through the air.

[FCH]

Ypres, 29 September 1967. Fifty years later a woman calmly proceeds on a shopping expedition.

Ypres, 29 September 1917. Looking out toward the Menin Gate with the ruins of the Cloth Hall to the left. In the foreground are the remains of ammunition limbers and horses caught by shell fire. The shrouded objects on the ground and the shovel in the middle of the picture suggest that the limber drivers did not escape unscathed. The sergeant (to the left) is carrying a gas mask on his chest and the horsemen in the rear has a horse mask (for the same purpose) slung over his back. [IWM].

29TH JUNE 1915

C and D Companies left billets at the Water Tower for rest in the Vlamertinghe Woods. We were glad to leave Ypres. Shell-fire in the front line is expected, and one is prepared for it, but shell-fire in billets is most unpleasant. We were usually shelled at night when we were all asleep. One would be wakened by yells and screams for stretcher-bearers and go out to find a billet had fallen in on top of some men. D Company were very unlucky, for besides losing numbers of men on the working parties at night, they lost many in billets from shell-fire. There is rarely any cover in a town from shell-fire. There were cellars in Ypres, but to take refuge in them meant running the risk of having the house collapse on top of one. It is always advisable to leave a town which is being badly shelled, but what can be done when surprised in the middle of the night? 'C'est la guerre,' as the Flemish peasants used to say when they went back to Ypres to salve some of the household goods, only to find their old home completely demolished. Turning their horses' heads once more towards Vlamertinghe, they would drive away repeating: 'C'est la guerre! C'est la guerre!'

[FCH]

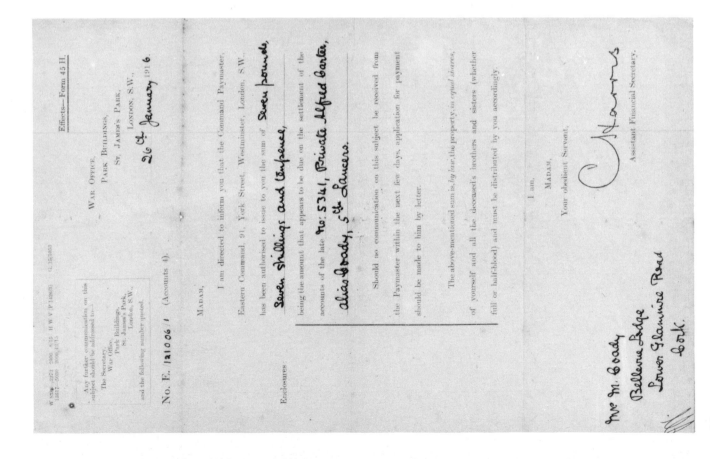

[Contributed by Lt-Comdr. F.A. Costelloe RN (Ret'd) by permission of Mrs D.C. Costelloe].

44

The Desolate Acres. Aerial photograph of Ypres after the guns had done their deadly work. The Grand Place, and the ruins of St Martin's and the Cloth Hall can be seen in the centre of the photograph. The Menin Gate is out of sight to the right. [IWM]

A view of Ypres today taken from the cat-walk on the face of the Cloth Hall tower and looking in the general direction of Passchendaele which lies in the far distance beyond the top right of the picture. In the left centre portion of the photograph can be seen the famous Menin Gate.
The previously all-cobbled Grand Place was modernised in 1964 and now has a one-way traffic system and special parking facilities for coping with an ever increasing volume of traffic.

One morning last week, two of us came down through the morning barrage into the square across the canal. Deadbeat, we asked a policeman where we would get a decent sleep for about three hours. He pointed out to us the old Cloth Hall, and there, beneath that massive tower, so dented and bruised that it no more can be destroyed by shells, behind a wall of sandbags, we fell asleep. About nine o'clock I woke up and explored a little: just inside the arch hung a delicately-wrought iron lamp, quite intact, with some fragments of glass still in it and, below, a pair of wooden wheels belonging to an old type of gun. Just beyond lay the ruins of the church, a mere blur of a building. The Cloth Hall seemed to have been so battered that not a single sculptured figure, or shadow of a figure, remained, except one gargoyle at the end, which leered down as jauntily as ever. When I come back, this incident will remain one of the treasured memories, something to recount time and again, as happening in a land of horror and dread whence few return.

[HQ]

The shattered walls of the Cloth Hall, 1917. [IWM].

Mended walls, fifty years later.

46

I shall never forget that afternoon in Ypres, when every officer and man we met asked us how our Division did in the attack. I was proud of it, too, in some kind of perverse delight, not keen on fighting, yet glad to be in it. Even then, among all that sordid mass of ruins we call Ypres, memory and recollection have given a romantic aspect, as some monument worthy of valour and enshrined in our deeds, where our bravest fought to the last and never yielded. It may be a cemetery, a horrible cemetery at that, but an air of nobility blows round it yet. The horrible remains a characteristic, instance that story of 'Hell Fire Corner', where two battalions of an English regiment lie buried, shelled to death. In Ypres too, are some billets in cellars (the only safe ones we have), where the rats have become so accustomed to soldiers, and so glutted with their blood, that they won't move out of the way — loathsome, bloated creatures, half-blind and as big as cats.

[HQ]

Above:

Through the window. The crumbled ruins of the Cloth Hall tower seen through a window in the Courts of Justice building. British troops stand in front of a Crosley in the middle of the photograph; emerging from behind it is an early motorcycle — a Velocette. British howitzers with their limbers can be seen to the right. [IWM].

Below:

The same window, fifty years later. Belgian clerks in the Courts of Justice building obligingly moved desks and office equipment to permit the author to take this photograph.

47

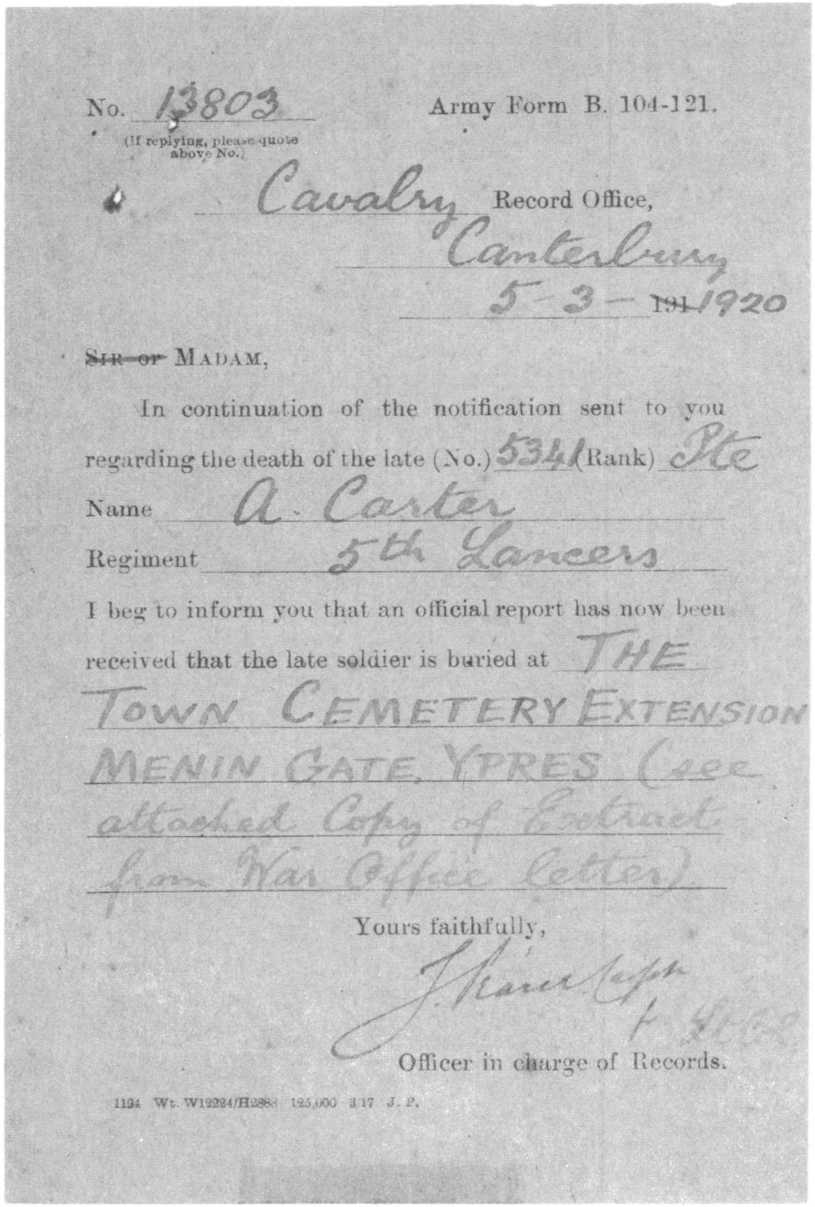

The resting place of Private 'A. Carter' in Ypres Town Cemetery Military Extension.

No. 13803
(If replying, please quote above No.)

Army Form B. 104-121.

Cavalry Record Office,
Canterbury
5 - 3 - 1920

Sir or Madam,

In continuation of the notification sent to you regarding the death of the late (No.) 5344 (Rank) Pte

Name A. Carter

Regiment 5th Lancers

I beg to inform you that an official report has now been received that the late soldier is buried at THE Town Cemetery Extension Menin Gate, Ypres (see attached copy of extract from War Office letter)

Yours faithfully,

Officer in charge of Records.

1194 Wt. W12284/R388 125,000 3.17 J.B.

Official notification of the grave location of 'Private Carter' dated 5th March 1920 and forwarded to Mrs M. Coady (his mother).
[By permission of Mrs D.C. Costelloe]

48

The Oude Veemarkt (Old Cattle Market), Ypres, June 1915. The lime trees have not yet been destroyed by later bombardments and scavenging troops. [IWM]

The Oude Veemarkt later in the war. (From an antique French postcard). The vault under the street, exposed by shelling, contained the river Yperlee. This vault started at a very old (Roman) casement at the Lille Gate and maintained the level of the moat as well as draining the Zillebeek (a name we shall hear again).

The Oude Veemarkt today taken from directly in front of the home of Dr A. Caenepeel who contributed the postcard above. Some of the railings have been restored, others are original; the lime trees are not.

ST GEORGE'S MEMORIAL CHURCH

In 1924 Field Marshall Earl Haig made an appeal for a British Church to serve as a memorial to the thousands of soldiers who died in the Salient during the four bitter years of 1914-18. On Sunday 24th July 1927 the foundation stone of the Church was laid by Field Marshal Lord Plumer and on 24th March 1929 a service of dedication was held by the Lord Bishop of Fulham.

A memorial to Field Marshall Sir John French, Commander of the British Forces in 1914, who later became Viscount French of Ypres, is in the church. During the 1939-45 war the regimental banners and the church plate were concealed from the Germans by the residents of Ypres who took care of these valuable items during the period of the occupation. German troops occasionally used St George's Church as a place of worship during the last war.

Field Marshall Sir Douglas Haig mounted on his charger 'Poperinghe' 1917.
[IWM]

50

St Martin's Cathedral, September 1917. German prisoners being marched past the ruined cathedral carrying their wounded. The lorry in the foreground is an AEC. [IWM]

St George's Memorial Church.

The same area September 1967. Part of St George's Memorial Church can be seen on the right.

The Interior of St George's Memorial Church. Regimental battle flags hang from the walls and the stained-glass windows bear British regimental insignia. Each chair has been purchased by relatives in honour of a soldier lost at Ypres and bears a brass plaque in his memory.

THE SOLDIER

If I should die, think only this of me:
    That there's some corner of a foreign field
That is for ever England. There shall be
    In that rich earth a richer dust concealed;
A dust whom England bore, shaped, made aware,
    Gave, once, her flowers to love, her ways to roam,
A body of England's breathing English air,
    Washed by the rivers, blest by suns of home.

And think, this heart, all evil shed away,
    A pulse in the eternal mind, no less
        Gives somewhere back the thoughts by England given;
Her sights and sounds; dreams happy as her day;
    And laughter, learnt of friends; and gentleness,
        In hearts at peace, under an English heaven.

                        Rupert Brooke

[By courtesy of Sidgwick & Jackson Ltd]

... age 20

*This spot
is forever England's*

St Martin's Cathedral. This beautiful church which originally dated from the 13th century was totally destroyed except for a small part of the south portal and a piece of the tower.

After the war it was completely rebuilt based on old plans except that a spire was added to the tower, the cost being offset by war reparations.

The Agony of Ypres. A shell-damaged relic recovered from the shattered town and now residing at the rear of the Cathedral. The stone figure appears to be expressing its own feelings at the inhumanity of that era.

The Company's rendezvous was at the Cross Roads near the Menin Gate; we had only to wait for a few minutes before we heard the tramp of the last platoon on the cobbles, and the jingle of their mess-tins on their equipment. We got the order to move, and marched off for Poperinghe across the silent square of Ypres, 'walking for all the world like a flock of old hens on hot bricks, and expecting a shell to land on top of one of the platoons at any minute.

We passed the Square safely, and the Cloth Hall, which loomed up in the moonlight, on our right flank. How we all dreaded Ypres, even Caulfield's charger seemed to have been infected with the Ypres fear, and shortened her usual striding steps, and turned her head from side to side, whinnying. We left silent Ypres; some of us were destined to see it again and some were not.

[FCH]

The Menin Gate Memorial. Inside, on each wall, is the inscription:
    'Here are recorded the names of officers and men who fell in the Ypres Salient but to whom the fortune of war denied the known and honoured burial given to their comrades in death.'

On the panels of this Memorial are engraved the names of nearly 55,000 officers and men of the armies of the British Empire who fell on the Ypres Front from the beginning of the war until 15th August 1917 and whose remains have either never been found or were beyond identification.

Approximately 34,000 more names of those missing in the Salient between 16th August 1917 and the end of the operations in this area are carved in the stonework of the Tyne Cot Memorial near Passchendaele.

54

The Menin Gate, 1917. The Ramparts to the left and right mark the actual location of the gate. German prisoners and Australian troops pass back through the gate towards the Cloth Hall. The stone lions which once posed belligerently on the Ramparts were presented to the Australian government after the war for their memorial at Canberra. One lion had only half a body left; the other was fairly sound, but had a wooden leg!

The mule leaders in the foreground were drawn from special transport platoons attached to each battalion (note that they are not carrying arms). The narrow-gauge railway was also used to bring forward supplies, usually in trucks pushed by hand. [IWM].

The Menin Gate, fifty years later. The rebuilt Cloth Hall framed in the carved stonework of the Menin Gate Memorial.

The pock marks on the right hand side of the memorial were made by German bullets in World War II, attracted probably by a British machine-gun sited on top of the Ramparts.
[Photo: Daniel, Ypres]

At the end of the evening. Every winter evening at 2000 hours and every summer evening at 2100 hours, members of the Ypres Fire Brigade play *The Last Post* from this spot. Traffic for that moment comes to a halt in memory of the thousands who passed through here on the way to their destinies.

III . THE DEAD

Blow out, you bugles, over the rich Dead!
   There's none of these so lonely and poor of old,
   But, dying, has made us rarer gifts than gold.
These laid the world away; poured out the red
Sweet wine of youth; gave up the years to be
   Of work and joy, and that unhoped serene,
   That men call age; and those who would have been,
Their sons, they gave, their immortality.

Blow, bugles, blow! They brought us, for our dearth,
   Holiness, lacked so long, and Love, and Pain.
Honour has come back, as a king, to earth,
   And paid his subjects with a royal wage;
And Nobleness walks in our ways again;
   And we have come into our heritage.

IV. THE DEAD

These hearts were woven of human joys and cares,
   Washed marvellously with sorrow, swift to mirth.
The years had given them kindness. Dawn was theirs,
   And sunset, and the colours of the earth.
These had seen movement, and heard music; known
   Slumber and waking; loved; gone proudly friended;
Felt the quick stir of wonder; sat alone;
   Touched flowers and furs and cheeks. All this is ended.

There are waters blown by changing winds to laughter
   And lit by the rich skies, all day. And after,
   Frost, with a gesture, stays the waves that dance
And wandering loveliness. He leaves a white
   Unbroken glory, a gathered radiance,
A width, a shining peace, under the night.

                              Rupert Brooke

[By courtesy of Sidgwick & Jackson Ltd]

Rest well, comrades. A most moving photograph by Antony of Ypres showing the Lille Gate British Military Cemetery as it once was. Taken in the late spring of 1919 the photograph shows how quickly the fertile soil of France tried to hide the desolation of war.

Lille Gate Cemetery today. The water in the background is part of the medieval moat which once surrounded Ypres and which are shown again in the next photographs.

11TH AUGUST 1915

These dug-outs had been cut out of the Ramparts. C and B Companies were on the right side of the Menin Gate leaving the city, and A and D Companies were on the left. We got the Company into quite a small area as the dug-outs were built tier upon tier up from the road which ran from the Menin to Lille Gates. Steps had been made out of filled sand-bags up to the parapet of the Ramparts.

We made a company mess out of an old ruined house. I reported on duty to Brigade Headquarters further down the Ramparts, where I met Brig-General Harper who stopped and talked to me. The C.O. had a 'pow-wow' with all the officers in the Battalion. He told us that we were ordered to consolidate the new position at Hooge. He said we would have to dig in and wire all night, and that we must be prepared for a counter-attack. His final orders were: 'Go and tell your platoons what they are up against, and what to expect.' The Ramparts were shelled all afternoon, the enemy was seaching for a battery which was hard by the moat beyond the duckboard track. We watched their howitzer shells falling in to the moat, and hitting the walls of the Ramparts below us.

[FCH]

Australian troops of the 6th Field Coy Engineers billeted in the Ramparts at Ypres, 2nd November 1917. [IWM].

The Lille Gate, September 1917. A British Officer in the foreground stands by the edge of the moat. Walking wounded can be seen straggling back along the road and to the right of them, under the Ramparts, is a Tommy dozing in the autumnal sun. In the Lille Gate itself is an ancient Thorneycroft, halted at a checkpoint while the driver seems to be fumbling papers from his pocket. [IWM]

Calm and peace where steel helmets are no longer necessary.

Although the old town fascinated me, I did not go into it, as it was being shelled. I had seen too much shell-fire for the past week; enough to last me for my life-time! I knew the town well. In June I had rambled from house to house with poor old Jim Marsland. We had roamed through the Cloth Hall and the Cathedral, and into the Church of St Martin's where all the vestments were lying about, covered in the powder of high explosive shells. Behind the altar, Marsland had raked out the second foundation coin, dated in the sixteenth century. It was a find gold plaque and he gave it to an old Abbe who was there salving what he could between the shell-fire. Graves of British soldiers lined the ramparts south of the Lille Gate. I returned to our billeting line, and Macartney had dinner with me, as I had the night off from working parties, Caulfield and 'Cherrie' having taken the Company up to Hooge.

[FCH]

19TH AUGUST

Had a long walk all round the Ramparts. There was no doubt that Ypres had been a beautiful city before the Boches started shelling it. Some of the houses had gabled fronts of timber; it was surrounded on three sides by high Ramparts, which looked very grim and forbidding from the canal bank, and above all rose the battered remnants of the Cloth Hall and the tower of St Martin's Cathedral. Only one of the old Gothic pinnacles remained of the famous tower of the Cloth Hall. Below lay the broad moat into which shells were plunging every few minutes. Except for the khaki figures which were darting in and out of the Ramparts, and the scream of the shells as they passed overhead to explode in the centre of the city, Ypres was a city of the dead.

[FCH]

Above, left: The Lille Gate, 1917. A British Officer (note riding boots and swagger stick) looks out over the calm of the moat. What seems to be a line of washing in the centre of the photograph is more probably a camouflage screen, hiding an exposed portion of the road on the far bank from the always interested observation of German gunners. [IWM]

Below, left: Shrapnel Corner, 30th October 1917. 1st Anzac Corps. The flatness of the countryside can readily be seen here for the ruins of Ypres are in the distance, the tower of the Cloth Hall to the left. [IWM]

Above, right: Moat and Ramparts, summertime 1968.

Below, right: Shrapnel Corner today.

At about 9 am we left our temporary sanctuary, l'Ecole de Ypres, and marched back to the company lines, via the Cloth Hall Square, the men still in bare feet and 1 in pyjamas! When we got back we found a shocking sight. Two more shells had landed slap into our dug-out lines, completely obliterating eight dug-outs, which, worse luck, were occupied. Sergt Price and Sergt Molloy, the sergeant cook, Privates Casey, Martin, Ross, Rutledge, and Reynolds had been killed, two of whom had been blown into the trees overhead, as no trace of them could be found, although we had the men digging up the earth all round the shell craters. Pte Griffin was so badly wounded that he died later, and Pte Prendergast of Piper's platoon had his leg off, and Pte Johnston of B Company had his arm hanging on by a piece of skin. Four others, including COMS Wall, were badly wounded. Total casualties eight killed and six wounded. B Company's HQ dug-out was completely blown up, including all Ducat's clothes. Our mess had also disappeared. We afterwards discovered that at 6.30 am a Boche aeroplane had come close over our dug-outs and had spotted the men out in the middle of this amphitheatre 'drumming up their char', and the Company cookers, which Molloy had left standing right in the road opposite our lines! It was a very sad sight, all these stout fellows lying out in a row waiting for the stretcher-bearers to take them off to the cemetery. Some of them hadn't a scratch on their bodies, and had been killed by concussion.

[FCH]

18TH AUGUST

We got up at about 11 am for breakfast. We were in dug-outs which were built tier upon tier, dug a re-entrant into the Ramparts beside the Lille Gate. Caulfield, 'Cherrie', and I shared a large dug-out, with beds taken out of the abandoned houses in the vicinity. B Company had their mess dug-out just opposite. Our mess was a kind of summer-house on the top of the Ramparts! We lazed about in the sun all day, and watched one of our 4.2 batteries getting crumped. At night 'Cherrie' and I brought the Company up to Hooge, to work for the North Staffords. I dug a new line in front of H 12 near the culvert. The North Staffords got bombed all night. A high explosive burst beside Corpl Sweeny and myself, knocking us down and covering us with earth. After midnight we had finished our task, and marched back along the Menin railway lines to the Lille Gate. It was very dark, and the men, utterly fatigued, kept stumbling and falling on the sleepers.

[FCH]

SECOND YPRES

After a winter huddled in flooded trenches or behind crumbling breastworks with little shelter from the elements and incessant shellfire, our troops in Flanders welcomed the first signs of spring. For months they had endured the appalling conditions with disciplined stoicism even though tours in the line often meant standing for hours – even days – up to their thighs and sometimes their waists, in muddy, bitterly cold water, conditions which made 'trench foot' commonplace.

Spring, however, heralded better times. Spring meant warmth and a change from the gloom of the flat, sodden countryside. The days grew longer and birds fluttered above the shell-holes and sang in the woods which had not yet become shattered stumps. The sap began to rise and life stirred anew despite the omnipresence of sudden death.

In the northern sector, the evening of Thursday 22nd April was calm and pleasant. Two days earlier though a warning of 'something to come' had been foreshadowed by the sudden bombardment of Ypres with German heavy guns. Huge shells burst with thunderous crashes in the Grand Place and amongst the buildings. The Cloth Hall was hit repeatedly and the frightened inhabitants of the doomed town hurriedly packed their belongings and left or cowered in cellars or other shelters which often became their tombs. No-one was aware of what that cannonade portended or the ghastly surprise that was in store for the Allies – a surprise that very nearly gave the Germans an important victory that could have proved crucial.

On 22nd April 1915, the northern part of the Salient was held by French troops of mainly colonial (Algerian) origin. On their right were the 3rd and 2nd Brigades of the Canadian Division (1st Brigade in reserve); farther right was the British 28th Division at the apex of the Salient (including Broodseinde) and then the British 27th Division.

At about 1730 hours on the 22nd, after heavy shelling of the French areas, British observers noted a mysterious cloud moving slowly across the French trenches helped by a light wind from the north-east. This phenomenon was duly reported, followed immediately by the news that Allied soldiers could be seen running to the rear. As dusk fell and enormous shells continued to tear out the heart of Ypres, terror-stricken French North African troops staggered along the roads to the city coughing and vomiting up blood and froth. Many fell on the roads and in the fields and ditches as they fled weaponless from the unknown horror. Field guns and other equipment littered the battlefield as gun-crews and others whipped horses into a frantic gallop away from the area. Roads became blocked with men and transport. Panic reigned supreme.

This first use of poison gas on the Western Front, it has been said, was initially condemned by the Kaiser but he was nevertheless, swayed by his advisers and his generals to allow its use. Surprise was complete yet Allied commanders (certainly the French and Belgians) had in fact received prior notice of the existence of this weapon – particularly from a German prisoner – but had ignored

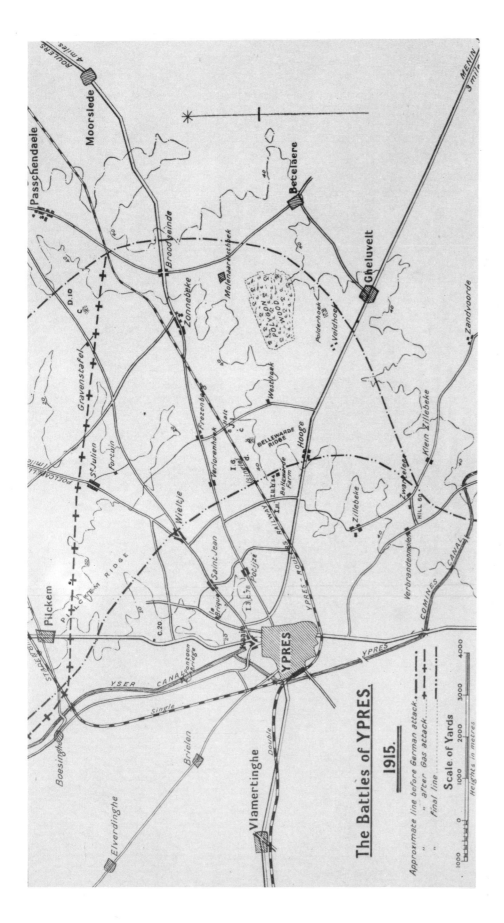

The Battles of YPRES.
1915.

Approximate line before German attack. —·—·—
" " after Gas attack ....++++
" " final line —·—·—·—

Scale of Yards

Heights in metres

[Map from *The Die-Hards in The Great War* by kind permission of Colonel F. Walden, DL, Secretary, Regimental Association of the Middlesex Regiment].

the threat. Not for the first time the troops bore the brunt of higher blunders. Thousands were blinded and thousands more died in dreadful agony while their bursting lungs gasped painfully for air. Worse still, from a strategic point of view, the line has been rent asunder, and a five-mile gap opened up. The enemy began to pour through. The way to Ypres was wide open, and the situation highly dangerous.

To the eternal credit of the Canadians, it was they who held fast until British reinforcements arrived with sorely needed help. Moreover, the Canadian 3rd Brigade which had also suffered to some degree from the effects of the gas, (although not as badly as the French) actually put in a counter-attack with the support of two of their reserve battalions. This was at a point east of the little village of St Julian known as Kitchener's Wood in which were located four captured British 4.7 howitzers. After a wild night struggle, the wood was carried and the guns recaptured. Owing to tremendous enemy pressure they were lost again but not before the pieces had been rendered unserviceable.

All night long the Canadians tenaciously held on against overwhelming numbers, but their left flank was exposed and they had no protection from the poisonous fumes (apart from a wet cloth tied around the nose and mouth). Struggling for breath, constantly bombarded, they were slowly forced to give ground, and, in spite of the arrival of British reinforcements, were eventually driven out to a new line through St Julian itself.

Another British force was rushed into the gap on the Canadians' left. It consisted of a mixture of units hastily assembled from all parts of the line and was commanded by Colonel Geddes of the Buffs. This makeshift unit became famous as 'Geddes Detachment' and it filled the gap bravely to the glory of the eight battalions involved – these being half of the 3rd Middlesex, about the same number of 2nd Shropshires, 4th Rifle Brigade, 2nd Cornwalls, 9th Royal Scots, 2nd Buffs, 1st Yorks and Lancasters, and 5th Lancasters. By regularly committing limited numbers of troops from each battalion an impression was given of continuous counter-offensive, thus giving others from the detachment an opportunity to prepare a new line in the rear. Few of the attackers lived to see the dawn and indeed one company of the Buffs disappeared entirely; many others paid a similar price for their bravery but all sold their lives dearly.

All that day, Friday, 23rd April, a mere 2,000 men covering a front 8,000 yards long barred the passage to Ypres. Once more the enemy was denied that beleaguered city.

It was not over yet. At about 0300 on the morning of Saturday, 24th April a violent bombardment commenced and half-an-hour later a second great cloud of gas was spread from cylinders within the German trenches. Once again the filthy poison reached the Allied trenches and this time the much weakened 3rd Canadian Brigade was compelled to fall back. A massive German attack was then ranged against the village of St Julian. Two battalions of the 2nd Brigade fought throughout the night until every man was killed, wounded, or taken. On Saturday the remnants of the 3rd Brigade were withdrawn followed on Sunday by the survivors of the 2nd. On the 29th April what was left of the Canadian Division was withdrawn from the Salient. Outflanked, outgunned, and stupified by gas they refused to break. Two Canadian Brigades together with the handful of British soldiers completely frustrated the attempt of four enemy divisions to take Ypres.

Second Ypres continued well into May with gas being used on numerous occasions, but that Friday, 23rd April, – St George's Day – was the most critical time of all. Colonel Geddes was killed a few days later but died with the knowledge that the mission entrusted to him had been successfully accomplished. The toll was heavy, and by the time Second Ypres finally ground to a halt the British had lost over 57,000 men killed, wounded and missing. Many too continued to suffer from the frightful effects of gassing, with seared internal organs, injuries from which some of them never fully recovered. In addition the perimeter of the Salient shrank by about two miles thus making that already battered town an even easier prey of the German artillery, and guns of all calibres continuing to pour in shells for over three more years from the arc of high ground surrounding Ypres.

The enemy was also grievously hurt. His casualties were at least as heavy as those of the Allies but, more importantly, his inhuman action aroused a fury in the hearts of the British soldiers and people, that bred a grim determination to continue the war to the bitter end.

The Memorial at Steenstraat, 1942. This memorial cross stood at the site of the first major gas attack in World War I. The inscription read:

To the dead
of the
418th infantry regiment
and to the first
victims of asphyxiating gas

The Yser Canal by the Steenstraat Bridge. On a pleasant evening in April 1915 choking clouds of gas crept forward over land and water at the commencement of Second Ypres. It was the first main gas attack of the war and was delivered by the Germans against French Colonial and Territorial troops. Later the opposing front lines were stabilised on opposite sides of the canal where they remained until Third Ypres in 1917. This photograph was taken looking in the direction of Boesinghe which was the left flank of the British front.

Above: St Julian. Crops being sprayed from a cylinder where in 1915 the ground was bleached by fumes sprayed from larger, more evil cylinders. These farmers will soon harvest their crops from fields where once death was the reaper.

Right: The Canadian Memorial at St Julian. This striking memorial commemorates the 2,000 Canadian victims of the first gas attacks in 1915. The Canadians were on the right of the French troops.

Below: Tablet let into the stonework of the column. The words are slightly misleading as the impression is given of the 2,000 victims being buried at the base of the memorial, which is not actually the case.

THIS·COLUMN·MARKS·THE
BATTLEFIELD·WHERE·18,000
CANADIANS·ON·THE·BRITISH
LEFT·WITHSTOOD·THE·FIRST
GERMAN·GAS·ATTACKS·THE
22=24ⁿᵈ·OF·APRIL·1915·2,000
FELL·AND·HERE·LIE·BURIED

STEENSTRAAT

These photographs are unique and as far as is known have never been published before. They were taken by a member of the German Occupation Forces in Belgium during the Second World War and show (1) the memorial being prepared for demolition (2) the actual explosion (3) the wrecked memorial after the main charge had been fired.

The monument, which was unveiled in 1929 in the presence of Belgian dignitaries, was blown up by the Germans on 8th May 1941 following an abortive attempt at partial destruction the day before. The mysterious disappearance of tools and explosives from the site during the night infuriated the German Commandant and led to accusations of sabotage. The unusual story behind this operation is that the Germans not only objected to the original monument which depicted the suffering and death caused through the introduction of poison gas by their predecessors in 1915, but refused to accept that they were the first to use this horror weapon. Orders were accordingly issued for the Belgians to obliterate the inscription on the memorial and also the agonised figures of asphyxiated soldiers. The Burgomaster of the district accordingly instructed civilian workers to cover the offending words with cement, but the senior German officer involved was not satisfied, for the accusing figures still remained. Because of this it was decided to destroy the monument completely and at 5.30 pm residents of the district heard a loud explosion as the stone-work shattered to pieces. Another version of the story suggests that, following the German complaints, arrangements were made for the whole monument to be thoroughly faced with cement and concrete. The Belgians however disobeyed instructions and used only a thin layer of cement that could easily be chipped off when their country was liberated. Unfortunately, due to deterioration by weather, the cement cracked and finally collapsed altogether causing the original carvings to once again become exposed. Following this the Germans decided to take no more chances and took the extreme measure already described.

[Photographs and principal details contributed by Monsieur Daniel of Ypres. (Photo Daniel)]

The Memorial Cross at Steenstraat, twenty-five years later. The cross still honours the memory of the 'first victims of asphyxiating gas'.

Above: *The Ypres-Boesinghe road* on the outskirts of that small town. On the right can be seen the memorial to the 49th West Riding Division surmounting the canal bank at Essex Farm Military Cemetery.

Above right: *A pleasant scene on the Yser Canal* by Essex Farm, north of Noordhofwijk, — a very different aspect compared to that described overleaf!

Right: Concrete shelters built into the canal bank at Essex Farm and which were used as a Dressing Station during Third Ypres.

F

Breakfast at 10 am. Splendid day. We were on the east side of the Yser Canal. Our dug-outs were built into the bank which overlooked the canal and led out on to the towpath. The canal was about fifty yards in breadth and about fifteen feet deep in the centre. It ran due north to Dixmude from Ypres, and was connected with the Ypres-Comines Canal at Kaai due north of the city. It had high banks on both sides, which were thickly belted by bushy-topped poplar trees. It ran parallel with the main road to Boesinghe, which was on its western side. The country was typically Flemish, barren wastes, fields of rotten corn, grass, or stubble, with dykes and ditches separating them. The ruins of old burnt-out homesteads were studded about here and there. The canal was crossed by four pontoons, one large one known as No 4 Bridge opposite Noordhofwijk, and three others of duckboard breadth only. The water was black and slimy. Padre Moloney and some men stripped and swam about in it. They had some nerve as it must have been very 'fruity' from corpses!

[FCH]

April 1915

Five Seaforth Highlanders
Believed to be buried in this cemetery.

At Essex Farm a German Gotha dropped a splinter bomb right on a lorry . . . There were many casualties.

[WF Chapman]

THE CENTRE SECTOR

The Menin Road – highway of fear. An aerial view of the long, straight road and the surrounding shell-pocked countryside. Hell Fire Corner can be seen on the lower right and in the top centre are Birr cross-roads and Hooge. Bellewaarde Lake is at the top left. [IWM].

When we left the Menin Road and took to the duckboards at a time when the enemy placed a barrage on them, the most careless of us cursed the man in front of him if he happened to pause a minute. It seemed the best solace for excited nerves to keep going, no matter whether into or out of danger. Yet, luck stood by us; in spite of our over-zealous artillery, not a shell dropped near us until we reached our trenches, and then we had it stiff. A sergeant and two privates were blown to pieces twenty yards from me: all that night and early morning we lay in the shallow trench, trying vainly to keep knees from shaking and teeth from chattering, with a deadly sick feeling in the stomach as bits of shrapnel hit the side of the trench with a dull thud and earth was shaken over our fence. I tried to sleep, but nervous excitement kept me awake all day until night, when we dug out a new trench. While plying the spade, I encountered what looked like a branch sticking out of the sand. I hacked and hacked at it until it fell severed, and I was picking it up prior to throwing it over the parapet when a sickness, or rather nausea, came over me. It was a human arm.

[HQ]

I am right in the thick of it again, in this historic place which I shall describe some time. When I think of the glorious weather, sunlight shimmering in a molten sky and slow winds just breathing over the wilderness of shell-holes, it seems so hard throwing it all aside for an uncertain end. Yet it must be done. Perhaps Fate may have some kindness in store for me. Last night I had a strangely poignant dream: I was lying in hospital, trying madly to move my legs, both tied down in splints, and biting my lips to overcome pain coming from the right groin. A comfortable wound might be the outcome of this premonition. Let us hope so: then I can see again the Old Country I had given up for lost, hear the old voices, look at the friendly glad faces.

[HQ]

Menin Road Cemetery, October 1916. Graves of officers, NCO's and men of the 8th Staffs grouped around a water-filled shell hole. [IWM].

Menin Road Military Cemetery. A beautiful, green, close-cut sward. The grave of Private F.W. Dicken (see above) is in the centre foreground.

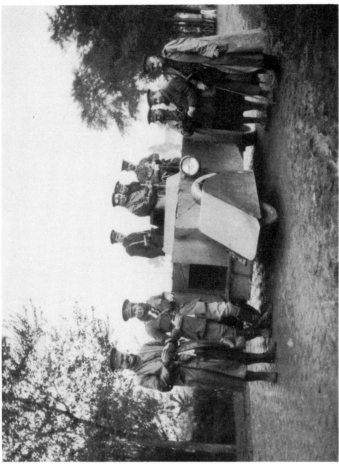

First Battle of Ypres, 1914. Naval armoured car on the Menin Road at a spot which afterwards became known as Hell Fire Corner. This photograph was taken on the 14th October, the day on which the 2nd Battalion of the Scots Guards marched into Ypres from Roulers. Part of the battalion did not go into Ypres, but turned off along the Menin Road to bivouac in a chateau. A party of Uhlans were seen in the distance and were immediately fired at, said to be the first shots fired by the 7th Division during the war. The car seen in the photograph rushed forward on hearing the shots, but no further action ensued. With its exposed radiator, pneumatic tyres, and vulnerable head-lamp, the armoured car (probably an old Daimler) seems naive by today's standards.

The faces of the men, confident and cheerful, seem naive too in hindsight of what the next four years was to bring them. [IWM].

First Battle of Ypres, 1914. HQ of the 2nd Scots Guards. The White Chateau (west of Hell Fire Corner). [IWM].

The Chateau now on the site of the original White Chateau which was completely destroyed.

The fields of Bellewaarde Ridge. The Princess Pat's Memorial on the ridge where desperate fighting took place. The tablet is inscribed:

Here in May 1915
The 'Originals' of
Princess Patricia's Canadian Light Infantry
Commanded by the Founder
Major A. Hamilton Gault D.S.O.
Held firm and counted not the cost.

10TH AUGUST 1915

Germans attempted a counter-attack, but were driven back. All the gains were held with the exception of A3, a trench running towards Bellwaarde Farm, which had to be vacated owing to enfilade fire. At 6.30 we got orders to move up to Hooge to work under the Sappers, Barnett and two platoons of A Company being attached to us. Marched off by platoons at 200 paces interval, and at the Water Tower we drew picks and shovels from one of our GS wagons. A few shells fell as we marched on through Ypres. When crossing the square we passed companies of the 2nd York and Lancs returning from Hooge to rest. Quite a number of them had German helmets stuck on the end of their rifles as souvenirs. They yelled out 'Good luck, Micks.' We were the only Irish regiment in the 6th Division. It was quite dark when we got to Birr cross roads. Shrapnell burst over us when crossing the railway line at Hell Fire Corner without inflicting any casualties.

Hell Fire Corner was a station of 'halt' on the Ypres-Menin road, the railway lines crossing it in the Roulers direction. It was also an important cross-roads, which led off to Potijze and Zillebeke, and the enemy was, therefore, perpetually shelling this junction. A few houses, and a small chapel, had once stood close by, but only a few heaps of red bricks remained, and a Crucifix, or Calvary, as the peasants called it, which stood up intact amidst the debris of brick and timber. We made a fine job of a communication trench, which ran parallel with the Menin Road, and a support line called H 12, near the culvert. Throughout our task we were heavily shelled. At 2 am we formed up and marched back to Ypres, where we billeted in dug-outs on the Ramparts beside the Menin Gate.

[FCH]

Just as we got back from the working party at 2.30 am it started to rain heavily, and we got soaked through. I thanked my lucky stars that I had made my batman, McCafferty, roof my dug-out with a sheet of corrugated iron the day before. Algeo came up to my dug-out as his had been flooded out, and he was drenched. It rained a deluge for hours; the men's dug-outs caved in one by one, and their rations and packs were carried away down the slope. This torrential rain created a young river in the trench.

The rain stopped at 8 am and the line, or what was left of it, was in a terrible state. We spent the morning draining the trench by digging big sump pits. In one place I had the parapet pulled down, and let the water off down the slope towards English Farm.

[FCH]

Death at Hell Fire Corner. Dead horses and wrecked wagon, the result of a direct hit by a German 5.9-inch Howitzer. Hell Fire Corner, Menin Road, 15th September 1917. [IWM].

Life at Hell Fire Corner – September 1967.

JULY 1915

The enemy had three captive balloons up observing our lines. At 7 pm when at dinner, we were all suddenly thrown on the ground by a colossal vibration. Getting up, we rushed out of the dug-out, to see, as it seemed, the whole of Hooge in the air!

A mine had been sprung by the 3rd Division, right under the German lines. The whole area had become quite dark, and we could still see the debris and earth falling from the sky from the explosion. The mine had made a deafening roar. Simultaneously, all our batteries opened. We then saw our troops getting out of their trenches and attacking in extended order. They disappeared into a great cloud of smoke, which was lit up now and then by the bursting of shrapnel shells. The Huns resented this bit of frightfulness on our part, and retaliated on all our front lines and back areas, 'crumping' Railway and Potijze Woods considerably.

We next saw our supports going up through Railway Wood in artillery formation towards the Bellewaarde Ridge. The objective for the attack was the enemy line which ran along the crest of this ridge from Bellewaarde Farm to Hooge inclusive. Then the rattle of musketry and staccato of machine-guns firing could be heard above the bursting of the shells. Within a short time the hiatus seemed to die down at Hooge, the 3rd Division had captured their objectives. This was a most successful attack and brilliantly carried out. In the fighting the 2nd Battalion Royal Irish Rifles* greatly distinguished themselves.

The mine made a record crater right beneath the enemy front line, which included a strongly held redoubt. One hundred and forty-five dead Germans were counted, and many more were killed by the 1st Gordon Highlanders as they were endeavouring to extricate themselves from the debris of shattered woodwork and earth. Throughout the attack we were severely shelled. Every minute one of our well-revetted parapets went sky-high. However, our traverses being very formidable, afforded us great cover. Although

we were bombarded for six hours, and our trenches were blown in in many places, yet the company had only one casualty! The Machine-Gun Section lost some men; one gunner who was up in Stink Post had his head blown off. The 3rd Rifle Brigade had some knocked out, and I met Padre Talbot going up to administer the last rites of the Church to the mortally wounded.

[FCH]

[*Now Royal Ulster Rifles]

80

A famous photograph. Hell Fire Corner was the most dangerous spot in a dangerous area, where no-one ever loitered. It was at the junction of the Menin Road with the Potijze-Zillebeke Road close to the Ypres-Roulers railway crossing. The German gunners knew the range to a yard and it was suicidal to waste time in passing this unhealthy location, as can be sensed by the urgency of the men and horses in the foreground. Camouflage screens stand to the left behind the 'Hell Fire Corner' notice which is on the same spot as the marker in the photograph below. [IWM].

Hell Fire Corner today (with the only danger being fast moving cars.) In the foreground is a small monument which marks the furthermost point reached by the enemy during the Battle of the Lys (1918) when all the ground won by our troops during Third Ypres — at such enormous cost — was given up virtually overnight and our lines were withdrawn to the very outskirts of the town. At no time before had our trenches been so close to the city or the enemy so near to his original goal except for a brief period in 1914 when some of his cavalry had passed through on reconnaissance patrol. The horizon marks the slight ridge along which the trenches were situated for so long and where so much bitter fighting took place. Chateau Wood is at the top left and Sanctuary Wood is on the distant right. The tiny hamlet of Hooge stands where the road fades into the distance.

THE ROAD TO HOOGE

On parade! get your spade,
fall in the pick & shovel Bde,
there's a 'carry-fatigue'
for half a league
and a trench to dig
with a spade:

Through the dust and ruin
of Ypres town,
and the 17"
still battering down
sprewing death
with it's fiery breath
on the red red road to Hooge.

Who is the one
whose time has come,
who won't return
when the work is done?
Who will leave his bones
on the blood-stained stones
on the red red road to Hooge.

Onward the Artillery
and 'not at the trot'
to the camouflaged guns
right up at the top;
though a 'packet' you may stop
on the red red road to Hooge.

The burst and the roar
of the 5-9 grenade
welcomed you on
to the death parade,
the pit of gloom
at the crater down at Hooge

List to the 'Stand
to fusilade'
sling your rifles
bring your spade,
and get away
before break of day
on the red red road to Hooge.

Call the Roll
and another name
is sent to fill
the 'Roll of Fame'
so we carve a cross
to mark the loss
of a Chum who fell at Hooge.

Not a deed
for the Press to write
no glorious charge
in the dawning light
and the Press who wait
won't tell the tale
of the night work out at Hooge

But, our General knows
and his praise we've won
and he's pleased with the work
that the boys have done,
in the shot and shell
at the gate of Hell
on the red red road to Hooge.

[Contributed by H.A. Bigel Esq.]

The Menin Road — September 1917. Shell-blasted trees, dead horses, and debris-strewn verges amidst fields of death. [IWM].

The Menin Road today: A broad smooth asphalt highway bounded by green cultivated fields and leafy trees.

Shell dumps at Birr cross-roads, 17th October 1917. A working party dismounts from an old Manchester. The actual cross-roads may be seen behind the two soldiers on the left.

The holes in the bottom of the shells fitted a special spanner which was used to screw on the baseplates after the charge had been inserted. The rings on the ends of the shells were used for carrying; they were unscrewed and replaced by fuses when the shell was to be fired.

The anti-aircraft gun in the background and the strained skyward attention of the party on the right suggest that the area may have been under aerial observation. [IWM].

The Menin Road at Birr cross-roads. The German front line was at the top of the slight incline in the far distance. This point was named after the Regimental Depot of the Leinster Regiment, one of the five Southern Irish regiments disbanded in 1922 following the establishment of the Irish Free State. Leinster Farm, so named by the 1st Battalion, is close by on the Zillebeke road.

84

The enemy blew a mine at Hooge and attacked. Their attack was a failure, but all night long there was tremendous activity; shells, bombs, star-shells, and bursts of rapid fire. I saw one of our aeroplanes brought down near Birr cross roads. Corpl Coghlan and I went out on patrol, and on our return got some rum which we brought out to the listening posts. (These listening posts consisted of a NCO, 2 bayonet men, and a bomber.)

[FCH]

The Mine Craters of Bellewaarde
Right: Aerial view of an area where mining and violent death were commonplace. Bitter fighting took place on the Bellewaarde Ridge, particularly during 1915, and in the area of Railway Wood — Hooge. This location had an evil repute and was hated by our soldiers who fought there. [IWM].

Below right: Cross of Sacrifice near a mine crater with Railway Wood in the background and the spires of Ypres in the left distance. This is known as the 'R.E. Grave, Railway Wood' and on the base of the cross are inscribed the words, 'Beneath this spot lie the bodies of an officer, three NCO's and eight men of, or attached to, 177th Tunnelling Company, Royal Engineers, who were killed in action underground during the defence of Ypres between November 1915 and August 1917.'

Below left: A line of craters stretches from the foreground towards Belle-waarde Farm which can be seen at the rear.

the barricade, so that the Huns could not approach this post under cover. Within fifteen yards of our barricade the enemy switched off their old front line into their old support line. Throughout the night, the enemy were very offensive with bombs and snipers. We did not retaliate, as we were too busily employed reversing the parapets, making fire-steps and deepening the trench everywhere, as we were anticipating a bombardment and a counter-attack on the morrow.

The place reeked with the smell of decomposed bodies. They lay about in hundreds, on top of the parapets, in our trenches, in No-Man's-Land, and behind the parados. The British dead mostly belong to the 2nd York and Lancs, and the 2nd DLI. The dug-outs were full of dead Germans, those that were not, two only, were strengthened for occupation. While we were working bullets spat viciously all round, and we had several casualties.

[FCH]

At 7 pm we marched off for Hooge in battle order, each man carried sand-bags, and a pick or shovel. We got to the front line at Hooge after a rough journey under shell-fire, over dead men and round countless shell-holes. At 11 pm we had taken over the Hooge sector and the mine crater from the 1st Battalion, The Buffs-16th Brigade. The order of the Battalion in the line was C and D Companies front line, with A and B in support and reserve. We had hardly taken over the line, when the Huns attacked our left flank, which was exposed. However, Algeo had posted the Company Bombers there, and with a handful of men armed with jam-tin bombs, succeeded in beating them back. By the light of the moon and the glow from the green-white star-shells one could make out the course of the trenches of both sides, and could just distinguish the serpentine course of the German lines running along the near side of the Bellewaarde or Chateau Wood, only fifty yards away. The leafless trees stood out in their shattered forms, and behind them was the lake reflecting the moonlight.

D Company connected with the 1st Royal Fusiliers, who held the line running through the Zouave Wood. My left flank was in the air, a barricade only separating us from the Germans. We actually shared our front line with the enemy! How this strange fact came about was as follows: The continuation of our front line running up the Bellewaarde ridge which had been captured by the 16th Brigade on the 9th had to be abandoned the same evening, as the trench was untenable owing to the enfilade fire which caused terrible havoc to the troops holding it. This enfilade fire came from the German positions on the high ground, on the extreme left flank at Bellewaarde Farm.

The 16th Brigade, therefore, evacuated this enfiladed section and erected a strong, sand-bagged barrier in the trench with a good field of fire. After about twelve hours, the Huns cautiously worked their way along their old front line, from Bellewaarde Farm, and found that our troops had withdrawn. After the bombing attack had been successfully repulsed, Algeo and his bombers flattened out the old German parapets, and filled in the trench in front of

Hooge in March 1917. The Menin Road (or what was left of it at that point) can be seen running from the bottom left to the top right of the photograph and the ground is criss-crossed with trenches. Bellewaarde Lake is at the top centre.

Hooge was probably the worst section of the whole salient and it was there that the British experienced the first German liquid fire attack which resulted in the death, in a counter-attack, of Gilbert Talbot (after whom 'TOC H' was named). [IWM]

Above left:
Near Hooge Crater and looking along Bellewaarde Ridge towards Railway Wood. This ground was once covered with trenches, barbed wire and bodies, soaked with blood and saturated with gas, constantly swept with machine-gun fire and high explosives.

Below left:
Hooge Crater Military Cemetery, which holds the remains of nearly 6000 soldiers, over 3500 of whom are unidentified. The cemetery is located approximately to the right of the dark bean shaped patch in the upper photo-graph.

Dawn broke at 4 am and within half an hour I had two casualties. Pte Bowes was killed by an explosive bullet in the head, and Pte Duffey was wounded by an enfilade bullet from the Bellewaarde Farm. We buried Bowes in a disused trench behind our line. One could now make out the country all round perfectly, and what an appalling sight it was. Everywhere lay the dead. The ridge in our rear was covered with dead men who had been wiped out in the final assault on the German position; their faces were blackened and swollen from the three days' exposure to the August sun, and quite unrecognisable. Some of the bodies were badly dismembered; here and there a huddled up heap of khaki on the brink of a shell-crater told of a direct hit. Haversacks, tangled heaps of webbing equipment, splintered rifles, and broken stretchers, lay scattered about. The ground was pitted with shell-holes of all sizes. A few solitary stakes and strands of barbed wire were all that was left of the dense mass of German entanglements by our artillery. Several khaki figures were hanging on these few strands in hideous attitudes. In front of us, in No-Man's-Land, lay a line of our dead, and ahead of them on the German parapet lay a DLI officer. They had advanced too far, and had got caught by a withering machine-gun fire from the Bellewaarde Wood. There was not a blade of grass to be seen in No Man's Land or on the ridge, the ground had been completely churned up by the shells, and any of the few patches of grass which had escaped had been burnt up by the liquid fire. Some fifty yards away, around the edge of the German Bellewaarde Wood, ran the sand-bagged parapet of the German line on its serpentine course towards the shattered remains of Hooge.

The wood itself had suffered severely from the shell-fire. Most of the trees were badly splintered, and some had been torn up by the roots. There was little foliage to be seen on any of the trees. All that was left of the once bushy topped trees which lined the Menin Road were shattered stumps, and the telegraph poles stood drunkenly at all angles. Although numbers of the Durhams and the York and Lancs lay about in the open, yet our trench was full of

German dead belonging to the Wurtembergers.

They lay in the dug-outs, where they had gone to seek refuge from our guns, in fours and in fives. Some had been killed by concussion, others had had their dug-outs blown in on top of them and had suffocated. Our gunners had done their work admirably, and the strong cover made with railway lines and sleepers and with trunks of trees had collapsed under the fierce onslaught of our shells. The faces of the enemy dead, who had thus been caught or pinned down by the remnants and shattered timber of their death-traps, wore agonised expressions.

Here and there, where portions of the trench had been obliterated by the shells, legs and arms in the German field-grey uniform stuck out between piles of sand-bags. Thousands of rounds of fired and unexpended cartridges lay about the parapets, and ground into the bottom of the trench. German Mausers, equipment, helmets, and their peculiar skin-covered packs lay everywhere. The ground was littered with portions of the enemy uniforms saturated in blood. Serving in the Ypres salient one was not unaccustomed to seeing men blown to pieces and, therefore, I expected to see bad sights on a battle-field, but I had never anticipated such a dreadful and desolate sight as Hooge presented, and I never saw anything like it again during my service at the front. The reason that Hooge was such a particularly bloody battle-field was due to the fact that it covered such a small area in the most easterly portion of the salient, and was not spread out over miles of open country like those battle-fields on the Somme in 1916. Hooge had been continually under shell-fire since the First Battle of Ypres in October, and the ridge which we had dug into had been captured and recaptured five times since April.

At 3 pm exactly, the enemy started a second bombardment of our line. All along our trench they put down a terrific barrage of shells of every description. High explosives and crumps exploded on our parapets, leaving burning and smoking craters, and torn flesh, and above, screeching and whining shrapnel burst over us. We were shelled from all sides by guns of every calibre. We could not have been in a worse position, and it seemed that every enemy gun around the Salient was turned on to our 400 yards of trench-on the left of the Menin Road. Shells from the Bellewaarde direction enfiladed us, and blew in our few traverses; shells from Hill 60 direction ploughed great rifts in our parados, and broke down our only protection from back-bursts, and now and then some horrible fragments of mortality were blown back from the ridge with lyddite wreaths.

The whole place had become quite dark from the shells and the clouds of earth which went spouting up to the sky. We could barely see twenty yards ahead throughout this terrible tornado of fire. Our casualties increased at such a rapid rate that we were all greatly alarmed, our trench had ceased to exist as such and the enemy shrapnel caused dreadful havoc amongst the practically exposed company. L/Corpl Leonard, Privates Keenan, McKenna, Digan, and Shea of my platoon had been hit, and Algeo got a direct hit on his platoon, killing 6032 Pte Fay, and 3642 Pte Lysaght, and wounding Privates Healy and Rattigan badly, and four of his NCO's. If this went on much longer, the Boches would walk into our position without any opposition, as we would all be casualties. The shells came down with tantalising regularity, which was nerve-racking.

The blackened bodies of our dead, and the badly wounded, lay about at the bottom of the trench, and it was impossible to move without treading on them. Every few minutes the call for the stretcher bearers would be heard. Then along came Morrissey with his first-aid bag, closely followed by Reid. 'Steady, me lad,' they'd say to a man who had lost his leg, but could still feel the toes of the lost limb tingling, ''tis a grand cushy one you've got. Sure you're grand entirely, and when darkness sets in we'll carry you off to the dressing station, and then ye'll get your ticket for Blighty.' How they stuck it, those company stretcher bearers, Morrissey, Reid, Dooley, and Neary. White men all! Sometimes a direct hit on the parapet would bury the occupants.

A most demoralising effect is that of being smothered in sandbags. Twice I emerged out of a heap of demolished sand-bags to find men hit on either side of me. It was extraordinary how one got to know and understand the men under shell-fire.

It was exasperating, sitting there getting crumped to blazes, while our own guns kept silent. Nothing puts more life into weary troops under a fierce bombardment than the sound of their own shells screaming over them, but ours were obviously saving their ammunition to repel a counter-attack.

Suddenly and unexpectedly our guns from away back at Ypres started firing. The enemy must have been massing for a counter-attack. 'Swish, swish, swish, bang, bang, bang,' over went out shells, crashing on the enemy parapets. They went so low over us that we imagined they were hitting our own parapets. Shells of all calibres burst over the Boches' lines. The noise of them split our ears, and we all felt quite dazed by the brain-racking concussions. This retaliation was perfect, and cheered us immensely. Our howitzers raised great columns of earth and debris from the enemy trenches into the sky. The trees of the Bellewaarde Wood were being blown into the air and across the enemy parapets. Shells fell into the Chateau lake, and sent the water spouting up like fountains.

A battery of French .75's lent to the Division was also in action. Their discharges were so rapid that they sounded as if they came from some supernatural machine-gun, their trajectory being low, it seemed that these wonderful .75's passed close over our heads. The German lines on our left and in front were covered in a cloud of green lyddite fumes. What pleased us more than anything was that the Huns were showing unmistakable signs of 'wind up', behind this curtain of smoke and fire we saw their SOS rockets shooting up all along his front to Hooge! Evidently they expected us to attack. We, who had lost 65 men out of 120 (strength of the three platoons in the front line) within the last seven hours!

As suddenly as the bombardment had opened at 3 pm it ceased at 5.30 pm. We all stood to, and Sergt Bennett mounted the tripod of

his wounds. Jim Marsland came round the line and visited the bombing post. I went along to see Orpen-Palmer, and found him asleep in a fire bay, with two days' growth on his face. Shaving was out of the question. Later, he woke up, and he, Macartney, and I sat chatting in an old dug-out for some time. D Company's advanced post at the crater captured two men of the 132nd Wurtembergers, and they were brought round to Company Headquarters to be interrogated by Macartney, who spoke German fluently.

[FCH]

his Vickers on a hastily built emplacement. But the Germans did not leave their lines. It appeared that they counted on us evacuating the position owing to the intense shell fire.

Right along the Company front, the men and the slightly wounded stood to arms for some time in case an enemy attack should materialise. The bombardment was over; everything was very calm except for the rumbling of artillery engaged in counter-battery work. One of our aeroplanes flew up from Ypres and across the lines towards Menin, to observe and direct fire for our gunners. Having posted night sentries, we attended to the wounded and buried the dead. We were all thirsty, and our water-bottles were empty, but not hungry, although we had had no food whatsoever since we had left Ypres the night before. The sickening stench of the charred human flesh had driven away all pangs of hunger. The men of the Company were very bitter to think they had been shelled all day by an invisible foe, and had lost some of their best pals, without a chance of retaliation. Nothing would have pleased C and D Companies more than an order for attack on the 132nd Wurtembergers.

With the exception of sniping everything was calm until 9.30 pm, when the Boches launched a fierce bombing attack on our left flank, which was still in the air. They surrounded our small post and hurled bombs into it. I opened rapid fire on my left front to help Algeo, and prevented the Huns from coming further up on the outside of the trench. Algeo and his half-dozen bombers did wonders. With cigarettes in their mouths for lighting the fuses of their jam-tin bombs, they drove back over thirty Huns armed with Krupp's latest pattern bomb. Some of this gallant little band were wounded by bomb splinters, but they refused to leave Algeo.

Sergt Flaherty got a bullet through the ear, but remained on duty with his 'souvenir shot' as he called it. 8212 Brown got a bullet through the neck.

The Boches seemed to have suffered equally from the bombardment and through a periscope I watched some Huns in their shirt-sleeves mending their parapets. I heard that O'Neill had died of

Baron Yves de Vinck, owner of the present Hooge Chateau, standing on the site of the original Chateau which was utterly destroyed.

The Baron remembers returning to the area of his former home when not a blade of grass was to be seen and in all directions was complete desolation as far as the eye could see.

For a while after the war the de Vinck family lived in wooden huts by the side of the Hooge crater. Eventually the whole area was re-forested until now in fact the trees have to be thinned out.

HOOGE

It was not far out of Ypres, to the left of the Menin Road, and to the north of Zouave Wood and Sanctuary Wood. For a time there was a chateau there, called the White Chateau, with excellent stables, and good accommodation for one or our Brigade Staffs, until one of our generals was killed and others wounded by a shell which broke up their conference. Afterwards there was no chateau, but only a rubble of bricks banked up with sand-bags and deep mine-craters filled with stinking water slopping over from the Bellewaarde Lake and low-lying pools. Bodies, and bits of bodies, and clots of blood, and green, metallic-looking slime, made by explosive gases, were floating on the surface of that water below the crater banks when I first passed that way, and so it was always. Our men lived there and died there within a few yards of the enemy, crouched below the sand-bags and burrowed in the sides of the crater. Lice crawled over them in legions. Human flesh, rotting and stinking, mere pulp, was pasted into the mud-banks. If they dug to get deeper cover, their shovels went into the softness of dead bodies who had been their comrades. Scraps of flesh, booted legs, blackened hands, eyeless heads, came falling over them when the enemy tench-mortared their position or blew up a new mine-shaft.

[Realities of War, Philip Gibbs]

ATTACK ON HOOGE

The men deployed before dawn broke, waiting for the preliminary bombardment which would smash a way for them. The officers struck matches now and then to glance at their wrist-watches, set very carefully to those of the gunners. Then our artillery burst forth with an enormous violence of shell-fire, so that the night was shattered with the tumult of it. Guns of every calibre mingled their explosions, and the long screech of the shells rushed through the air as though thousands of engines were chasing each other madly through a vast junction in that black vault.

The men listened and waited. As soon as the guns lengthened their fuses the infantry advance would begin. Their nerves were getting jangled. It was just the torture of human animals . There was an indrawing of breath when suddenly the enemy began to fire rockets, sending up flares which made white waves of light. If they were seen, there would be a shambles.

The company officers blew their whistles, and there was a sudden clatter from trench-spades slung to rifle-barrels, and from men girdled with hand-grenades, as the advancing companies deployed and made their first rush forward. The ground had been churned up by our shells, and the trenches had been battered into shapelessness strewn with broken wire and heaps of loose stones and fragments of steel.

It seemed impossible that any Germans should be left alive in this quagmire, but there was still a rattle of machine-guns from holes and hillocks. Not for long. The bombing-parties searched, and found them, and silenced them. From the heaps of earth which had once been trenches, German soldiers rose and staggered in a dazed, drunken way, stupefied by the bombardment beneath which they had crouched.

Our men spitted them on their bayonets, or hurled hand-grenades and swept the ground before them. Some Germans screeched like pigs in a slaughter-house.

The men went on in short rushes. They were across the Menin

Road now, and were first to the crater, though other troops were advancing quickly from the left. They went down into the crater, shouting hoarsely, and hurling bombs at Germans, who were caught like rats in a trap, and scurried up the steep sides beyond, firing before rolling down again, until at least two hundred bodies lay at the bottom of this pit of hell.

While some of the men dug themselves into the crater or held the dug-outs already made by the enemy, others climbed up to the ridge beyond, and, with a final rush, almost winded and spent, reached the extreme limit of their line of assault and achieved the task which had been set them. They were mad now, not human in their senses. They saw red through bloodshot eyes. They were beasts of prey.

Round the stables themselves, three hundred Germans were bayoneted, until not a single enemy lived on this ground, and the light of day on 9th August revealed a bloody and terrible scene, not decent for words to tell. Not decent, but a shambles of human flesh, which had been a panic-stricken crowd of living men crying for mercy, with that dreadful screech of terror from German boys who saw the white gleam of steel at their stomachs before they were spitted. Not many of those lads remain alive now with that memory. The few who do must have thrust it out of their vision, unless at night it haunts them.

[Realities of War, Philip Gibbs]

Top right: *First Battle of Ypres, 1914.* The left wing of Hooge Chateau, as seen from the road. The destruction was caused by the bursting of an 11-inch shell, killing or wounding several staff officers, among whom was Colonel Percival. Baron Vinck the owner, had left the chateau a few moments before the shell burst.

Lower: *Hooge Chateau* during the early part of the war before it was totally destroyed. Right: *The rear of the rebuilt Chateau* which is not in exactly the same position as the original building. The tree on the right is one of three which grew from original trench support stakes.

HOOGE

Today the rebuilt Chateau stands amidst beautiful scenery and the vast mine crater has become a lovely lake nestled against a background of fine trees, green grass and shrubs. Old pieces of shrapnel can even now be picked up from the potato field of Baron de Vinck who owns the Chateau and surrounding land. Other small pieces of 'iron', which have worked their way to the surface, can also be collected without much difficulty although they have oxidised over the years and easily crumble into fragments. Other reminders of the past are two tall trees which grew from original trench support stakes.

Until a year or so ago, in another part of the estate, was a private memorial erected by the parents of an officer believed to have been killed at that spot. The cross previously stood by a huge shell hole but now rests outside the entrance to Sanctuary Wood Cemetery where it is tended by the Commonwealth War Graves Commission. Meanwhile, the shell-hole has merged into the vegetation of the garden as time and nature combine in healing the scars of war as they have done throughout the whole Salient.

The enemy were at Hooge too. From the diary of Friederich Kressis of the 6th Company, 132nd Regiment who helped in the capture of Hooge Chateau on 25th May 1915. Kressis was slightly wounded at Hooge on 16th June.

5.0 marched off to the Witches' Cauldron, Hooge. A terrible night again. HE and shrapnel without number. Oh, thrice cursed Hooge! In one hour 11 killed and 23 wounded and the fire unceasing. It is enough to drive one mad, and we have to spend three days and three nights here. It is worse than an earthquake, and anyone who has not experienced it can have no idea of what it is like. The English fired a mine, a hole 15 metres deep and 50 to 60 broad, and this 'cauldron' has to be occupied at night. At present it isn't too badly shelled. At every shot the dug-outs sway to and fro like weather-cocks. This life we have to stick for months. One needs nerves of steel and iron. Now I must crawl into our hole as trunks and branches of trees fly in our trench like spray.

Tonight moved to the crater again half running and half crawling. At seven a sudden burst of fire from the whole of the artillery. From about 11.00 yesterday evening we lie out in the sap on our stomachs whilst the artillery fires as if possessed. This morning at 4.00 we fall back. We find the 126th have no communications with the rear as the communication trenches have been completely blown in. The smoke and thirst are enough to drive one mad. Our cooker does not come up. The 126th give us bread and coffee from the little they have. If only it would stop! We get direct hits one after another and lie in a sort of dead-end cut off from all communication. If only it were night! What a feeling to be thinking every second when shall I get it! . . . has just fallen, the third man in our platoon. Since 8.00 the fire has been unceasing; the earth shakes and we with it. Will God ever bring us out of this fire? I have said the Lord's Prayer and am resigned.

One prisoner was badly wounded in the arm, and said he was afraid that we would shoot him. He said that on the 1st August his Regiment, the 132nd Wurtembergers, had been sent up to reinforce the 3rd Battalion of the 126th, as the latter had lost half their men in our bombardment. He complained bitterly of the accuracy of our shrapnel and the French ·75's. The FOO* for the Gunners was a very good fellow, belonging to the Territorials. He and I went along D Company's line to see the crater. What a sight we saw! At least two hundred German corpses in every imaginable shape and form; the place was one mass of torn and charred flesh!

The enemy had worked like ants in this vast mine crater since the 30th July, when they took it from the 14th Division. It resembled an ampitheatre, with its tiers of bomb-proof shelters scooped out of the crumbling sides of the chasm, and shored up with tree trunks.

But all shelters and dug-outs had collapsed under our terrific barrage on the 9th August. The 3rd Rifle Brigade were filling it in with chloride of lime. The little Cockneys were revelling in their task searching the corpses for souvenirs, and then rolling them into the vast depths of the crater. The Chateau of Hooge and its stables had practically disappeared, only a few crumbling walls and heaps of red bricks remained.

[FCH]

[*Forward observation officer, RFA]

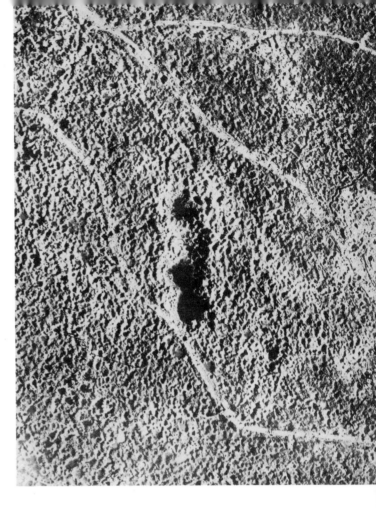

Hooge Crater with tracks through the shell-holes and mud. [IWM].

The same crater fifty years later. The rebuilt chateau forms a background to this setting of peace and beauty. Only the ominous, ivy covered shape of a German pill box at the right centre recalls the horror of the past.

Shrapnel was drumming overhead, along the line of the duckboard track. Nothing frightens one more than high shrapnel, a blow from it is almost certain death, for the bullets strike the head first and there remains no way of escaping. With a high-explosive one can side-slip or lie down beside it, letting the stuff go over. An old soldier can tell to a nicety where a shell will land, and makes off to suit, but high shrapnel bursts around one before the hearing or even instinct can warn. I saw two men carrying a wounded High-lander killed at the same time, while the latter got off scot-free; the only trouble was his being dropped into a stinking shell-hole.

[HQ]

Spent the day revetting the trench as well as we could, without exposing ourselves over the parapets. We also dug sump pits to drain off the stagnant water which lay in the bottom of the trench. In the evening I went down to Railway Wood to see A Company. Their line ran through the wood, and through numerous mine craters like a jig-saw puzzle, and then over the railway line where there was a sand-bagged barricade which had rows of 'knife rests' in front of it. The trench at Railway Wood formed an ugly little salient before it swung back towards Hooge, less than forty yards separated from the enemy line, and it was so close that the barbed wire entanglements put up by one side answered equally well for the other!

[FCH]

Above left: *An artillery position by Chateau Wood and Bellewaarde Lake, November 1917.* The covers over the guns served more as camouflage from aerial observation than as protection from the rain. Note the dump of expended 18-pounder shells to the right. [IWM].

Below left: *Bellewaarde Lake and woods fifty years later.* The scene now reveals nothing more evil than an electric fence in the middle of the field to contain straying cattle.

Above right: *The ravages of battle.* Soldier collecting papers from a fallen comrade by the side of a duck-board track in shell-shattered Chateau Wood. 1st Anzac Corps, 29th October 1917. [IWM].

Below right: *Serenity and Peace.* A path in Chateau Wood.

The setting of the old Corduroy road through Chateau Wood to Westhoek.

5th November 1917. Blasted trees stand like sentinels over the road that lead through Chateau Wood to Westhoek Ridge. [WM].

15TH AUGUST

At 5.30 B Company got heavily shelled for over one and a half hours. The shrapnel-fire was terrific, and their line was completely enveloped in a dense mass of smoke from the bursting shells.

We stood to in case of an attack, but the shell-fire did not materialise into anything. Daly's casualties were seven killed and twenty-one wounded. These numbers included most of his NCO's.

When it was dark I set off with two platoons to bury the dead. It was a most unpleasant duty, as they were all men of the Durhams and York and Lancasters, who had been killed on the 9th in the charge. There were many other bodies lying out in this shell-churned area, and the ghastly stench of mangled corpses gripped us all by the throat as we carried out our task. It was very sad, but headless and armless got exactly the same treatment. We searched all for their identity discs, and their Army Books 64, and any other personal belongings for their next-of-kin. We salved their webbing equipment and rifles, and buried them in threes and fours in large graves.

[FCH]

Above: 1st October 1918. Artillery limbers and pack mules pick their way around an enormous shell crater on the Menin Road at Hooge. They are proceeding towards Gheluvelt.
The frightening looking weapon near the roll of telephone wire in the centre of the photograph is in fact a portable field kitchen. [IWM]

Below: The Menin Road at Hooge today.

16TH AUGUST

Barnett died of his wounds. The Doctor told us that he stuck his wound splendidly, and that men who were only hit in the arms and legs were groaning all round him in the dressing-station. Barnett had a presentiment that he would get killed, and told us so when we got orders for Hooge. I relieved 'Cherrie' Piper and Caulfield at 9 am in the fire trench. The Brig-General came round to inspect the line with the C.O. The Brigadier said the Battalion had done splendidly, and that the place was thoroughly consolidated; he, however, objected to a German's leg which was protruding out of parapet, and I was told by the C.O. to have it buried forthwith. I called Finnegan, and told him to remove the offending limb. As it would have meant pulling down the whole parapet to bury it, he took up a shovel and slashed at it with the sharp edge of the tool. After some hard bangs, he managed to sever the limb. I had turned away and was standing in the next fire bay, when I overhead Finnegan remarking to another man: 'And what the bloody hell will I hang me equipment on now?'

17TH AUGUST

On duty all morning in the advanced trench. The C.O. brought the C.O. of the North Staffords, Lieut-Colonel de Falbe, up to look around the line. He gave me orders about burying some dead. In a hollow he had discovered three unburied. This was a sad sight as the trio consisted of a patient lying on a stretcher and the two stretcher bearers lying across him, with the slings of the stretcher still across their shoulders. All had been knocked out by the same shell.

We were only shelled in the support trench and at Railway Wood. At 10 pm we were relieved by the 1st North Staffords, and I handed over my line with its flank in the air joyfully! After relief we did not return to billets, but found carrying parties for RE material to the Hooge crater. So back again we toiled along the Menin Road in Indian file, with duckboards, stakes, planks, and sand-bags. To make matters worse, it was raining hard and very dark. It was a tedious job; fallen trees had to be negotiated and numerous shell-holes full of water had to be avoided. The enemy was sending up star-shells, and we had to halt until the flare fell and had burnt itself out. To have been seen by the enemy would have been fatal, as we were on the exposed Menin Road, right away from cover of any description. We finished our work at 1.30 am and moved off for Ypres in the dark, and in heavy rain.

More fighting at Hooge. At 6 am the Huns tried another form of frightfulness, *flammenwerfer*, on the front-line troops astride the Menin Road. The troops, 8th and 9th Service Battalions of the RBs and 60th Rifles, who belonged to the 14th Division, were driven out of their trenches, and the positions gained by the 3rd Division on the 19th July were lost. The 14th Division carried out a counter-attack which did not meet with any success and incurred heavy casualties. Our 16th Brigade were pulled out of their rest billets to hold the new line. Daly's Company had a perfect view of the fighting from their positions round Wieltje, which was on the high ground. They stated that the 'liquid fire' attack looked most demoralising.

[FCH]

Above right: Sanctuary Wood. The maze of trenches and the shell-pocked ground where now all is quiet and peaceful. [IWM]

Above: Sanctuary Wood. Relics of old trenches.

Right: Sanctuary Wood Cemetery. The grave of Lieutenant Gilbert Talbot, killed in a counter-attack after the first enemy liquid fire attack at Hooge at the end of July 1915. 'Toc H' was named after this officer. (See p. 138)

(See p. 138)

Past and Present. A shell-shattered trunk amongst the young saplings of Sanctuary Wood.

Good weather. We were shelled all evening by large crumps. Corpl Maher of my platoon narrowly missed being blown up by a direct hit on the parapet of fire bay he was in. His rifle was turned into a piece of twisted iron. More shell-fire at Hooge. Enemy air-craft very active all day.

We were supplied with full particulars regarding the 'liquid fire' attack.. It appeared that the enemy's method of launching this attack was with a number of men carrying on their backs a tank similar to a potato-spraying device with a hose. From this jet issued forth a flame of liquid which was estimated could shoot some 30–50 yards.

The defenders of this sector had lost few men from actual burns, but the demoralising element was very great. We were instructed to aim at those who carried the flame-spraying device, who made a good target.

It was reported that a Hun who had his cargo of frightfulness hit by a bullet blew up with a colossal burst. Counter measures against an attack were with rapid fire and machine-gun fire. As the flames shot forward they created a smoke-screen, so we realised that we would have to fire into 'the brown'.

[FCH]

102

Sanctuary Wood, October 1917. [IWM]

Past and Present. Sanctuary Wood from the same vantage point. The wood now lives up to its name.

H

103

JULY 1915

Good weather again. Marsland, Piper and I went up to see 'Stink Post' in the evening. It was quite a job getting out to the end of the sap as the communication trench was frightfully low, and we had to crawl along as the enemy snipers were particularly hostile.

This cut ran through some old ruined houses, under which were the graves of the late owners, killed in the second battle. Horses' hoofs too, stuck out at odd intervals from the parapets. The sickly smell of decaying flesh hung all about the place. No wonder it had been called 'Stink Post', but it was marked on the maps as Odour Houses. We found the garrison sitting down, their rifles across their knees, and gazing into periscopes which were stuck up along the parados. There were no sniping places of any description, and our snipers had to 'chance their arm' and fire over the parapets. Whilst we were in the post, two of the Battalion snipers, 5970 Pte Flanaghan, and 3784 Pte Ward, were shot clean through the head. The former lived for just twenty minutes and the latter for about the same time.

[FCH]

There were French Turcos on our left; they were a great nuisance as they kept up a rapid fire all night. The enemy retaliated on us, catching our working and wiring parties. These Turcos were quaint-looking troops in their short blue tunics and picturesque baggy red trousers. In the day-time numbers of them used to leave their trenches and go back at large to loot in Ypres.

[FCH]

THE LEFT SECTOR

6TH JULY 1915

The 4th Division carried out an attack which did not materialise into any great success. They advanced, taking 200 yards of enemy trenches and a bag of 80 prisoners.

Working from 9 pm to 1 am carrying RE material up to A Company from the Battalion dump in Potijze. We had just got clear of the village when the enemy started strafing. Potijze had had its share of shell-fire up to this time in the War. It was only a mere hamlet on a cross-roads, most of the houses were roofless, the jagged beams and rafters projected into the void, and fragments of cottage furniture and cooking utensils were strewn across the road. Here and there were twisted rifles and torn bits of khaki uniform. One house had a large pile of un-opened bully beef tins.

[FCH]

9TH JULY 1915

Relieved A Company at midnight. Before going up I took my platoon to the Company dump in Potijze for SAA, sand-bags, and barbed wire. We narrowly missed being blown up; just as we had moved off, over came some '8-inchers', and blew up the dump and the cross-roads. Some men of the 3rd RBs were hit, and the back of their water-cart was blown in. The horses bolted and went careering off towards Ypres without a driver!

[FCH]

How Old is this Face? Twenty-five? Thirty? It is, in fact, the face of a *sixteen* year old German prisoner, wounded and captured in the Battle of the Menin Ridge Road. More than 2,000 prisoners were captured by Scottish and South African troops near Potijze, 20th September 1917. [IWM]

4TH AUGUST 1915

Orders issued for relief. Not unexpected, although we had been given to understand we were in this sector for a long tour. Hooge seemed a certainty. The Regiment which was to relieve us got held up by shell-fire. L/Corpl Jenkins brought our relieving Company up across country. At 1.45 am we had handed over our sector to the 1st Battalion Wiltshire Regiment of the 7th Brigade, 3rd Division. We got out behind the trenches and cut across to the St Jean road. It was a fine moonlight night, and only a few solitary shells were whining over our heads towards Ypres. We marched past the crumbling ruins of the St Jean Church and its torn-up graveyard.

This graveyard had been badly shelled. All the crosses and tombstones had been smashed, and dead bodies and coffins were lying exposed on the brink of large craters. I fell out my platoon at the Menin Gate, the rendezvous, to wait for the Company.

We marched through Ypres, which was being spasmodically shelled. A few crumps landed uncomfortably close as we marched over the Cross Roads beside the Water Tower. Rain fell just after we had got clear of the town and the Poperinghe road seemed longer and uglier than ever as we marched along its uneven pave. We got drenched, and when it stopped, a thick mist hung all round, which obliterated the countless poplars which belted the road ahead of us. We were tired and depressed.

[FCH]

Potijze Chateau, 20th September 1917. More prisoners after the successful attack on Iberian Farm, Frezenberg, by the **West Lancashire Territorials** and **English county troops.** Rolls of barbed wire and camouflage netting (such as that used to conceal the bunker on the left) are in the foreground. [IWM]

French Military Cemetery near Potijze which contains about 4000 graves.

Site of Potijze Chateau today. In former days parties were held and there was gaiety and laughter with the chateau ablaze with lights. Now it is a hushed, solemn place — the resting place of so many of our soldiers.

ST JEAN

This little village is situated about a mile from the Ypres ramparts and these days practically forms the north-eastern outskirts of the town on the St Julian road.

As with so many other villages in the Salient it underwent heavy bombardment with the inevitable toll of death and destruction.

St Jean is still known by some old inhabitants as 'Hooghozieken'. There are two schools of thought as to the exact meaning of this name, some saying that it describes a high place (i.e. a hill) while others think that it has a connection with 'high sickness' or, in other words, 'serious sickness' stemming from a plague in the Middle Ages.

The Potijze – St Jean Road.

St Jean, 31 July 1917. Pack mules passing a wrecked artillery limber and dead mules on the road at St Jean. The brush in the RE dump was used for mending roads. [IWM]

The Village of St Jean from the same position.

22ND SEPTEMBER

Took the Company out digging, working on a new line east of St Jean, running parallel with the St Jean–Potijze road. O-P came round to inspect the work. He had just got his Majority and had been appointed second in command. There was great activity in sniping, but I had no men hit.

[FCH]

WIELTJE

Wieltje, which is about two miles north-east of Ypres, is situated at the fork of the St Julian—Gravenstafel roads although it is now by-passed by a modern concrete highway. It is surrounded by lovely farmland where heavy fighting took place, particularly during Second Ypres and Third Ypres. Nearby are farms previously given the names of Mouse-Trap (Shell Trap) Farm, Hampshire Farm, Canadian Farm, Kultur Farm, Civilisation Farm, Irish Farm, English Farm and Argyle Farm.

Occupied modern residence and unoccupied old residence.

Returned from fatigue at 4 am. We were all pretty jaded and disgruntled with this task. Every night on the same work, hacking through corpses and filling sand-bags! The ground was a swamp, and churned up by shell-fire which prevented drainage. Nothing broke the monotony of this working party; the same smell of gas, and sickening smell of decomposing human flesh hung round the locality. Every now and then shrapnel would burst over us to break the stillness of the night. Otherwise the only sounds were the sighing poplars and the everlasting croaking of the frogs. In the morning we built up the line which had been blown and, as usual, we dug up some bodies and had to re-bury them. At dark, we often cut the standing meadows in No-Man's-Land in order to get a better field of fire, in case the front line had to withdrawn to out support line. On these grass-cutting expeditions we often came across the bodies of dead Canadians, which we buried.

[FCH]

Above: Wieltje. A working party going up at night on a duckboard track through the flooded shell-holes. Wieltje, 11 January 1918. [IWM]

Below: The Fields of Wieltje. Once this was no-man's land; British trenches were to the left and German to the right.

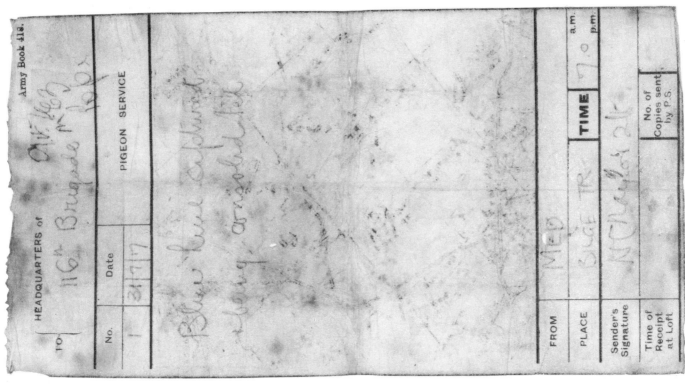

Army Book 418.

HEADQUARTERS of

TO

PIGEON SERVICE

No.	Date
1	31/7/17

Blue line captured
doing original LOL

FROM MED

PLACE BDE TR   TIME 7.0 a.m. / p.m.

Sender's Signature N° Taylor 2/Lt

Time of Receipt at Loft

No. of Copies sent by P.S.

Army Book

HEADQUARTERS of

TO

PIGEON SERVICE

No.	Date
	31/7/17

FROM MED

PLACE BDE TR   TIME a.m. / p.m.

Sender's Signature

Time of Receipt at Loft

No. of Copies sent by P.S.

At 5 am the enemy started shelling the advanced post of D Company which surrounded some old ruins called Stink Post. I watched them sending over trench mortars for some time. They then burst salvoes of shrapnel and 'whiz-bangs' over the position. The place was covered in smoke and red brick-dust from the already demolished houses in the vicinity, which completely obliterated the post from view. After a furious bombardment in which the garrison were all either killed or wounded, the enemy rushed the post and bayoneted the few who happened to be badly wounded. Captain Orpen-Palmer organised a counter-attack and drove the Germans out in less than ten minutes 'scrapping'.

At 9 am we were watching one of our aeroplanes reconnoitring the enemy lines (from 4000 feet up). It was being shelled by larger anti-aircraft shells than usual. The third shell got a direct hit, and it suddenly crumpled up, and came crashing down behind the enemy lines. It made a dreadful roaring noise, and we saw one man fall out. It crashed just out of view from our trenches as the Huns were on the high ground, but we saw the flames shoot up when it struck earth. The enemy cheered like blazes. A demoralising sight. Reilly died from his wounds. The Germans attacked the 47th Division (Territorial), but got repulsed. The canal bank was gassed all day by gas shells. The Salient commenced getting very lively from this date onwards.

The Huns strafed the tower of Ypres Cathedral all morning. Our artillery observation post found! Our Press used to amuse us immensely with its accounts of the Huns' 'frightfulness' in bombarding churches. Both sides invariably used church towers as artillery observation posts.

[FCH]

The view from Shell Trap Farm. Looking towards Ypres (the tower of the Cloth Hall can be seen in the left centre) from just behind the German front lines (the cows mark the actual line of the trenches). Hampshire farm is out of the picture to the right and Irish Farm is in the direction of the trees in the right distance.

A map and message contained on wafer thin paper and sent by carrier pigeon at the beginning of Third Ypres.

This was addressed to the 116th Brigade Headquarters and was sent by a Second Lieutenant Naylor at 0700 hours on 31st July 1917.

The message read 'Blue Line captured and being consolidated' and originated from Bilge Trench which was in the old German lines.

The pigeon was found dead in our lines and the message was received too late to be of any real value.

Mouse Trap (formerly Shell Trap) Farm is located in the centre-right portion of the map.

[Contributed by Mr S. T. H. Ross]

113

We got doors and rafters from Irish Farm. Daly climbed up on the roof and started taking down a window shutter which looked due north, towards the Hun lines. He was spotted instantly, and we were shelled heavily for an hour with 'Black Marias' and 'Jack Johnsons'.

Moved my platoon farther along the trench, as they were getting direct hits on my parapet near the road.

After the smoke and debris of one shell had cleared away Daly emerged from the farm gate with the shutter on his shoulder. Our artillery, the 42nd and 112th Batteries, retaliated on the Hun lines at Canadian, Hampshire and Shell Trap Farms.* There was a terrible shortage of shells, at this period each gun was rationed to three shells per day. When Algeo rang up the gunners for retaliation, the answer he invariably got was: 'Sorry, but we have expended our allowance, and if we fire any more shells off today, we will be left with none to repulse attacks with tomorrow! Company still on fatigue digging the communication trench near English Farm. As we had dug right through a swamp, the trench welled water, and we had to bale it out. Commencing our work at 8 pm, we rarely finished until after 3 am. The smell from dead bodies lying round was ghastly, and in digging the trench we often had to dig up a corpse. Shells came over at intervals, but we had no casualties.

[FCH]

* Later in the war this farm was renamed Mouse Trap Farm, as the name Shell Trap, it was considered, might have a demoralising effect on troops taking over that sector.

St Julien, 13th March 1918. A water-filled shell crater bordered with crosses. The cross on the left bears eight name-plates. [IWM]

Other men working the same fields fifty years later.

ST JULIEN

The village lies about three and a half miles north-east of Ypres and is famous in the annals of Canadian history.

It was originally lost during the surprise enemy gas attacks of April 1915 after much bitter fighting at the time of Second Ypres. St Julian once more came under British control on 3rd August 1917 after having been initially entered a few days earlier at the opening of Third Ypres, but temporarily abandoned following strong enemy counter attacks.

The Battalion was in support to the Royal Fusiliers. Our support line ran from a point 300 yds west of Irish Farm, and across to some 200 yards south-west of English Farm, and back towards St Jean. Company Headquarters was situated on top of the ridge where this village stood, which gave us a good view of the surrounding country, flat, barren wastes studded here and there with derelict farm-houses. There was practically no timber of any kind, with the exception of the usual few willow trees, which grow at random all over Flanders. Most of the land was in meadow, now bleached by the gas. It was a depressing sight; behind us was the deserted and battered village of St Jean, and off in the distance we could see the tower and pinnacle of the Church and Cloth Hall of Ypres. Everywhere there was the sickly smell of the gas which had been used on the Canadians in the 2nd Battle of Ypres. The Company was employed making a support line around the wood north of English Farm all night, and we got shelled.

[FCH]

Our line was 350 yds away from the enemy. In the middle of No-Man's-Land were the remains of a Canadian ammunition column which had got blown up in May. Marsland, Sergt T. Flaherty and O'Leary were on patrol all night. They found the bodies of three men of the 2nd Royal Dublin Fusiliers, and collected their identity discs and pay books, and sent them in to Battalion Headquarters.

[FCH]

At 5 am Sergt Bennett woke me up, saying that one of our aeroplanes was landing near us on fire. I got out of the dug-out in time to see it crashing near our reserve trenches north-east of La Brique. It had been scrapping with an enemy Taube, which it sent down over the lines near Poelcappelle. Under heavy fire from hostile anti-aircraft guns our pilot turned towards our lines to continue his reconnaissance, when his petrol tank was hit. His machine then burst into flames, and he started to descend. The observer was seen getting out on to the wings to escape from the flames. When the plane crashed, both fell clear and we picked them up, badly burnt. The rounds in their revolvers had all gone off. The plane was now burning fiercely and the unexpended ammunition was going off. We salved the machine-gun and the 'skull and cross-bones' which was in front of the body. The pilot was one of our 'aces', and had got this honour for having downed many enemy machines. The men carried the pilot and observer off to the dressing-station, where our MO attended to them. They were both terribly burnt. The Huns, seeing the plane landing, and expecting we would go out to help the occupants, sent over shrapnel, but we all managed to get away in time. Six months afterwards the pilot died from his injuries.

[FCH]

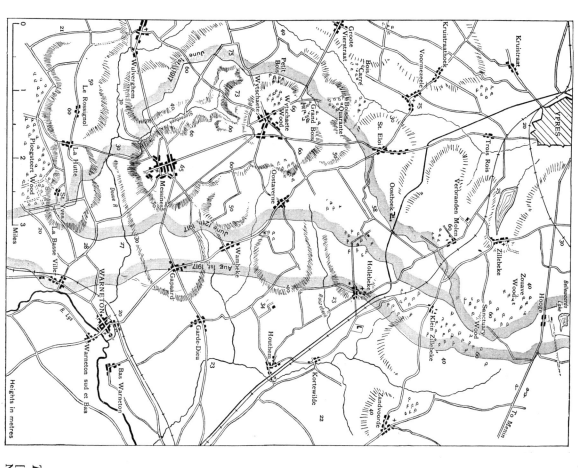

The Messines Ridge.
[Map from *Nelson's History of the War* (John Buchan). By permission of Thomas Nelson & Sons Ltd.]

THE RIGHT SECTOR

Facing page: Zillebeke Lake at the end of the War. The streams which normally feed the lake have been diverted from their courses by the heavy shellfire. [IWM]

Above: Zillebeke Lake, 29th September 1917. A panorama of water-filled Zillebeke Lake. 1st Anzac Corps. [IWM]

Below: Modern Panorama. Advertisements replace the watchers of old.

Maple Copse from Observatory Ridge. The spires of Ypres are in the distance.

MAPLE COPSE

This area at the southern end of the Sanctuary Wood became an inferno when at the beginning of June 1916, the German XIII Wurtemburg Corps attacked in force along that part of the Canadian Corps front. At 0830 hours on 2nd June an enemy artillery barrage opened up from three directions on the trenches in Sanctuary Wood and Maple Copse, which were held by Princess Patricia's Light Infantry and other Canadian Units.

Although bombarded for hours the Canadians held on grimly and eventually met the inevitable infantry attack with great gallantry. Much slaughter ensued on both sides. The enemy succeeded in capturing what little remained of the British front line trenches but was unable to advance beyond the support lines. Within a very short time the whole area was littered with dead and dying and the Canadian regiments were reduced to a shadow of their former numbers.

Eleven days later the Canadians counter-attacked at night, across the shattered ground including Observatory Ridge and Armagh Wood, and once more savage hand-to-hand fighting took place with the enemy bravely endeavouring to hold on to his earlier gains. Eventually the Canadians attacks forced back the Germans to their original positions and Maple Copse once more became a Canadian possession although at the cost of heavy losses.

Thus ended yet another of the see-saw battles which were commonplace during the First World War when, on both sides, a few yards of broken ground were won and then all too often lost again, the only noticeable result being higher casualty figures.

120

Right: Armagh Wood from Observatory Ridge near Ypres, July 1916. [IWM]

Below Right: Wounded Germans at a dressing station near Zillebeke. [IWM]

Below: Looking down from Observatory Ridge towards part of a sunlit Armagh Wood with farmworkers haymaking in the foreground. July 1968.

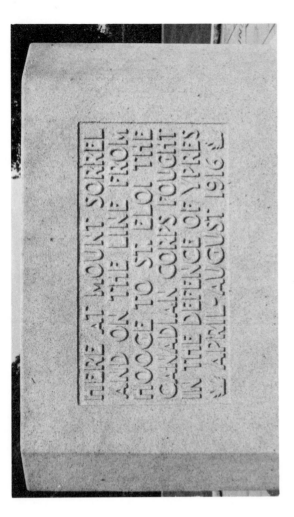

Memorial surmounting Hill 62. Some confusion arises over this hill and Mount Sorrel. In fact the latter lies a short distance farther south.

HERE AT MOUNT SORREL
AND ON THE LINE FROM
HOOGE TO ST ELOI THE
CANADIAN CORPS FOUGHT
IN THE DEFENCE OF YPRES
APRIL-AUGUST 1916

Greater Love. Grave of a Canadian soldier whose epitaph reads 'Past the military age he responded to the Mother Country's call.'

A changed identity.

Unidentified.

122

George Murray and I went up to the front line, and then along to see the Canadians on A Company's left. They were the 21st Battalion and were a fine-looking body of men. Their trenches were in splendid condition. At night we revetted the parapets of our redoubt. I also had a party of men digging out in front of the redoubt and throwing up more earth to broaden the parapets. We left them wide enough to allow GS waggons to drive along them, as the men said! Got machine-gunned several times while at work.

[FCH]

View over no-man's land from Hill 62. The spires of the Cloth Hall and St Martin's are in the distance.

Hill 62. The Canadian front lines ran across this cabbage patch to the hill in the background. Just visible above the trees is a Belgian jet fighter.

THE BATTLE OF MOUNT SORREL

The first Canadian deliberately-planned attack in any force resulted in an unqualified success.' — British Official History.

In June, 1916, the 3rd Canadian Division, as the 2nd Division had done at St Eloi two months before, fought its first battle. The other divisions of the Corps took part before the fight was over.

The 3rd Division began its life on Christmas Day, 1915, under Major-General M. S. Mercer whose brigades — the 7th, 8th, and 9th — were commanded by Brigadier-Generals Macdonell, Williams and Hill. As yet the Division had no artillery of its own. Until July, 1916, it was provided by the Indian 3rd (Lahore) Division.

The 7th Brigade consisted of Princess Patricia's Canadian Light Infantry (a veteran battalion, having had a year's distinguished service with the British), the Royal Canadian Regiment (fresh from Bermuda and with only a month's experience on the Western Front), and the 42nd (RHC) and 49th (Edmonton) Battalions (which had both undergone a tour of non-operational duty but had not yet been tried in battle).

The 1st, 2nd, 4th and 5th Battalions, Canadian Mounted Rifles, made up the 8th Brigade. These units had been formed by converting to infantry the six CMR regiments which had crossed to France in September and October, 1915.

The 9th Brigade did not join the Division until February, 1916. Its units were the 43rd, 52nd, 58th and 60th Battalions (all new arrivals in France) from Winnipeg, Port Arthur, the Niagara area and Montreal.

The beginning of June found the Canadian Corps, still in the Ypres Salient, holding an arc of front that stretched from St Eloi on the right to, on the left, the village of Hooge. The 2nd Division held the St Eloi sector. In the centre the 1st Division faced Hill 60. On the left, where the line projected most sharply into enemy territory, the 3rd Division held the only part of the Ypres ridge that still remained in Allied hands. The high ground in this sector included Mount Sorrel, Hill 61 and Hill 62, before falling away through Sanctuary Wood, across an open valley known as 'the Gap', to the village of Hooge on the Menin Road. Hills 61 and 62 were also known as 'Tor Top'. From Hill 62 a spur named Observatory Ridge thrust west between Armagh Wood (on the southern flank of the spur) and Sanctuary Wood, while to the north of the spur, farther back, was Maple Copse.

Opposite the 3rd Division the 26th and 27th German Infantry Divisions of the 13th Wurttemberg Corps had rehearsed the seizure of the high ground for the past six weeks. Possession of it might compel a withdrawal from the

Salient; and it would help delay preparations for the Somme offensive which the Germans knew to be impending.

The second half of May had been unusually tranquil. In June, however, the unnatural calm was broken by an intermittent bombardment from the direction of enemy-held Hill 60. This died at nightfall, allaying suspicions that it might be a prelude to attack; but it was no more than a temporary lull ordered to avoid interference with gapping parties which that night breached the Canadian wire.

TORNADO OF FIRE

Early on the morning of 2nd June the enemy bombardment burst out again with redoubled fury, falling on the 7th Canadian Infantry Brigade and, more heavily, on the 8th (CMR) Brigade. Hardest hit of all was the 4th CMR in front of Armagh Wood, when only 76 men came through unscathed. Spouting earth and flame pulsed through the shell-torn stumps of Armagh Wood, Sanctuary Wood and Maple Copse. Black shrapnel bursts enveloped Mount Sorrel, Tor Top and Observatory Ridge, and for four hours this violent tornado of fire ravaged the Canadian positions, hurling into the air 'tree trunks, weapons and equipment . . and, occasionally, human bodies,' General Mercer and Brigadier-General Williams, who were in the 4th Canadian Mounted Rifles' area when the fire came down, both became casualties — Mercer killed, and Williams, who was wounded, taken prisoner when the German infantry at last came forward.

This the enemy did in the Mount Sorrel sector, after exploding four mines just short of the Canadian positions, at about 1 pm. Trenches had been wrecked and whole garrisons annihilated even before the mines were sprung; the Germans could not be held. Four waves of the grey-clad enemy came leisurely forward — confident that their artillery had wiped out resistance — in the bright sunshine of early afternoon. Small bands of survivors from the 1st and 4th CMR — but these were few — fought with bombs and bayonets; machine-guns of the Patricias and the 5th CMR Battalion, on the flanks, raked the enemy lines, but only on the right was the enemy temporarily held. There a company of Patricias, which had escaped the worst of the bombardment, held out in Sanctuary Wood for eighteen hours, while two companies of Patricias to the rear held the Germans from the support line until it had been reinforced. When the Germans at last advanced it was over PPCLI dead — the battalion had 150 killed alone, including the Commanding Officer, Lieutenant-Colonel H. C. Buller, former Military Secretary to HRH the Duke of Connaught, Governor-General of Canada.

To the east and southeast sides of Maple Copse, German thrusts were checked by the accurate shooting of the 5th CMR holding strongpoints behind the 1st and 4th CMR Battalions, but a section of the 5th Battery,

CFA, was overrun. All the gunners were killed or wounded and the two 18-pounders fell into German hands but were recovered in the later fighting.

Late that afternoon the Germans halted, digging in 600-700 yards west of their former line. They had captured Mount Sorrel, Hill 61, Hill 62 and most of Armagh and Sanctuary Woods. Machine-guns of the 10th Battalion and the Canadian Motor Machine Gun Brigade sealed off the enemy encroachment. Sir Julian Byng, who had succeeded General Alderson as Corps Commander after the April battle at St Eloi, ordered all the lost ground to be recovered that night.

BYNG'S BATTLE PLAN

The 3rd Division had suffered heavily; therefore Byng placed two brigades of the 1st Division at its disposal. The 2nd Brigade would operate against Mount Sorrel and the 3rd against Hills 61 and 61. But the attacks, carried out by the 7th, 14th, 15th and 49th Battalions, were improvised and uneven, and in any case did not go in until daylight on 3rd June. Though they achieved some success, they failed in their ultimate objectives. The 49th Battalion captured, and held, some trenches near the old German line. The main result was the closing of a gap between Square Wood (a western appendage of Armagh Wood) across Observatory Ridge to Maple Copse.

The enemy made the next move on 6th June. He exploded four mines directly under the 6th Brigade (brought up from the 2nd Division's reserve) at Hooge and then wrested the forward trenches from the dazed troops of the 28th (Saskatchewan) Battalion on whom the blow had fallen. The 31st Battalion, on the right, kept the Germans out of the support line. Thus the enemy had merely gained a few yards, and the forward trenches were left in his possession.

Byng was still determined to drive the enemy from the lost high ground; he nominated the 1st Division which, on 8th June, withdrew from the line to rest and prepare. Again the 2nd Brigade (Brigadier-General Lipsett) would attack Mount Sorrel and the 3rd Brigade (Brigadier-General Tuxford) the hills, but this time there was a thorough plan. Both the attacking formations were to be composite brigades made up of the stronger battalions. Lipsett had the 1st, 3rd, 7th and 8th Battalions; Tuxford commanded the 2nd, 4th, 13th and 16th Battalions. In addition the 58th Battalion (9th Brigade) plus a company of the 52nd would assault on the left. The 5th, 10th, 14th and 15th Battalions formed a reserve brigade under Brigadier-General Garnet Hughes.

HEAVY ARTILLERY SUPPORT

The attacking battalions carefully rehearsed their co-ordinated roles, and every day reconnaissance parties reported on the enemy defences for comparison with aerial photographs of his trenches. Above all, though the ground

would have to be recovered by the Canadians' own efforts (a brigade of British infantry only was provided to assist, but this remained in reserve), Byng had arranged for powerful artillery support. Altogether 218 pieces were at the Canadian Corps' disposal (including 116 eighteen-pounders, heavy guns and howitzers), representing the Canadian Corps Heavy Artillery; the 1st and 2nd Divisional Artilleries; the Lahore Divisional Artillery; the British 5th, 10th, 11th Heavy Artillery Groups, 3rd Divisional Artillery, 51st Howitzer Battery and 89th Siege Battery; and the South African 71st and 72nd Howitzer Batteries. In addition, the Heavy Artillery of the British 5th and 14th Corps, on the flanks, would co-operate.

The operation was timed for 1.30 am on 13th June. Thus there was time for the proper planning of a 'set-piece' attack. Between the 9th and 12th of June four intense bombardments hurled steel on the German positions for periods of short duration to delude the enemy into expecting an immediate assault; when none materialized the real one, it was hoped, would be thought to be merely another feint.

For ten hours on 12th June the German positions between Hill 60 and Sanctuary Wood were pounded heavily, and still there was no infantry attack. A half-hour's shelling in the late evening followed, under cover of which the well-rehearsed infantry moved forward to their jumping off positions — many of them out in No-Man's-Land — where the men waited in damp and clammy clothes for their time to come. For the last forty-five minutes before zero hour the heavies poured down a final torrent of shells, and then the infantry sprang forward to attack.

It was a pitch-black night with wind and rain. Even so, smoke-shells were fired to conceal the flashes of small-arms weapons from the watchful German machine-gunners on Hill 60.

There was little uncertainty, despite the darkness, and the battalions that had been chosen to attack (the 3rd, 16th, 13th and 58th) moved steadily forward through the mud in four long waves. Brigadier-General Brustall, the CRA of the Corps, had predicted that his guns would permit the infantry to reach the objectives 'with slung rifles'. He was nearly right.

Some machine-gunners had escaped destruction; isolated pockets of Germans still survived. The fighting was bitter here. But the majority of the Wurttembergers, taken by surprise and badly shaken by the accurate artillery fire, either fell back to their old frontline or gave themselves up to the fresh Canadians. Prisoners came stumbling back enroute to ruined Zillebeke, which stood by its stagnant, triangular lake not far from Ypres behind the lines. These men 'were in small groups', an eye-witness (Captain, later Colonel, W. W. Murray) wrote, 'and were obviously suffering also from exposure, for during the past few days the artillery supporting the attack had been considerably reinforced, and their barrages were devastating.'

THE BATTLE IS WON

In an hour the battle was over. The 3rd Battalion swept onto Mount Sorrel; the 16th cleared Armagh Wood; the 13th advanced along Observatory Ridge to occupy the twin eminences, Hills 61 and 62; and the attached 58th Battalion reached the former line through Sanctuary Wood.

What had once been a system of trenches had been obliterated by the overwhelming gun-fire. This was not the Somme where the Germans, in deep dug-outs, remained relatively immune from shells. The Canadians consolidated the soggy ground on what was thought to have been the old forward line.

'The first Canadian deliberately-planned attack in any force,' reports the British Official History, 'had resulted in an unqualified success.' It had been due to allowing time for careful planning, resolute infantry, and strong artillery support on a narrow front.

The weather remained wet and raw; throughout the 13th a steady rain cleared to a light drizzle and then began again. The forward troops, completely exposed to the depressing weather, held trenches deep in mud. In the aftermath of the attack the men lived on cold food without a chance of rest; heavy German artillery fire lashed and flayed the new-won line.

COUNTER-ATTACKS FAIL

Early on 14th June the inevitable counter-attacks took place. There were two of them, both directed on Mount Sorrel, but each one failed. Thereafter the sector settled down into the surly stalemate of static warfare, with the Germans dug in between one and two hundred yards away.

The Canadian line held firm, and continued to do so throughout the summer when the Canadian Corps left the Ypres Salient for the fighting on the Somme.

Reprinted with the kind permission of Mr John Swettenham, Historian, Canadian War Museum and Mr Lorne Manchester, Managing Editor of Legion, the national magazine of the Royal Canadian Legion.

Hill 60. The hill is a mass of shell holes and trenches. On the right can be seen a large crater which was one of the nineteen mines blown by the British during the Battle of Messines. Note how the German trenches follow the edge of the crater.

What looks like a large ditch on the right of the photograph is the Ypres—Comines railway cutting; Hill 60, in fact, was formed by the waste materials taken from the cut. [IWM]

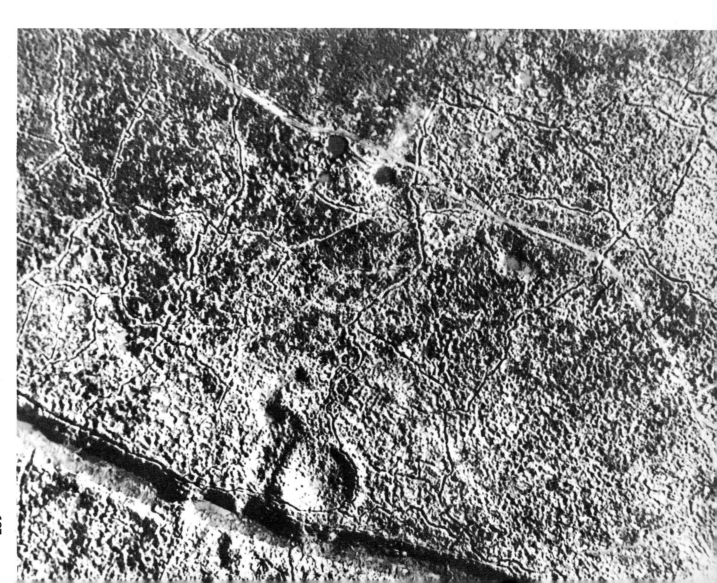

HILL 60

A few miles south-east of Ypres is a small hill about 150 yards wide by 250 yards long. The hill is flanked on one side by a railway cutting through which runs the single track that connects Ypres with the rail junction town of Comines. This minor prominence, no higher than about the fifth floor of the Post Office Tower, in London, is Hill 60, once of major importance as an observation position overlooking the surrounding flat countryside and where occurred some of the most bitter and savage fighting ever to take place in the whole bloodsoaked Ypres Salient.

Control of this insignificant but vital hill first passed to the Germans in December 1914, when they captured it from the French. When this part of the front line was subsequently taken over by the British, GHQ promptly decided that Hill 60 would have to be re-taken.

Plans for mining operations were initiated, and at the beginning of March 1915 three tunnels were commenced by 171 Tunnelling Company in the wet sandy clay. Under immensely difficult conditions (including enemy countermining), these excavations slowly proceeded towards the German lines and by 15th April a total of six mines, created from the three galleries, were ready to be blown.

At about five minutes past seven on the evening of 17th April after a lovely spring day, the mines were exploded. Enormous eruptions ripped out the heart of Hill 60 and huge clods of earth, debris, and the shattered bodies of Germans were flung hundreds of yards around. Simultaneously a crushing bombardment poured from British, French, and Belgian guns. Then units of the 13th Infantry Brigade (comprised mainly of the 1st Royal West Kents and the 2nd Scottish Borderers) went over the top to the sound of bugles. The dazed and shocked survivors were quickly overwhelmed at a cost of very few British lives and the attack appeared to be a complete success.

Then the Germans unleashed a thunderous counter-bombardment on the Tommies desperately digging themselves in on the crest of the hill. Later, in the early hours of the morning and headed by

bomb-throwers, came the first of the inevitable counter-attacks and the bombers inflicted severe casualties upon our troops in their shallow defence positions. By daylight fresh battalions had been rushed forward to support our hard-pressed men and murderous fighting continued with bomb and bayonet at close quarters. Slowly the Germans forced back the defenders. Each shell hole and each mine crater became a battleground and blood soaked into the ground from the many corpses now littering the hill.

Fresh British attacks were followed by yet more enemy counter-attacks. Time and again the crest changed hands in head-on clashes of the utmost severity. After forty-eight hours of incessant battle, a short lull found the British still in control of the hill, which was by now a bloody shambles. But on 19th April a concentrated bombardment crashed down on the defenders. All day long this nerve-wracking and destructive shellfire continued as it did all the next day and the next save for the limited intervals during which the enemy assaulted our half-stupified troops with clusters of bombs thrown from shell holes and folds in the ground that had been used as cover by the attackers. Casualties steadily mounted. Trenches became ready-made graves and men were buried alive, but still our troops held fast. Companies lost practically all of their officers and the battered survivors reeled from the hammer-blows of the monstrous *minnenwerfers* and a multitude of other projectiles. Hill 60 was a volcano of flames, smoke, and flying metal but still our men clung to the summit and still they fought off the counter-attacks hurled against them.

For five long days and nights the vicious fighting blazed on. Seven fresh British battalions had been thrown into the cauldron and four VCs had been won, including one by a young officer, Lieutenant Wooley, of the 9th (Queen Victoria) Rifles, a London Territorial unit. This battalion's part in the action is commemorated by a tablet on the crest of the hill but no memorial can possibly tell of the valour shown by these 'week-end soldiers' during the fight for Hill 60. More than 5000 bodies lay within the limited boundaries of the ghastly hill. British and German corpses were

Hill 60 in 1967. Sun warmed and quiet. The ruins of a machine-gun post can be seen on top of the hill, to the left of the memorial.

Shell-strafed Hill 60, 1917. [IWM]

jumbled together in the attitudes of violent death and virtually every shell hole was filled with dead and dying.

Then German field guns were brought up to fire at short range and in turn more British guns were hastened into the arena. The German artillery was forced back. At long last, on 21st April, the bitter trial of strength passed its peak and as the afternoon drew on the sound of battle slowly faded away. The weary, decimated battalions were withdrawn and passed to the comparative safety of the rear whilst the smashed and battered defences were entrusted to the 2nd Cameron Highlanders.

The German battering ram had once more been outclassed by the courage and tenacity of the British soldier as was acclaimed by Sir John French in a general order which praised all concerned in the brilliant direction, capture, and retention of the hill.

Sadly this was not the end of the matter. Although the enemy had fought with courage and bravery in a fair but bloody fight, his next attack was barbaric. Poison gas.

April 22nd saw the commencement of the protracted and widespread struggle called Second Ypres and, as has been stated elsewhere in this book, it was then that gas was used for the first time by the Germans on the Western Front. At the beginning of May it was the turn of Hill 60 to undergo this ordeal by poison. Early on the morning of 5th May the horrible cloud of death spread around and over the hill slowly enveloping the trenches and their occupants. Many men died valiantly at their posts that grim day and various battalions of famous English County regiments suffered grievous losses by refusing, in spite of having practically no means of protection, to retreat before this new terror. German

infantry attacked shortly after the gas had finished its work and, with resistance now almost non-existent, again took the crest and dug themselves in.

There they stayed until over two years later when the hill fell to the British during the Battle of Messines.

That, then, was Hill 60. Even now the multitude of grass-covered shell holes and the old mine craters can be seen as a reminder of what happened there over five decades ago.

The hill has been left as much as possible in its original state as a perpetual memorial to those who fought and died there. The smashed concrete shelters, the British pill-box on the crest, the huge bowl-shaped crater of the 1917 mine, and the hundreds upon hundred of high explosive indentations in the ground remain for all to see and wonder how such an insignificant hill could have been the scene of such appalling carnage.

At the entrance to the hill, and close to the narrow concrete roadway which now passes through what was once the centre of No-Man's-Land, is another plaque in memory of the many men still entombed in the depth of the hill (which was at one time a veritable rabbit warren of tunnels). Thus are remembered those who fought their own particular war in the darkness of underground galleries. Some of them may have been present when the original Hill 60 mines were fired; some of them may have helped to prepare the massive mine which shattered the German trenches in 1917. All of them have long since been at peace, as has the ill-famed hill itself.

Right: Hill 60. Road bridge over the railway cutting from the German trenches and looking towards the British front line. [Courtesy of Dr A. Caenepeel]

Below: Hill 60. Relic of a British trench with relics picked up from the battlefield — helmets, broken shell casements, the tail of an old mortar bomb, a mess tin.

Below Right: The road bridge today. Approximately the position of the old German 1st line.

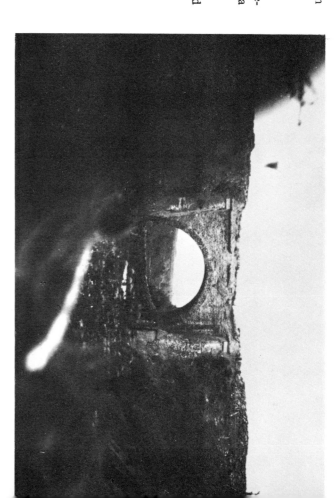

Opposite: Hill 60. German trench and troops. The *pickel-hauber* on the parapet in the middle helps date this photograph at about 1915. [Courtesy of Dr A. Caenepeel]

Below Right: Hill 60. The Ypres–Roulers line, looking toward Ypres from the road bridge. 10th November 1918. [IWM]

Below: The same view a half century later. The railway line follows the line of the communication trench in the opposite photograph.

December 1968.
[By courtesy of The Daily Telegraph]

Obituary

G. H. Woolley, Territorial VC of Hill 60

THE Rev. Geoffrey Harold Woolley, who has died at West Chiltington, Pulborough, Sussex, aged 76, won the Victoria Cross at Hill 60, on the Western Front, in April, 1915.

He was the first Territorial Army officer to receive the award in the 1914-18 war.

In 1943 he was appointed O.B.E, "in recognition of gallant and distinguished services in North Africa," where he was known as "the Woodbine Willie of Algiers."

Mr. Woolley joined the Army on the outbreak of war on Aug. 4, 1914, and went to France with the 9th Bn., The London Regt. (Queen Victoria's Rifles) that November.

The name "Hill 60," where his VC was won, became a household word during the war. It was really just a heap of earth near Ypres, but was important because it afforded an artillery observation post which commanded a large portion of the front.

Resisted attacks

The only officer on Hill 60 at the time, and with very few men, Second Lt. Woolley resisted all attacks on his trench and continued throwing bombs and encouraging his men until relief came.

Mr. Woolley was educated at St. John's School, Leatherhead, and Queen's College, Oxford. After the war he was ordained and became an assistant master at Rugby and then vicar of Monk Sherborne, near Basingstoke. From 1927 to 1939 he was assistant master and chaplain at Harrow.

During the 1939-45 war he was senior chaplain to the troops in Algiers. He was vicar of Harrow from 1944 to 1952.

Mr. Woolley was a former vice-chairman of the Victoria Cross and George Cross Association. He wrote several books, including "Sometimes a Soldier".

132

Hill 60. Details cut into the stonework of a memorial tablet at the foot of the hill.

'Hill 60, the scene of bitter fighting, was held by German troops from 10th December 1914 to 17th April 1915 when it was captured after the explosion of five mines by the British 5th Division. On the 5th May it was recaptured by the German XV Corps. It remained in German hands until the Battle of Messines, 7th June 1917; after many months of underground fighting two mines were exploded here and, at the end of April 1918 after the Battle of the Lys, it passed into German hands again. It was finally re-taken by British troops under the command of H.M. King of the Belgians on the 28th September 1918. In the broken tunnels beneath this enclosure many British and German dead were buried and the hill is therefore preserved so far as nature will permit in the state in which it was left after the Great War.'

The years between. The author's son (left) and a friend, both of whom were born well after the Second World War, survey the terrain of Hill 60 in August 1969 from the top of a British pill-box, the base of which was formed by a German concrete shelter.

As can be seen the pill-box received a direct hit from what must have been a fairly heavy shell but the main structure still held firm, as was so often the case with its German counterparts.

Right: Memorial on Hill 60 to the officers and men of the 1st Australian Tunnelling Company.

134

Hollebeke Village and Church. Limit of advance in that area during the Battle of Messines, June 1917.

That quality of horror pervades the canal bank: there must have been dreadful fighting there at one time, for both sides of the canal, high banks just raised like mounds above the surrounding country, are still strewn with men dead years ago and burnt up like mummies by the weather. On the enemy side of the bank stretch miles of water-logged shell-holes and craters, where men lie thickly, obscene masses of decay, shapeless distorted, some bunched up, others with legs or arms rising blackly above the mud, others buried to the head with horrible faces on a level with the ground. The atmosphere dwells heavy, and a slight but penetrating smell of decay spreads over everything; the water of the canal itself rolls along sluggishly as if weighted with blood. The reeds cluster more rankly and thickly, the grass twists more intricately, and nature has a strong growth, unhealthy in rottenness.

[HQ]

The Bluff and Ypres–Comines Canal. A grim place where considerable mining activity took place. This was a much disputed area of bitter fighting.
[IWM]

Area of The Bluff. A lovely sylvan setting across the old disused and overgrown Ypres—Comines Canal. This is now a bird sanctuary where previously it was bullets that whistled through the air and the cries were those of wounded and dying men.

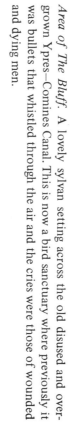

Across the fields. Looking towards Hollebeke Church and the line of the now disused Ypres—Comines Canal (centre of picture) across smooth fields which were once slashed with German trenches and covered with the debris of war. Photograph taken near The Bluff and north of the canal.

The name of Talbot House was a tribute to Gilbert Talbot, a subaltern in the Rifle Brigade who was killed while leading his men in an effort to regain trenches lost at Hooge. Philip ('Tubby') Clayton, padre in the 6th Division was chosen as warden and with willing helpers he created an oasis for weary front-line soldiers who sought a little peace and tranquillity in a mad world.

Tubby Clayton gathered around him a team of men and inspired them with his own faith and enthusiasm. Today Toc H still flourishes and its oil-burning lamp is seen by travellers in far away places where men and women still endeavour to carry on the tradition of comradeship and good-will which sprang up in the small township of Poperinghe so many years ago.

30TH SEPTEMBER

At 8.30 pm I fainted in the support trench! I had not felt well all day, but CSM Morgan brought me into his dug-out and gave me a strong tot of rum, and I felt better. Caulfield sent me down to the dressing-station in the Potijze Chateau to get a lift back to Poperinghe, so as to avoid the march of ten miles to billets. When the shelling had ceased on the building and woods, the ambulances crept up with muffled lights and drove me off with some casualties to Vlamertinghe. The roads were being badly strafed all the way to Ypres, and two shells exploded in the square of Ypres as we drove through. It was a bad night, pitch dark and raining heavily. I wondered when the Company would get relieved. At Vlamertinghe we halted at the CCS and I watched an MO extracting splinters from a man's face and chest. Another ambulance came along, and took us to Poperinghe.

[FCH]

138

Above: Poperinghe. The little town of Poperinghe, famous for its association with 'Toc H' and known by so many of our soldiers for its welcome relief from the firing lines, was occupied by the Germans on 15th October 1914. Their stay was shortlived as the French arrived on 4th October 1914, followed a few days later by the British 1st Division. Poperinghe then grew into a major rest centre for British troops although later in the war it was shelled by enemy long range guns. Talbot House was itself hit by a shell, but survived major damage to carry on its good work.

Above Right: The Grande Place at Poperinghe. This is 1917 and as a sign of the times, perhaps, there are more motor vehicles than horses. AECs, Dennises, Model T's, and Maudsley's thunder around with busy purpose. The chauffeur-driven staff cars in the foreground are almost certainly waiting for a very high-ranking officer. Kilted soldiers of a Scottish unit add to the congested scene. Note the marks on the building at the right — probably caused by shell fragments from a German long range gun. [IWM]

Right: The Grande Place at Poperinghe, 1968. The square is still cobblestoned but on this warm sunny Sunday, all available parking spaces have been filled with cars and there is not a horse to be seen.

MESSINES

At 0300 hours, on 7th June, 1917 a tense hush descended on the battlefield of Messines, to the south of Ypres. The night had turned warm and overcast after a violent thunderstorm and for some hours the torn earth had been shrouded in a mist which obscured the widespread litter of war. The skies had cleared about half an hour earlier and a full moon strode out from behind the clouds and spread a luminous glow over the cratered landscape. From the German lines flares streaked through the moonlit night as the enemy kept an uneasy watch on our positions having earlier experienced a pitiless artillery barrage to which he had replied, less vigourously, with gas, shrapnel and high explosive.

Precisely at 0310 hours the nervous calm was shattered by the noise of nineteen enormous mines exploding along the length of the Messines Ridge. From Hill 60 at the northern end to a place near Ploegsteert Wood in the south, volcanoes of flame belched skyward followed by clouds of black smoke and, shortly afterwards, a thunderclap of sound. Then came a violent earthquake and the ground rocked and heaved from the effects of the 933,200 pounds of ammonal which had ripped out the heart of the ridge. Simultaneously, massed British guns opened up a heavy bombardment on the enemy lines and rear areas and thousands of shell-flashes sparkled in the wall of dust created by the firing of the mines. In the wake of the barrage 100,000 British troops clambered from their trenches and went forward as the sun rose over the horizon.

Unlike previous battles, the shattered remnants of enemy trenches and strong points had been overrun in an incredibly short time. There was little resistance. Dazed German soldiers crawled around on hands and knees in utter confusion, many were weeping, and others were terror-stricken. Except in rare instances the dreaded machine guns were silent and the gunners dead or wounded or too shaken to operate their weapons.

Within a few hours the ridge was taken; in the short space of time since the mines had been exploded the southern arc of the Ypres

General Sir H. Plumer, General Lawrence, and Field Marshall Sir Douglas Haig on the steps of GHQ. General Plumer is wearing the arm band of an Army staff officer. [IWM]

Salient had ceased to exist. At long last, after years of suffering in the waterlogged trenches in the swamp below the ridge, our men could emerge from their holes without fear of being observed or shot at from the higher ground in front. At the same time an important enfilading artillery base had been denied the Germans who had been exploiting the ridge for this purpose ever since Messines had fallen to them in November 1914, during First Ypres. Messines was the first outright British victory since the war began and the first time we had attacked without incurring staggering losses that far outweighed the value of the ground won. Unlike Neuve Chappelle, Loos, the Somme, or Passchendaele, the battle of Messines saved British lives and was a strategic success.

The mines of Messines were the brain-child of an outspoken Member of Parliament and engineer named J. Norton-Griffiths. It was this man who saw the possibility of breaking the stranglehold of the Germans on the Salient by blowing him out of his defensive positions with vast underground explosions. Norton-Griffiths was dissatisfied with the Royal Engineers' attitude toward mining warfare and set out to change the situation in his own inimitable way, which meant cutting red tape and getting things done in the shortest possible time. Not surprisingly his methods were resented by some regular officers but Norton-Griffiths cared little about correct military procedure and lost little sleep over upsetting anyone who preferred to work strictly according to the rules.

In May 1915 Norton-Griffiths first gave serious consideration to the destruction of the formidable German defences on the Messines Ridge. Full of enthusiasm he put a tentative plan to his superiors by whom it was immediately rejected. Not until January 1916 was the plan reconsidered and then finally accepted. In due course work was begun. By the end of 1916 fifteen enormous mines were in position beneath the ridge and by dint of frantic toil a further six mines were completed before the deadline fixed by General Sir Herbert-Plumer — 7th June 1917. One mine had been discovered in the course of preparation by the Germans and

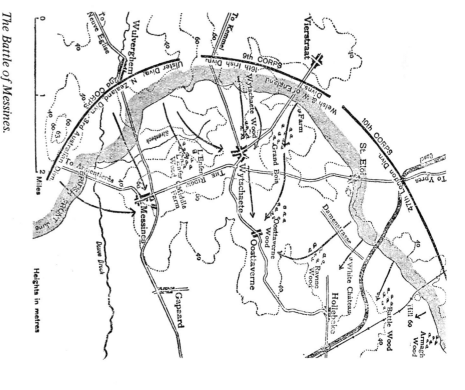

The Battle of Messines.
sketch map from *Nelson's History of the War.* By John Buchan, with permission of Thomas Nelson and Sons Ltd.

the biggest — Spanbroeckmolen — had been badly damaged by an enemy camouflet which necessitated considerable additional work until literally the last available minute.

Prior to the time of the attack officers and men of the mining companies — including Canadians, Australians, and New Zealanders — had sweated to put the finishing touches to the preparations. Two of the mines were not to be used for they were beyond the area of the main assault and were subsequently abandoned. Later, in 1918, they were overrun during the Battle of the Lys (Fourth

Ypres) and details of their locations were mislaid. One blew up of its own accord – some say through lightning – on 17th June 1955 without causing any material damage. To this day the other remains buried somewhere beneath the soil of Flanders.

The principal objective of the British forces on 7th June was the Oosttaverne Line – the actual chord of the Salient on which was sited, a little to the east of the village of Oosttaverne and approximately 2½ miles from our front line, the third German defence system. The whole area including woods and buildings (in particular the famous White Chateau of Hollebeke), was heavily fortified with skilfully sited redoubts, from which flanking fire could be poured upon attacking troops, and numbers of pill-boxes.

The Messines front was held by General Sir Herbert Plumer's Second Army and for a whole year this very able Commander (later to become Field Marshall Lord Plumer of Messines) had been preparing for this offensive with immense care and patience. Staff work was impeccable and played a major part in the successful outcome of the battle. Opposing Plumer was part of General Sixt von Armin's Fourth Army with Otto von Below's Sixth Army on his left. Von Armin correctly anticipated an assault on the Messines Ridge and one of his subordinates, General von Laffort, Commander of the 4th German Corps at Messines, accurately defined the limits of the anticipated attack. Neither, however, was aware of exactly when the blow would fall and, although it was known that there had been much British mining activity in the area, the sheer scale of the subsequent eruptions came as a staggering surprise.

At the northernmost point of the British front (opposite Mount Sorrel) lay the 10th Corps under General Morland, then facing Wytschaete, the 9th Corps under General Hamilton-Gordon, and on the right, the 2nd Anzac Corps under General Godley. The main direct assault was to be carried out by the two southern corps. The 10th Corps was to advance on the ridge and the Oosttaverne Line from the northern flank. The 16th Irish Division and the Ulster Division were included in these three Corps but for once

political and religious differences were forgotten and both divisions were united by a common bond that stood them in good stead in the heat of battle.

One famous Southern Irishman, the Nationalist MP, Major William Redmond, fell at the very start of the battle and his body was subsequently carried from the field by Ulstermen. This was a sad loss of a sincere man who had long striven for Irish unity yet who gave his life for another cause he believed to be right. Major Redmond was well beyond the age for fighting but pleaded to be allowed to go over the top with his men. Reluctantly permission was granted but on the understanding that it would be the last time. Fate tragically decreed that it was so.

By 0800 hours on 7th June the Ulstermen and the 16th (Southern Ireland) Division had smashed their way through the wire in Wytschaete Wood; before midday they had captured the heap of rubble that had been Wytschaete village and were moving onwards towards Oosttaverne, routing all opposition and overrunning strongpoints in their forward rush.

To the north, the top of Hill 60 had disappeared in a separate mine explosion and British casualties had been light. More to the right, however, the 47th London Division had encountered unharmed machine-guns sited on the canal banks and in a strongly fortified location called the Damm Strasse. In other places, such as Ravine Wood, Battle Wood, and the grounds of the White Chateau, fierce fighting took place but by early afternoon most of 10th Corps' objectives had been gained. At 1545 the Welsh entered Oosttaverne village and a quarter of an hour later English County troops had taken the Oosttaverne Line east of the village.

On the Southern flank, the men of the 3rd Australian Division had assaulted at zero hour across the River Douve on bridges formed from duckboards and swarmed up the slopes of Messines Ridge. At their side men of the New Zealand Division fought their way from across the Steenbeek and by 0700 hours had reached the ruins of Messines village. In company with the Australians, the

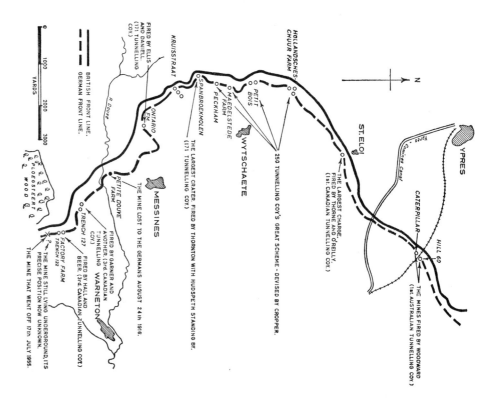

The Messines Mines. Of the 21 mines ready for action on 7th June, 1917, 19 were fired, in the positions shown here. Two (at the southern end) were not fired. Another (black circle) was earlier lost to the Germans. Sketch map and chart from *War Underground* (Frederick Muller Ltd., London) by permission of the author, Alexander Barrie.

Name of Mine	Date of Completion of Charging	Depth of Charge in Feet	Charge in Lbs.	Crater Dimensions in Feet — Diameter at Ground Level	Width of Rim	Diameter of Complete Obliteration	Length of Gallery in Feet
Hill 60							
A Left	1.8.16	90	45,700 Am. / 7,800 Gc. = 53,500	191	47	285	Branch 240
B Caterpillar	18.10.16	100	Ammonal 70,000	260	77	380	1,380
St. Eloi	28.5.17	125	Ammonal 95,000	176	77	330	825
Hollandscheschour							
No. 1	20.6.16	60	30,000 Am. / 4,200 Blas. = 34,200	183	80	343	Branch 45
No. 2	11.7.16	55	12,500 Am. / 2,400 Bla. = 14,900	105	55	215	45
No. 3	20.8.16	55	15,000 Am. / 2,500 Bla. = 17,500	215	30	201	395
Petit Bois							
No. 2 Left	15.8.16	57	21,000 Am. / 9,000 Bla. = 30,000	141	30	201	Branch 210
No. 1 Right	30.7.16	70	27,000 Am. / 3,000 Bla. = 30,000	175	100	417	2,070
Maedelstede Fm.	2.6.17	100	90,000 Am. / 4,000 Gc. = 94,000	205	90	385	1,610
Peckham	19.7.16	70	65,000 Am. / 15,000 Blas. / 7,000 Gc. Dyn. = 87,000	240	45	330	1,145
Spanbroekmolen	28.6.16 (Recovered 6.6.17)	88	Ammonal 91,000	250	90	430	1,710
Kruisstraat							
Nos. 1 and 4	5.7.16	57	Ammonal 30,000	235	80	395	—
No. 2	11.4.17	57	18,500 Am. / 1,000 Gc. = 19,500	217	75	367	Branch 170
No. 3	5.7.16	57	Ammonal 30,000	202	65	332	2,160
Ontario Fm.	6.6.17	104	Ammonal 60,000	200	10	220	1,290
Trench 127							
No. 7 Left	20.4.16	75	Ammonal 36,000	182	25	232	Branch 250
No. 8 Right	9.5.16	76	Ammonal 50,000	210	65	342	1,355
Trench 122							
No. 5 Left	14.5.16	60	Ammonal 20,000	195	64	323	Branch 440
No. 6 Right	11.6.16	75	Ammonal 40,000	228	64	356	970

New Zealanders continued forward until checked by machine guns from a strong-point called Fanny's Farm. Here a tank came to their aid and cleared out the defenders; by midday the Second Anzac Corps had also reached their main goal.

Before night fell Sir Hubert Plumer's Army had reached its final objectives and the night was spent in securing their gains against the expected counter-attacks. Owing to the devastation and disorientation caused by the mines, the counter-attack was slow in coming and not until the evening of the 8th did the Germans attack in force along almost the whole of the new line. Everywhere the enemy was repulsed and apart from localised fighting near the Lys and other odd spots of resistance the task was completed.

Messines was a brilliantly planned operation accomplished against positions which had been regarded by the enemy as impregnable. Our losses were light, particularly during the initial stages of the advance and although gains of two and a half miles on a front of nearly ten miles may seem minimal, it was, under the conditions of the Western Front, a splendid and clear-cut victory.

Messines was the curtain-raiser to Third Ypres and is generally grouped as part of that more widespread series of battles (which began on 31st July 1917). But in effect it was a separate conflict since a different strategy was employed in the later battle. No mines were dug during Third Ypres and Plumer's 'limited objective' method was not used again until the later stages of the advance towards Passchendaele when Plumer himself was moved up from the south to take charge of the situation. Strangely, perhaps, the use of mines on a major scale was discontinued by both sides after Messines.

'The worst part of the Salient' today. Lock Number Eight on the old Ypres—Comines Canal, looking toward Lock Number Seven. In the distance is Spoil Bank. Photograph taken from the Ypres—St Eloi Road, August 1969.

Opposite top left: St Eloi, fifty years later. The largest crater in the photograph at the right as it is today. This serene lake with its pond lilies and green banks was riven from the earth in a giant explosion at the start of the Battle of Messines, June 1917.

Below left: Peckham Crater. Another of the mines exploded on 7th June 1917. At the top right can be seen the trees and shrubs which grow around the vast Spanbroekmolen crater. The German front trenches ran on a direct line between the two craters.

Top right: 'The Mound of Death', as the St Eloi mine craters were known to our men, in 1917. The ruins of St Eloi and the road junction can be seen at the bottom left. [IWM]

Below right: The First Battalion, Royal Northumberland Fusiliers wearing German helmets and gas masks captured at St Eloi, 27th March 1916. A star shell and a Very pistol can be seen in the middle of the photograph and a Lewis gun at the left. [IWM]

144

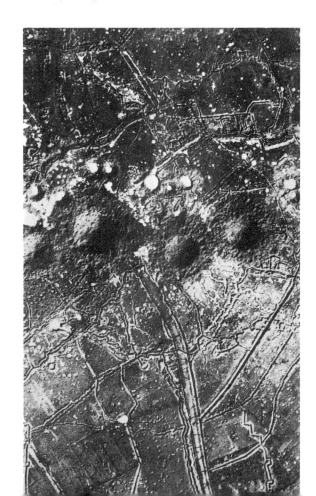

145

The Spanbroekmolen Crater (Pool of Peace) Memorial Tablet. The text reads:

Spanbroekmolen or Lone Tree Crater

This Crater was one of the 19 blown up by the Second Army on 7th June, 1917.

Following the explosion of these mines Lord Plumer's Army was able to capture the Messines Ridge.

Particulars

Sap started 1st January, 1916. Completed 26th June, 1916.
Depth of charge 88 feet. Charge 91,000 lbs Ammonal.
Length of gallery 1,710 feet.
Blown 7th June, 1917.

Dimensions

Diameter at ground level, 250 ft. Width of rim 90 feet.
Depth below normal ground level 40 feet. Height of rim 13 feet.
Diameter of complete obliteration 430 feet.
The crater is the property of Toc H Poperinghe.

TOPOGRAPHY OF THE ST ELOI SECTOR

The German lines ran along the top of the predominating ridge, which lay east of Ypres from Hooge to Wytschaete. Just below ran the British trenches, but never any further distant than 150 yards. At St Eloi at the neck of the Salient, the lines came very close together and ran astride the main Ypres—Wytschaete road, with not more than 50 yards separating them. The village of St Eloi itself, now reduced to a small cluster of ruins, stood at the junction of the cross-roads Ypres—Wytschaete and Voormezeele—Warneton, on the highest part of the commanding ground, and was held by the enemy. Constant shell-fire had reduced the ridge to a state of nakedness. It was devoid of all trees, and all signs of vegetation. The scene which met the eyes on looking over the parapets was that of the enemy's dense wire entanglements, mostly consisting of large *chevaux de frise*, behind which the jagged silhouette of the crumbling ruins of St Eloi stuck out against the sky, and slightly to the left, or south-east of the village, stood a large mound of earth, or tumultus, known as the 'Mound of Death'.

St Eloi was a most important part of the line, and had the enemy been able to advance their line in this locality our trenches running round Ypres would have become untenable. Owing to its importance strategically St Eloi had witnessed many fierce battles, and since October '14 the ridge had been occupied alternatively by British and Germans.

[FCH]

1ST NOVEMBER

Ordinary day in billets. Orders circulated to companies for the relief of the 1st North Staffords in the front line at the 'Mound of Death' on the morrow. Company commanders went off on reconnaissance and returned at night with a bad account of our new line. For the past month the area around the ruins of St Eloi had witnessed much fighting. Three mines had been exploded and there was the usual scrapping for possession of the craters.

Our Division expected an attack, and we were detailed to hold the position. Platoon commanders were given maps, and were told to explain the situation to the men.

ST ELOI. 2ND NOVEMBER

At 3 pm paraded for the trenches, and the Battalion, headed by the pipers, marched to Dickebusch, which we reached at dusk. At Voormezeele I remained behind with Sergt Flaherty to bring up the bombers and their bombs. Leaving Voormezeele after darkness had set in, we took to the communication trench. However, using it was out of the question as it was under water from the recent heavy rains.

As the heavily laden bombers slid and staggered at every step owing to the duckboards tilting sideways underfoot, we left the CT and marched up to the trenches by road. At the barrier at St Eloi we got into the front line, and branched off to the left.

We discovered that the line was equally as bad as the CT. It was waterlogged, and the inky darkness of the night added to our difficulties. This sector of the line was held by the North Staffords,

View from Spanbroekmolen Crater. Looking over the Douve Valley across no-man's land, to what was once British territory. Wulverghem Church is on the left and the spire of Neuve Eglise Church is on the horizon at the right.

The 'Pool of Peace.' Looking over the still waters of Spanbroekmolen crater—the largest of them all—towards Kemmel Hill. The poles in the middle distance mark the British trenches and the crater, of course, the German ones.

and the fire bays were fully occupied. Gradually the line became worse, and when we got to our Company flank we found practically no trench at all. We seemed to have been in one continuous nightmare of mud. Many of my heavily laden bombers were engulfed in the trench, and had to be helped out.

Words cannot describe the state of our new line, and rain was falling heavily to complete our discomfort. Practically the whole company front was under water, and the floating duckboards would fly up and hit the unwary one in the face when stood upon. At 9 pm we relieved A Company of the 1st North Staffordshire Regiment. In our company front there were three mine craters to hold. The North Staffords reported the Huns particularly hostile. All the craters were in the middle of No-Man's-Land as the mines had in every case failed to reach the lines, and both sides held the near lips by saps run for about fifty yards from the main trench. Wet up to my waist, I put out the unfortunate bombers in the listening posts. The enemy hurled bombs for some time and then became silent. Having been warned of an expected attack, we kept very much on the alert throughout the night. There were only a dozen dug-outs in the whole line. Caulfield and Plowman shared one, and Burns and I another. One of our advanced posts was very difficult to get to; going over the open was impossible, owing to the mud and wire entanglements. There was, however, a fallen tree trunk lying across the trench which was flooded to a depth of two feet. By hanging on to the so-called parapet, one managed to reach to the post without getting drowned.

Burns and I sat up for the remainder of the night, taking turns to visit the posts every hour. A rum ration was issued; also smelly goat-skins which had got soaked being brought up with the rations and the mail.

It poured throughout the night, and Sergt Ginn kept reporting that a dug-out or parapet had fallen in on top of one of the men, and then we would have to muster a rescue party. It was truly a terrible night.

[FCH]

3RD NOVEMBER

At 6 o'clock Sergt Ginn called me to say that the enemy were walking about on their parapets. Burns and I went out to find that some Germans were walking about in the mist, swinging coke braziers to and fro to keep them alight! Like us, they were caked in mud. We did not fire, as they, being on the brow of the ridge, had the advantage over us. At 'stand to' I went round the Company and found the men wonderfully cheery, in spite of the terrible conditions. The rain had stopped, and it had started to freeze hard.

During the morning gum boots were issued out to all ranks. However, as they only came up to one's knees, and as in most places the water came well up the thighs, they welled water at every step. The result was that the owners often preferred to pull their feet out of them by the aid of the suction of the mud, and carry on in their socks!

All morning spent in trying to drain out the water. Sump pits were dug, as the only trench pump available would not function. Fatigue parties worked away with old biscuit tins, and baled the water out over the parados. We all walked about in the open as the Saxons were also walking out on their parapets. Their trenches, although on the high ground, were water-logged, and we watched them bailing and pumping water into the large mine crater.

5TH NOVEMBER

About dawn the frost broke, and the trenches became as bad as ever. The sand-bags of the few remaining revetments bulged outwards and collapsed. The cold was intense, at 'stand to' I found the men so benumbed that some were unable to pull back the bolts of their rifles.

At dawn throughout this tour I went round all posts armed with a rum jar. After the NCO in charge had reported his command present and his rifles clean, each man of the post filed up to me, and I issued him his 'tot' in a small metal sup. I never saw the rum more appreciated than it was during this tour.

Messines from the air. This photograph shows the trenches of the opposing armies before the whole area became saturated with shell fire and mine craters. The trenches run from right to left across the photograph; the British trenches are in the immediate foreground and the German ones slightly above them, but below the village. [IWM]

At 6 am our line was systematically shelled with 'whiz-bangs'. On going round one of the traverses into a fire bay I found that there had been a direct hit. Drummer Spencer was killed; Pte Farrell was bleeding badly from the head and had his eye out, and Pte Richards was wounded in the ear. They had been sitting round a brazier, making tea for their breakfasts, and had no doubt, drawn fire with the smoke. When I got to them, the poor fellows were lying half submerged in the liquid mud, with pools of blood all round.

[FCH]

MESSINES

This famous village is about five and a quarter miles south of Ypres and dominates much of the surrounding countryside. It fell to the Germans on 1st November 1914 after heroic resistance by British cavalry and lies close to the scene of the brilliant action of the London Scottish Territorials. The ruined village was recaptured by the New Zealand Division of the Anzac Corps after the explosion of the Messines mines on 7th June 1917 but again passed into enemy hands during April of 1918. At the end of September 1918 the shattered remnants of the village reverted once more to British control after being taken by troops of the 34th Division.

View across the Douve Valley, showing an artillery bombardment in progress, 8th June 1917. The shell burst on the horizon marks the location of the church in the photograph below. [IWM]

Messines today. The church, rebuilt from rubble, marks the location of the village.

150

Battle of Messines. Horses and mules taking up small arms ammunition through the devastated German front lines, 11th June 1917. Note the German 'potato-mashers' on the parapet of the trench at the lower left. This area was lost to the enemy again during Fourth Ypres in 1918. [IWM]

Messines, August 1969. A horse grazing on the Messines Ridge. This photograph was taken at a spot slightly to the left of the scene above and looking more towards Hill 63 and across the Douve Valley.

Six soldiers, five soldiers, six soldiers . . of the Great War.

As a stretcher-bearer one saw many many ghastly sights at 'Plugstreet' — men with dreadful wounds, gassed men, etc. . . . I took several of my friends down to be buried at Ploegsteert Cemetery. . . . In Plugstreet Wood an officer and twenty-three men were wiped out by 'whizz-bangs'. One man had all his chest blown away. His identity disc was where his heart should have been. . . .

[WF Chapman]

A shell fell in a trench in Plugstreet Wood and the only thing they could find of the parapet sentry was his bottom jaw sticking in the sandbags. He was literally blown to pieces.

[WF Chapman]

Known unto God

The Memorial at Oosttaverne

OOSTTAVERNE

The objective of our troops in the Battle of Messines was the German third defence system a little east of the village itself. This was known as the 'Oosttaverne Line' and it was reached on the afternoon of 7th June 1917 (following the firing of the Messines mines) by English County troops. Welsh soldiers captured Oosttaverne village a little earlier.

The memorial Oosttaverne is to men of the 19th (Western) Division who fell near this spot at the time and during later fighting in 1918.

Ploegsteert (*Plugstreet*). Photograph taken in pouring rain, August 1969, of a famous spot known as 'Mud Corner' with Ploegsteert Wood in the background. Mud Corner Military Cemetery can be seen on the right. Close to this area, which is near St Yves, Bruce Bairnsfather served during the winter of 1914–15 and commenced the drawings which led to his famous 'Old Bill' caricatures. Near here too were the trenches from which, in company with others, he climbed out to fraternise with the Germans on Christmas Day 1914, during the unofficial 'truce'.

WYTSCHAETE

This village, which is located about four miles south of Ypres and just over a mile north of Messines, was prominent in the fighting of 1914 and 1917 and once more became a scene of fierce combat in April 1918 during which the South African Brigade of the 9th Division fought off heavy enemy attacks. After further ebb-and-flow struggles Wytschaete was abandoned by our troops until finally regained at the end of September 1918 in the course of the Anglo-Belgian attack in Flanders.

The crater of the 'Lost Mine' in 1969. No damage was done as farm workers had left the fields to shelter from a storm. Another mine, the exact location of which is unknown, still lies beneath the ground somewhere in this area.

Ploegsteert, July 1955. Two Belgians standing at the bottom of the large crater caused by the explosion of one of the lost mines near St Yves. The mine seemingly blew of its own accord but some claim it was triggered by lightning.

[Courtesy of the 'Family Delchambre', St Yvon, Warneton.]

154

Village of Wytschaete, 8th June 1917. Captured by 16th (Irish) and 36th (Ulster) Divisions, 7th June 1917. [IWM]

Wytschaete Village (known to our troops as 'Whitesheet') as it is today.

KEMMEL

Kemmel village is about five miles south-west of Ypres and two and a half miles west of Wytschaete. It was well known as a 'behind the lines' billet for our men but was lost to the Germans on 25th April 1918 during Fourth Ypres.

The main weight of the enemy attack upon the village fell upon troops of the South African Brigade of the 9th Division. Kemmel Hill which was then being held by the French was also overrun by the Germans who stormed over the crest and beyond to the village of Locre where their advance lost impetus and finally ground to a halt.

A Man of God and His Charge. The grave of Major William Redmond stands a few yards from the official British Military Cemetery at Locre. Attempts were made at one time to move the grave there, but these were resisted by his family and also by Monsieur Debevere, the former (now retired) priest of Locre Church. He has personally looked after the grave of this well loved son of Ireland for many years and regularly prays by it, and ensures that it is tended with loving care. With him is Madame Delau Van Uxem of Ypres who died in February 1970.

Major Redmond was killed at the start of Third Ypres.

Panorama from the crest of Mount Kemmel, looking down towards Kemmel Village. From the top of this hill can be seen the whole arc of the old Salient from Ypres right round to Armentieres and beyond. The village suffered considerable damage and shells regularly whistled past the spot from where this photograph was taken.

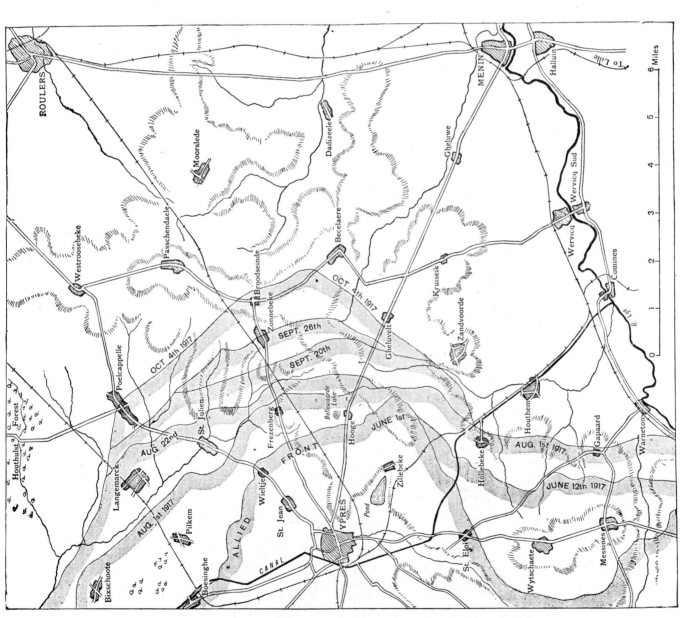

The country between the Ypres Salient and the Roulers–Menin Line, showing the progress of the Offensive up to the first week of October 1917. Map from *Nelson's History of the War*, (John Buchan) by permission of Thomas Nelson & Sons Ltd.

THIRD YPRES
AND PASSCHENDAELE

On 30th October 1917, in a clear cold dawn, Canadian troops commenced an attack on the shattered ruins of a small village in Flanders against desperate resistance by the 5th and 11th Bavarian Divisions of the German Fourth Army. This attack on Passchendaele, supported on the left by London Territorials and the Royal Naval Division, constituted the closing stages of the three months of bloody and extended fighting known as Third Ypres.

Passchendaele even now arouses fierce controversy and arguments on the merits of the strategy of Field-Marshal Sir Douglas Haig. Was he – as many people believe – a withdrawn unapproachable man, unaware of the suffering of his soldiers and the shocking condition of the ground over which they had to struggle, or was he – as others think – a man of vision, brave and determined, with a first class plan which, had luck (and the weather) been on his side, would have shortened the war and saved many lives in the process?

Was he genuinely trying to help the French by occupying the full attention of the enemy after the serious mutinies in the French armies following the dismal failure of General Nivelle's offensive in April, and was he fed too optimistic information by his intelligence staff, or were these merely excuses for a continuance of the offensive which, combined with the earlier Somme battles, had destroyed the flower of British manhood and for the first time caused a serious loss of confidence in British generalship? Did Haig have an obsession to prove himself in Flanders before the Americans arrived in sufficient numbers to take over the main

Third Ypres. A typical battlefield scene. British and German dead. A broken rifle with bayonet. Shell holes. Stagnant water. Denuded trees. Mud. [IWM]

burden of the fighting (which could not be before 1918 (or is this just another smear by his opponents?

No-one can give a definite answer to those questions but the evidence is available for all to examine and judge. Without doubt Haig believed that an attack through Flanders, combined with an amphibious landing near Ostend, would roll up the German right wing, clear the Channel coast, and present the possibility of open warfare. Indeed, he planned such an offensive for 1916 but was subsequently persuaded by the French to transfer his main thrust to the proposed Somme battlefields. In the event the Somme was mainly a British action for, although forty French divisions were due to take part, less than twenty were able to do so because of the immense drain on French reserves caused by the blood-path of Verdun.

Many factors militated against the success of Haig's offensive. Because of the Somme and Arras, the battle of Third Ypres were long delayed and the weather correspondingly degenerated later in the year; besides this, the low, marshy ground with the water table lying just below its heavily shelled surface, coupled with the many small streams meandering through the whole area, was not conducive to easy movement. Moreover, even after the battle of Messines the enemy still commanded many of the heights above the Salient and retained excellent observation of our activities. The recent introduction of concrete pillboxes bristling with machine guns, in conjunction with the usual masses of barbed wire and the waterlogged ground, presented formidable obstacles. And time was against us. The Russian front was crumbling, a number of German divisions and batteries had already been transported to the west and this disposition was rapidly gathering momentum. Surprise was out of the question for the enemy was well aware of the impending offensive (which, incidentally, had previously been condemned by the French, by several British generals, and by Lloyd George and other politicians).

According to Haig's plan the rising ground to the east, north-east, and north of Ypres – including Passchendaele itself – was to be

captured by our forces within a fortnight. This would enable a move to be made against German bases in West Flanders. It was not until early November, however, that Passchendaele was finally taken and even then the northern-most part of that ridge remained in enemy hands.

The tragedy of Ypres was not yet finished, however, for during the last desperate gamble of the Germans in the spring of 1918 all of the ground won at such high cost was abandoned overnight and the British lines withdrawn almost to the walls of the town. Fighting outside Ypres in 1917, turned into a bloody war of attrition. Whether it achieved anything worthwhile is still open to doubt; the toll was enormous and estimates of British casualties vary from 250,000 to 300,000. (In Lloyd George's memoirs, in fact, there is a hint that the casualties were nearer to 400,000. No unequivocal estimate has yet been given and, as with other queries surrounding this tragic issue, the real truth may never be known.

THE THIRD BATTLE OF YPRES

Third Ypres was not a single battle but a series of separate struggles which culminated in the grim fight for Passchendaele in late October and early November. These assaults are known in history under the following names:

Battle of Pilckem Ridge	(31st July)
Battle of Gheluvelt Plateau	(10th August)
Battle of Langemarck	(16th August)
Battle of Menin Road Ridge	(20th September)
Battle of Polygon Wood	(26th September)
Battle of Broodseinde	(4th October)
Battle of Poelcapelle	(9th October)
First Battle of Passchendaele	(12th October)
Second Battle of Passchendaele	(26th October –
	10th November)

Prior to the start of Third Ypres a major re-distribution of British Forces took place on the Western Front and the subsequent line-up in the Salient was as follows: on the extreme left, between the sea and St Georges (territory taken over from the French) was Sir Henry Rawlinson's Fourth Army. On his right were the Belgians and on their right the French First Army under General Anthoine. Then came the British Fifth Army, commanded by Sir Hubert Gough, which covered the ground from Boesinghe to the Zillebecke-Zandvoorde road south-east of Ypres, and finally Sir Herbert Plumer's Second Army stretching down to the Lys. Ground beyond the boundaries of the Salient was the responsibility of Sir Henry Horne's First Army and General Byng's Third Army.

Commanding the enemy's Fourth Army in the Salient, was General Sixt von Armin, the losing general at the Battle of Messines two months earlier but nonetheless a clever and determined fighter. Because of the swampy ground in Flanders and the consequent difficulty in digging deep fortifications, von Armin had devised an extremely effective alternative – the concrete 'pill-box'. The pillbox had made its debut at Messines but in the Salient it truly came into its own; the Germans used these thick-walled machinegun forts to considerable advantage in their 'elastic defence' method and with them inflicted heavy casualties on our troops. Von Armin's strategy was to hold his front line thinly with infantrymen who would fall back when assaulted. The attackers would then get involved in the pill-box zone after which special counter-attack troops, backed by artillery bombardments, would repel the advance. For some time this system was used successfully but it was temporarily abandoned in the later stages of Third Ypres in favour of the older technique of the strongly manned front.

Included in Haig's original plan was a landing from the sea behind the enemy lines in conjunction with the main assault. With the appearance of the Fourth Army near the coast, the Germans realised that such a move was imminent particularly since they were well aware of the impending offensive in the Salient. They decided, therefore, to act first and on Tuesday, 10th July they attacked in strength against our breastwork defences on the east

bank of the Yser opposite Nieuport. In a very short time the bridgehead was overwhelmed and two battalions of our troops were destroyed or captured.

Throughout July the build-up of men, materials, and guns continued and our aircraft were constantly engaged on reconnaissance flights and in stopping hostile planes from learning too much. From the middle of the month our artillery maintained a steady bombardment, which covered the whole of the Salient including back areas and enemy artillery, with explosives and gas.

The main burden of the coming battle fell on the four assault corps (ten divisions) of the Fifth Army, attacking on the seven mile front. Plumer's five divisions (including the 3rd Australian Division and the New Zealand Division) had limited objectives and were to act mainly on a holding basis. On the left, General Anthoine's First French Army would also commit two divisions thus spreading the total frontage of the offensive to fifteen miles from just north of Steenstraat down to the Lys. Approximately 100,000 men were involved with an additional seventeen divisions in reserve.

The German forces consisted of fifteen front line and close support divisions with others fanned out behind. Ground advantage lay with the enemy (as it did throughout the Salient).

As the time of the assault drew nearer, hopes of good weather (imperative for success) sank as grey clouds scudded across the sky. The last week in July was dull and cloudy and on 30th July heavy rain fell for a time; darkness fell with a steady drizzle which ceased towards the early hours of the morning. The air was damp and misty when, precisely at 0850 hours on the morning of 31st July, the Allied front erupted with flame.

The Third Battle of Ypres had begun. The Allies went over the top and behind a heavy barrage smashed their way into the German positions. In most places they met with almost immediate success; the French took Steenstraat on the left and St Julian was entered by English County troops (although it was not captured until several days later). Pilckem fell to the 38th Welsh Division and crossings on the Steenbeek were seized by the 51st Highland Division and the Guards. In the centre, the remains of Hooge Chateau and the village were captured and, after fierce fighting, Frezenberg was won by the 15th Division. A strongpoint called 'Pommern Castle', a short distance north of Frezenberg, was carried by the 55th Division (West Lancashire Territorials).

The 2nd Corps under General Jacobs, however, encountered strong opposition and the advance along the axis of the Menin Road was slow and painful as enemy machine gunners took a heavy toll from outposts in shell-shattered Chateau Wood, ill-named Sanctuary Wood, and Shrewsbury Forest. 'Stirling Castle' fell into our hands after stiff fighting but the attackers were then halted by heavy fire from concentrations of enemy troops in front of Inverness Copse and Glencorse Wood. The Germans had massed troops there in order to bar the way to the Gheluvelt Plateau — the key to their defence system.

Tanks were used in the assault but owing to the soft ground and the many obstacles they failed to get forward and quickly became victims of the German guns. An enemy anti-tank gun enclosed in a pill-box and sited along the Menin Road knocked out seventeen of the steel monsters with ease. This area became known as the Tank Graveyard. It also became the graveyard of the crews, who were often wiped out as they tried to leave their machines.

Early in the afternoon the drizzle started again and within two or three hours developed into a heavy, soaking downpour. Streams began to flood and the mud became stickier and more widespread. That which had been most dreaded was becoming a reality. Flanders was slowly reverting to a swamp.

In the afternoon of the 31st the enemy carried out his first major counter attacks but apart from some limited withdrawals by our troops — mainly in the north — they were unsuccessful. At the end of the day the German first line had been breached along two thirds of the front. On the right, the New Zealand Division had captured La Basse Ville. The ruins of Hollebeke had fallen into our hands as had

Klein Zillebeke (where almost three years earlier the Brigade of Guards and the dismounted Household Cavalry had put up the determined resistance which had smashed back the last major effort of the Germans during 'First Ypres'. Overshadowing these successes, however, was the failure of II Corps to break through along the Menin Road — a foretaste of what was to come. Additionally, heavy casualties had already been incurred by Gough's army. Worst of all, the weather turned against us on 1st August and prevented any further significant movement. For four days and four nights heavy rain fell, turning the whole battlefield into a quagmire. During that time parties of Germans attacked with bombs and bayonets; fierce, bloody, fighting took place in the wet gloom and mud. In shell holes, around pill-boxes and shattered woods, small groups of mud-covered men hacked indecisively at one another as the rain poured down on the sodden landscape.

Then, on the 5th August, the rain stopped leaving sullen skies and moisture-laden mists blanketing the battlefield. For two weeks the main offensive was bogged down whilst the rain intermittently poured or drizzled and the swamp grew larger. Small operations were still carried out whenever possible and on 3rd August our troops re-entered St Julian and elsewhere other positions were consolidated.

In the middle of the month Sir Douglas Haig instigated another subsidiary action further south with the object of detracting the enemy's attention from the Salient and ensuring that German strength was not entirely concentrated in the north. This attack was at Loos (where in 1915 men of the 15th Division had swarmed over Hill 70 but were wiped out and the hill subsequently remained in enemy hands). This time Canadians were the attacking forces. On 15th August they swept the Germans off the crest of Hill 70, reached all their objectives beyond that point, and held them against strong counter-attacks.

Other fighting took place during August especially by the French and by the troops on our own left sector but the pill-boxes took a heavy toll. Desperate fighting broke out again along the Menin Road in the region of Glencorse Wood and Inverness Copse,

Above:
Battle of Polygon Wood. 'Clapham Junction' on the Menin Road, 26th September 1917. Camouflaged tanks and infantry moving up to the attack. Shell bursts in the distance. A Lewis-gun crew may be seen at the lower left; the first man carrying the tripod, the second the barrel, and the third burdened down with ammunition panniers. [IWM]

Above right:
Menin Road near Ypres, 20th September 1917. Derelict Mark IVs — a male tank in the foreground and a female behind it. A wooden 'unditching' beam is on top of the female tank. Dead soldiers sprawl near both tanks. [IWM]

Right:
'Clapham Junction' looking toward Sanctuary Wood, 23rd September 1917. Derelict British tanks, probably Mark IIIs (identifiable by the enlarged track shoe at every sixth link, and by the elongated six-pounder [naval] gun in the sponson). The shorter Army gun was not available until the Mark IV.

Tanks were initially called 'landships' but for security reasons this was changed to 'water carriers' which inevitably was shortened to 'tanks'. Each model had a male and a female version — male tanks mounted six-pounders in the sponsons, and females mounted machine-guns. There was even a hermaphrodite machine which mounted a six-pounder in one sponson and machine-guns in the other. [IWM]

desolate areas in which merciless engagements were fought by mud-covered men. The troops of both sides fought like wild animals and time and again Inverness Copse changed ownership after bloody hand-to-hand encounters. The Germans continued to counter-attack fiercely and all our efforts to press through those dreadful woods failed.

It was at that time too, that a sense of depression permeated our front; not only were the Tommies exhausted but they had become embittered by the wasteful loss of life and the appalling conditions under which they were expected to fight. Although the enemy were undergoing the same hardships, Ludendorff knew that August — in spite of the initial British gains — had been a better month for the Germans than for the British. In fact Ludendorff had even found it possible to transfer a number of divisions from Flanders during August to help the Austrians.

The situation was indeed grim for the Allies and there was even talk of abandoning the offensive altogether. Haig, however, was convinced that the Germans were beginning to break and that further pressure would cause their collapse. He decided to continue the battle but to employ fresh strategy and so invited Sir Herbert Plumer to extend his Second Army front northwards to include the area of the bogged down II Corps. Somewhat reluctantly Plumer agreed but made it understood that future operations were to consist of limited objectives to be taken on a step-by-step basis.

During early September the weather became more favourable and the water-logged Salient dried out. Regular aerial operations again became possible and large formations of aircraft took to the bright skies.

Harassing attacks were made by Gough's soldiers towards Poelcapelle on three days during the first half of September. But, with little to show for them except casualties, further attempts were abandoned. Meanwhile Plumer had given careful thought to his future task of pushing along the Menin Road. Various methods of combating the well-sited enemy pill-boxes were given close consideration. On 13th September our guns opened up a heavy bombardment and the Germans, who had been wondering whether we had decided to forego further attempts in the Salient, realised that another big attack was coming. At 0540 hours on 20th September they became acutely aware of our intentions for an attack was launched on an eight-mile front by four divisions assisted by massed artillery and close air support. This was a controlled attack directed mainly against the Gheluvelt Plateau, that vitally important point intersected by the Menin Road. Inverness Copse and then the hamlet of Veldhoek fell at last to troops of the 23rd Division. The remains of Glencorse Wood and Nonne Boschen (Nun's Wood) were taken by the 1st Anzac Corps and in spite of a temporary hold-up at Black Watch corner the Australians went on to take about half of Polygon Wood, thus reaching their objective. South of the Menin Road, Welsh and English County troops cleared Shrewsbury Forest and, below that, other small woods lying north of the Ypres–Comines Canal. The appalling mud wastes of Dumbarton Lakes were also captured and advances made to the Tower Hamlets spur (over the other side of which lay Gheluvelt). In the north, the 55th West Lancashire Territorials succeeded in reaching their objective as did the 47th London Division, the 51st Highland Territorials, and the 9th Division (which included Scottish and South African brigades). Once again heavy rain had fallen during the night and once again the battlefields had reverted to swamps. Fortunately the rain ceased before the attack but it caused tremendous hardship to our men.

Fierce fighting occurred all along the line and brittle skirmishes took place when pill-boxes and other strongpoints were surrounded by our troops. Some frightened and badly shaken Germans, dazed by the tremendous weight of the artillery bombardment, ran to the rear or threw up their hands begging for mercy; in other places they fought on doggedly until finally overwhelmed.

Heavy machine-gun fire held up the advance at Tower Hamlets but elsewhere things proceeded smoothly and an advance of about a mile along the Menin Road was made. The battle had been a triumph for the British. Our soldiers had fought against a brave and determined enemy and, in spite of the terrain and deadly machine-gun fire, had won the day. Counter-attacks swiftly followed in the late afternoon and evening and during the next few days but apart from one or two short-lived successes they were repulsed.

The next major attack came on 26th September. The objectives were the remainder of Polygon Wood and Zonnebeke Village. At 0550 hours our infantry attacked along a front of about six miles and achieved almost total success. Practically all of Polygon Wood and the smashed ruins of Zonnebeke were cleared; on the left men from the North Midlands and a division of London Territorials advanced along the Wieltje–Passchendaele road. Other British troops fought their way beyond Veldhoek, relieving on the way two companies of Argyll and Sutherland Highlanders who had been surrounded the night before when the Germans had executed a surprise attack.

Powerful enemy counter-attacks followed the British success and in fact between 26th September and 3rd October numerous attempts were made by the Germans to recapture lost ground. *Flammenwerfers* were employed but nowhere, apart from minor and temporary – gains, was it possible to force back the British.

Then the old enemy returned. Heavy rain and drizzle, coupled with gale force winds set in. Once more rain had arrived just as a new attack was about to be launched – this time on a front of approximately seven miles and aiming at the Broodseinde heights, Gravenstafel, and Poelcapelle. The assault was due to commence at 0600 hours on the 4th of October. By an amazing coincidence the enemy had also prepared an attack with fresh divisions but timed to start at 0610 hours. Just as the Germans were forming up for the jump off our own preliminary artillery barrage burst upon them and in a short space of time deadly execution took place. Before the Germans could recover, our assault troops burst upon them causing more casualties and utter confusion in their ranks. Broodseinde and that part of the Zonnebeke area still in enemy hands fell to the Australians, Gravenstafel was captured by the New Zealanders, and the western half of Poelcapelle was occupied by the South Midland Division from Gough's Fifth Army against

fierce resistance and in grim conditions. The shattered remnants of Polygon Wood and the village of Reutal also came under British control. By early afternoon we had won. The German High Command was disturbed both at the success of our attack and the extent of the losses incurred by their own troops. The British forces also suffered heavy casualties and, although a major success (for those days) had been achieved, the maximum distance we advanced on 4th October was about one mile.

Inevitably German counter-attacks followed (with no less than eight being directed between the Menin Road and Reutal) but all were repulsed. Then in the afternoon it rained heavily. Captured pill-boxes and trenches flooded over and shell-holes filled with water to the very brim. Everywhere was mud, and the artillerymen found it increasingly difficult to stop their guns from sinking to their axles – in some cases to their muzzles – in the ooze.

Any thoughts of achieving the original objectives of the Flanders campaign had long been abandoned and what Haig now sought was a firm base on the Passchendaele Ridge for the coming winter months. The only alternative was to pull right back but this was not acceptable for a number of reasons – not the least being the enormous casualty lists. Haig decided to carry out further attacks and Tuesday, 9th October was the date chosen for a joint French–British assault. Rain fell heavily for two days before the assault but at 0520 hours on the Tuesday and in a horribly wet dawn Allied troops moved forward. The main effort was focused on a six mile front from east of Zonnebeke to north-west of Langemarck.

Advancing alongside the French in the north, the Guards Division captured a number of small villages and by early afternoon they and our Allies had arrived on the outskirts of the Houthulst Forest, a vast area of woodland of which, many years earlier, Marlborough had said, 'He who holds Houthulst commands Flanders.' This was the northern pillar of the enemy line and only a limited portion of the forest was penetrated by the Allies.

To the south, the ruins of Poelcapelle were taken by Yorkshiremen of the 11th Division after a savage fight (particularly near a brewery) where enemy machine-gunners again caused great trouble.

On the 11th Division's right, the main attack was carried out by Australians of General Plumer's Second Army together with British Territorial troops. Their orders were to move towards Passchendaele along two spurs between which was the valley of the Ravebeek. At one time a tiny watercourse, heavy rains and constant bombardment had swollen it to a small lake of filthy water and liquid mud which was virtually impassable. (Part of this area had already been designated on war maps as 'Marsh Bottom' and part 'Waterfields'; both are apt descriptions).

Conditions during and before the attack were beyond belief. Additionally several divisions had been thoroughly exhausted by a long nightmare march through mud, water and craters to attack under heavy enemy fire from artillery and machine-guns.

Incredibly another attack was fixed, this time for Friday, 12th October and yet again the heavens opened and added more floods to the pitiless wastelands. In this assault – the First Battle of Passchendaele – only very slight gains were made and heavy losses were caused to the attackers. No further attacks took place until 22nd October when more limited gains were made east of Poelcapelle and in Houthulst Forest. Three days later a drying wind set the stage for an assault along the Bellevue and Gravenstafel spurs which ran parallel towards Passchendaele. Canadian troops had recently moved into the area to relieve the exhausted Anzac Corps and to them fell the task of the final drive to Passchendaele.

The rain returned at 0545 hours on 25th October just as the Canadians edged forward along the line of advance. They met determined opposition on the Bellevue spur where many machine-guns were situated in blockhouses (some of which were built into the ruined houses surmounting the ridge). This too was where the old German Staden–Zonnebeke main defence line was located but despite this the Canadians won their objectives; their left was supported by the 63rd (Royal Naval) Division and a London Territorial Division; on the right the Canadians captured a small hill south of Passchendaele. At the other end of the Salient, British troops entered Gheluvelt for the first time since the deadly fighting of 1914. Unfortunately mud was clogging their rifles and, following fierce enemy counter-attacks, they were forced to withdraw. On the far left the French prepared to attack over the St Jansbeek and on the 27th, in company with the Belgians, they captured several villages. By the end of the next day Merckem Peninsular had been cleared and our Allies were menacing the western side of Houthulst Forest.

On 30th October the first main attack against Passchendaele village itself commenced, the Canadians jumping off at 0540 hours. For three days it had not rained but at 1000 hours it began to fall heavily. Slowly, but at the cost of many casualties, the Canadians forced their way past a number of pill-boxes whilst on their left, north of the Bellvue spur, the Territorials and the Naval Division endeavoured to keep pace. Due to the muddy conditions these troops floundered helplessly and became the target for well-directed fire which caused a large number of casualties. The Canadians, meanwhile, succeeded in forcing their way to Crest Farm, about 500 yards from Passchendaele Church. Their line ran across the valley with the left wing across the Bellvue spur and its apex actually forming a Salient in the outskirts of Passchendaele. From this position they held off numerous counter-attacks.

At long last came a few days of dry weather. On 6th November, at 0600 hours and under lowering skies, the Canadians plunged forward in the final headlong rush which carried them into Passchendaele. There was no village left: only rubble. Roads had virtually disappeared as had the church, and the whole area for miles around was a muddy desert of overlapping shell-holes filled to the brim with filthy water.

Several days later the Canadians pushed forward again and most of the main ridge fell into Allied hands. For once we looked down upon the enemy after years of his observing our every move and (for a few months only as it turned out) Ypres was free from his ever searching eyes.

Passchendaele had cost at least half a million human casualties.

God knows what cynical wit christened those splintered stumps Inverness Copse or Sanctuary Wood. Who named that stinking quagmire Dumbarton Lakes? And who ordained that those treacherous heaps of filth should be known as Stirling Castle or Northampton Farm?

['Warrior']

Stirling Castle. The Chateau east of the Menin Road near Clapham Junction. This is a fairly early photograph – probably after the first strike in 1915. By the time of Third Ypres, the Chateau had been reduced to a pile of rubble, but had been converted into a powerful defensive position which inflicted heavy casualties on our troops advancing from the direction of Sanctuary Wood. [IWM]

Below: The attractive house built on the site of Stirling Castle.

Our road to Company HQ from Ypres is shown in places by dead men in various postures, here three men lying together, there a dead 'Jock' lying across a trench, the only possible bridge, and we had to step on him to get across. The old German front-line, now behind our reserve, must be the most dreadful thing in existence, whether in reality or imagination, a stretch of slimy wicker-work bordering a noisome canal of brown water, where dead men float and fragments of bodies and limbs project hideously, as if in pickle. The remembrance of one attitude will always haunt me, a German doubled up with knees under his chin and hand clutching hair above the face of the ghastliest terror.

[HQ]

Garter Point. A stretcher party bringing in a wounded soldier over a duckboard track during Third Ypres, 10th October 1917. [IWM]

Garter Point. Poppies bloom by the Westhoek–Zonnebeke Road today.

168

The Butte De Polygon, in the heart of Polygon Wood, February 1918.

The distinctive shape of the Butte De Polygon today. Polygon Wood lies about three and a half miles east of Ypres and was the scene of fierce fighting during the attack of the Prussian Guards at First Ypres.

In September 1917 the wood was stormed by the Australians and a memorial to their 5th Division now surmounts the Butte. Below it, lie the graves of 2,000 British, Australians, Canadians, and New Zealanders. Records of New Zealand missing are in a memorial building near the spot from which this photograph was taken.

Fighting in this area during Third Ypres extended from 26th September to 3rd October 1917 and was known as the battle of Polygon Wood. Capture of the wood was vital to allow the continued advance of the British forces towards the main part of Passchendaele Ridge.

Every battle possessed its own peculiar Pageantry, but of them all the first was Third Ypres.

Here was stupendous spectacle, accompanied throughout by a Gargantuan symphony of sound. The thunderous roar of the guns exceeded pandemonium. The boom of cannon was accompanied by the ceaseless clang of metal, blasting masonry, and clattering against tree stumps.

It was as if giants beat ten thousand tomtoms, while raving fanatics smote all the instruments of death in wild disharmony.

Yet the steady beat of rhythmic uproar kept the feet of the players moving to an even thread. The chatter of machine-guns throbbed maniac melody to the peal of cannon.

Always, from somewhere out of the gloom, unseen voices chanted 'Water, give me water. For Christ's sake give me water'; and staccato voices shrieked through the night, 'Hell! . . . Damn! . . . God! . . . Kamerad! . . . Mein Gott! . . .' Cries so often silenced in a gurgle as the player sank beneath the soggy slime, drawing a last breath of gas, with oxygen twice laden with hydrogen. The urgent plea for water at last fulfilled.

The dulcet notes of spinning metal, and the hissing of spent bullets, made known their plaintive wail, accentuated against the din of gunfire.

The deep bass from the voice of active man commanding was carried away amidst the bellowing, the slightest variation of intonation producing a new ear-splitting note. The stricken commander, lying somewhere beyond human aid in a shell-hole, wailed piteously above the storm — 'Give me water!' And though his voice, and that of hundreds more, pierced the uproar, it came from a region unseen and undiscoverable. The whirring of aeroengines above, the tearing of the sticks of timber, once trees, added a fresh plane of note-sound to break and confuse the whipping melody of rifle-fire.

One sound alone for each man beat with deafening certainty, a heart knocking in a wheezing throat.

The solemn procession of men, mules, and horses, of wagons, limbers and crazy two-wheeled carts, man-hauled, streamed ever eastward across the broken tracks. Sometimes the columns checked to make way for an ambulance. Then men would lie, or sit, or squat just where they stood, from sheer fatigue. Or again, the columns would sway and stagger as some gust of shell-fire smote the track taking more, as if by design and appointment, to swell the chanting chorus of the wounded.

And in the forefront of the Pageant the players rolled and staggered through deep pits suffused with barbed wire, cursing the Universe, muttering incoherent refrain.

'Give 'em Hell! . . . My rifle's jammed! . . .'

And on the other side they whispered hoarsely 'Sie Kommen!'

'Two red rockets gone up on the right!'

Echo — 'For Christ's sake water, water.'

The Warrior wipes his rifle and presses a new clip into the breach. 'Strafe it!' he shrieks, looking to the east. 'Gerry's coming!' He raises his rifle, firing feverishly. Then the ground upheaves beneath him, and his body describes a wide parabola, one limb still clutching the rifle torn from the torso as it is hurled through the air. The body falls beside another, muttering as he works the rifle bolt, 'Hell, I'll give 'em Hell!' And the fallen body takes up the chant 'Water, water.'

The pale light of an evil day through dust and smoke of battle reveals the marching columns, as they move eastwards, broken into tiny groups, finally lost in haze, single men stumbling, wallowing, muttering, chanting.

['Warrior']

Above: Battle of Ypres. The Menin Road passing the site of Gheluvelt as it appeared three days after its capture by the 29th Division (1st October 1918). Note pill-boxes and Royal Engineers testing telephone, on left. [IWM]

Above right: Battle of Ypres. General view of the battlefield showing a row of German concrete strongpoints captured by the 3rd and 7th Infantry Brigades during the Australian attack at Nonne Bosschen, 20th September 1917. There were probably more concrete strongpoints to the acre in this area than on any part of the Western Front. [IWM]

Right: The Menin Road passing through the rebuilt village of Gheluvelt, July 1968. The spire of the church can be seen on the left. During the last phases of Third Ypres, Gheluvelt was entered by our troops but they were forced to withdraw after mud had clogged their weapons. The village remained in German hands until the final Allied advance of 1918.

BOESINGHE

This small town on the British left wing was the junction point with our French and Belgian Allies. Severe fighting took place in this area in 1915, during Second Ypres.

Near the town, which was completely destroyed as the war progressed, the opposing trenches ran along each side of the Yser Canal. About half a mile towards Ypres the British line crossed the canal and both fronts followed a course along the Pilckem Ridge in the direction of Wieltje and then onwards to Hooge, Sanctuary Wood, and Hill 60.

Near Boesinghe. Two Belgians inspecting an old shell dug up during road improvements, August 1969, and placed on the verge to await collection by The Belgian Army Bomb Disposal Squad.

Shortly after this photograph was taken the gentleman in the cloth cap decided to start tapping the shell with a hammer in order to remove some of the thick coating of mud and rust. At this point the author beat a hasty retreat but when the same spot was passed two hours later, the shell (and the Belgians) were still there.

During the height of the bombardment a young officer had been overcome with the most severe infliction of shell-shock which I had witnessed. Its symptoms were not unlike those of epilepsy. The eyes dilated and he foamed at the mouth, shrieking all the while, finally rushing in front of the guns towards the enemy. I called for fire to cease, and an NCO ran out and overpowered him. The brain obviously was unhinged. He fought like a madman, and no muffling would subdue his cries. The effect on troops whose sensibility was already pulverised by heavy shelling and casualties would have been disastrous, especially since reserves were continually passing near the flank of the gun position. The lad was stunned and died during the night.

The ferocity of the cannonade defied the senses. The British Batteries poured on incessant stream of shells overhead preparatory to the further attack on the morrow. The German artillery in titanic support of strong counter-attacks delivered by Bavarians hailed a most violent bombardment upon our support line and communications. So tremendous was the roar that its sound could clearly be heard in Boulogne, and even across the Channel in Kentish seaports and villages. The ground heaved and rocked. A tornado of earth clods and flying mud, splinters of timber, bricks and hot metal whistled all around. The swish and sigh of our own shells overhead was accompanied by unceasing crashes as the German shells thundered a gigantic defiance.

['Warrior']

172

I walked on to the east, then set my map. Gone were the chateaux, farms, and woods of which it spoke. To the east nothing but pools of yellow undulations. I guessed the quality of the churnings for along the horizon, and often round and about shrieked and dived great shells heaving volumes of mud into the air, accompanied by clouds of spray. I would watch the shells plunge. So deep, so yielding was the soil in its embrace that seconds passed before impact against anything solid which might detonate the metal mass. Then, as if by some angered reptile of the nether world, the earth's surface would heave and spout and flash with fire, emitting black fumes before delivering itself of a tempestuous diarrhoea. A shower of gangrenous metal and yellow mud.

With the aid of a compass I learned the general direction of the attack objective. We would go east from astride the Menin Road by Herenthage Chateau. I noted a derelict tank — thank Heavens for that landmark — and an unburied corpse or two, which marked the track from Holybone. Then I returned to my horse. The map sheet was a fair deceiver. But a bogged tank, unburied dead, and a spray vomiting mud along the horizon gave me the lie of the land. To this battleground on the morrow would I lead my troops.

[Warrior]

Third Ypres, 5th August 1917. Shattered German trenches and dug-outs near Boesinghe. A British working party resting in the foreground; troops at the upper left seem to be rigging a bridge across the Yser Canal. The inverted rifle in the middle of the photograph marks a hasty grave. [IWM]

The line of German trenches and dug-outs today. These lines were marked on British maps as 'Baboon Trench'. The trees still trace the line of the Yser Canal. Not far away to the right is Artillery Wood captured by the Guards Division on 31st July 1917. Today it is Artillery Wood Military Cemetery and contains some 1,300 graves. Steenstraat is in the far distance beyond the bend in the canal.

The British trenches were at about the same distance inland on the other side of the canal.

173

Report made out by 'Bert' Slack on the morning of the first day of Third Ypres. (*See p. 177*)

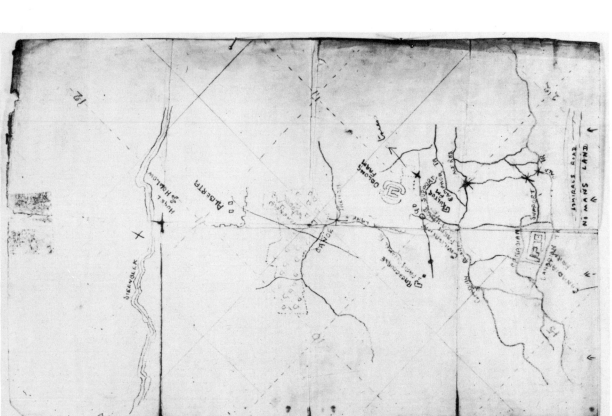

Sketch map used by 'Bert' Slack at the commencement of Third Ypres.

Above: Pilckem Ridge. Jacking and hauling an 18-pounder out of the mud, 2nd August 1917. [IWM]

Above right: Near Pilckem Ridge. The Battle of Langemarck, 17th August 1917. A monstrous shell burst in the distance; German concrete pill-box in the foreground. [IWM]

Right: Near Pilckem Ridge. A farm cart stands precisely on the old German front line which ran from the lower left to the building at the right.

The SOS signal was seen at every point along our lines. Our guns of all calibres and machine-guns immediately opened fire. Following this bombardment, the enemy attacked in massed formation upon our lines, no less than six Divisions being used in this attack upon our Divisional front. On the right the posts of the 1st Queen's were overwhelmed, the enemy debouching from the village of Gheluvelt armed with flame throwers. The stream of burning oil thrown from these devilish weapons reached a length of thirty yards and many feet in the air, and set fire to the trees, which being as dry as tinder immediately took fire.

I had already observed at the Hindenburg Line earlier in the year the gruesome effect of the *flammenwerfer* as a weapon of attack. Carried on the back of an infantry soldier it threw a stream of flaming spirit. This terrible apparatus could be brought up along covered ways, communicating the captured trench system of reserve lines, well known to the enemy, and was used as the first paralysing stroke to cover storm troops in their counter-attack upon exhausted troops. This was the role especially allotted to the *flammenwerfer gruppen* with infantry. Defenders were saturated, their bodies being charred to cinders.

The men of the 1st Middlesex and the 93rd Highlanders on the left flank met the Bavarian wave with Lewis guns, bombs, and at the point of the bayonet. The resistance was insufficient and the attack swept on.

But though the German attack had overrun the Divisional right, and had made a deep impress upon its left, two Companies, one of the 1st Middlesex, the other of 93rd Highlanders, held their ground. This was the second occasion in one year upon which a Company of this Battalion of Highlanders had refused ground to an enemy counter-attack, and, true to its Balaclava tradition, had fought again as 'The Thin Red Line'. There were enemy in front and rear, and on both flanks. Neither Middlesex nor Highlanders were in touch with one another. Assaults, assisted by *flammenwerfer*, were again and again made upon these isolated posts embarrassing the German advance. The air was filled with bombs which continually hailed upon the positions; the defenders being

obliged to husband their ammunition lest worse befall them. Not only did they become the continuous target for missiles of all kinds, but the aeroplanes, having disposed of the machine-gun batteries, turned their attention to these pockets which held up the progress of the counter-attack.

The plans for the original attack had now been abandoned, and until some definite news was received concerning the situation I ordered my batteries to cease fire and to recondition themselves for further action. We buried our dead, twenty-seven of them, in graves already prepared by shell burst, marking each position with a rifle, thrust bayonet first into the ground, a steel helmet covered the butt, the common practice. The idle teams fell to the task of refilling ammunition belts and changing worn guns barrels for renewed action.

It was during this lull in the attack that a dishevelled signaller from Headquarters, penetrating the barrage, arrived at my headquarters. I tore open the sealed envelope to discover not the information which I sought as to the position of the advance, but an order that I should forthwith report the number of tins of plum jam consumed by the units under my command since my last report. This served to remind me that I had eaten nothing all day. The irony of the matter so struck me that I recommended the signaller for the receipt of a Military Medal for 'conspicuous gallantry in the field whilst conveying messages under the heaviest bombardment.'

['Warrior']

THIRD BATTLE OF YPRES – JULY 31ST 1917

A month after the Messines Ridge battle, in which it had played an important part, 117 Machine Gun Coy was withdrawn from the line for rest and training for the next major attack.

During this latter period we were shown a piece of land about the size of a tennis court, which was a miniature layout of the ground over which our troops were to attack, with all the trenches and landmarks, etc, labelled. We also listened to a lecture – all highly secret – and questions were discussed and answered.

By 30th July we were in the line and carrying parties were taking boxes of ammunition for the machine guns, up to the front line. Zero hour was 3.50 am on 31st July and our job was to follow up the line of attack carrying the heavy tripod, Vickers Gun, ammunition and other supplies, then choose a position where we would have a good field of fire to beat off any counter-attack. Extra men had, meantime, been attached to us as carriers from the infantry. I had also been issued with a rough sketch map of the German trenches, all of which had been named with English names beginning with the letter 'C', such as 'Canadian', 'Calf' 'Camphor', etc, and there were other landmarks such as farms e.g. 'Oblong' and 'Kultur' and 'Kitchener's Wood' (of 1915 fame). Our final objective was to be a drainage dyke known as the 'Steenbeek'.

Precisely at 3.50 am our troops went over the top and as soon as the infantry advanced we picked up our gear and went forward into No-Man's-Land as fast as we could to avoid the German barrage which was soon falling behind us. As No 1 of the team I carried the heavy tripod, followed by my No 2 with the gun, and the others with belt boxes, etc, all in single file. The ground was an awful mess – shell holes, often half-full of water; tangled barbed wire, and patches of swamp where the drainage system had broken down.

Between the opposing trenches (according to the map) ran Admiral's Road. However, I had been warned that we should not be able to see it but if we felt firmer ground under the mud that would be Admiral's Road. This turned out to be the case, which

gave us more confidence, and we then passed over Calf trench Reserve, subsequently reaching Oblong farm. We then found that our infantry were held up by machine guns from Canoe trench on the edge of Kitchener's Wood, so we took refuge in several shell holes, mounted our gun and were ready to open fire if necessary. It had taken us just under an hour to advance about three-quarters of a mile. Three of the carriers were missing and one man was wounded in the thigh but we needed more ammunition and bombs. On the back of my map was a report from to fill in and send back to HQ, with eleven numbered paragraphs, such as 'From . . . To . . . Date and time; Am at place marked . . . on map; Situation Report, etc.' This I sent off by runner, timed 4.45 am.

Before he returned I had received a visit from our Officer and he noted the information. Later in the day the runner came back, having been unable to find our HQ and so I was able to keep a very good souvenir of that Report.

Very soon the infantry were able to capture the trenches in front of Kitchener's Wood known as Canoe and Canopus trenches. We followed them in and what a surprise awaited us for apart from being a foot deep in water and mud there were some 76 small concrete pill-boxes built into the front of the trench, all very close to each other. Rain had been falling steadily since about 9 am and it continued to do so for the next five days to the extreme discomfort of everyone!

Shelter was sought and very soon we found a dugout with only about a foot of water covering the base. Our next immediate task was to make a gun emplacement, which after completion was protected with a ground sheet and we then returned to the dugout. Shelling was frequent around us and our rations were exhausted. Moreover with all that water about we had none fit to drink! One of my team volunteered to go back to see what he could find – he was my best 'scrounger' – and he was not long in returning, laden with sand-bags crammed with food, including a large piece of boiled bacon, bread, sugar, tea, tins of milk and best of a bottle of SRD (Rum) plus a can of water. He had found a ration dump

177

Third Ypres. Mules and horses bringing up ammunition for the 18-pounders over Pilckem Ridge. An enemy shell bursts in the background. [IWM]

Beasts of burden at rest. A mare and her foal graze contentedly on Pilckem Ridge. The barbed wire in the foreground marks the site of the German front line near Turco Farm.

behind our lines that had been made by the ASC (with the aid of mules, because no ordinary transport could reach us) and as the custodian was absent — perhaps a casualty — my man just helped himself.

Although more than fifty years ago, I can still vividly remember that dugout, a foot deep in muddy water, with ammunition boxes spread around the floor, so that we could sit on one with our feet on another. A mess tin was being heated over a candle flame, wrapped around with sacking to give a better heat, and in the mess tin, water, Ideal Milk and rum. I am certain that the rum kept us alive and, needless to say, there were more visits to that dump! Shells fell around us from time to time but attacks were highly unlikely under such conditions. I sent a runner back most nights but no one came up to see us, and often the runner had to turn back either from sheer exhaustion or through having lost his way.

On 5th August I was hit in the back with a spent piece of shrapnel — painful but not serious — and the same night we were relieved by another team. After midnight we made a dash for it and I decided that instead of wading through the shell-holes full of water and sludge we would take the risk of moving as fast as we could down the St Julian Road during lulls in the shelling. The road, of course, had plenty of shell-holes and it was not long before my No 2, carrying the heavy gun, slipped when he heard a shell coming — and the gun fell into a deep shell hole and disappeared. On the spur of the moment, and influenced by the thought of the next shell, I dumped my heavy tripod into the same hole — and we moved much faster!

In the early hours of the morning we arrived at Richbourg Chateau Camp worn out, wet through, but still alive after an experience I have never forgotten.

Contributed by Mr A. E. Slack formerly of 117 Machine Gun Coy

178

At present danger is approaching again. From now onwards I shall have need of all your hopes and desires, even prayers. That passed, I shall have some sure prospect of coming home. I found in a 'Notizenbuch', taken from a German greatcoat, the diary of one of those earnest painstaking village schoolmasters, whose work remains their pride and whole centre of life, whose ideals set a glory round their memory. It seems such a tragedy that a man like that should be forced to fight at all. But that is the tragedy for all of us.

[HQ]

Third Ypres, 1917. Grenadier Guardsmen resting behind a smashed German pillbox. The use of steel girders to reinforce the concrete was typical of their construction.

The troops wearing an 'S' armband (such as the man on the extreme right) are stretcher bearers. [IWM]

Pilckem Ridge. The spires of Ypres seen from the site of the German front line emphasise the excellent observation enjoyed by the enemy. The British front trenches ran from left to right across the middle of the photograph. No Man's Cot Cemetery is to the right centre.

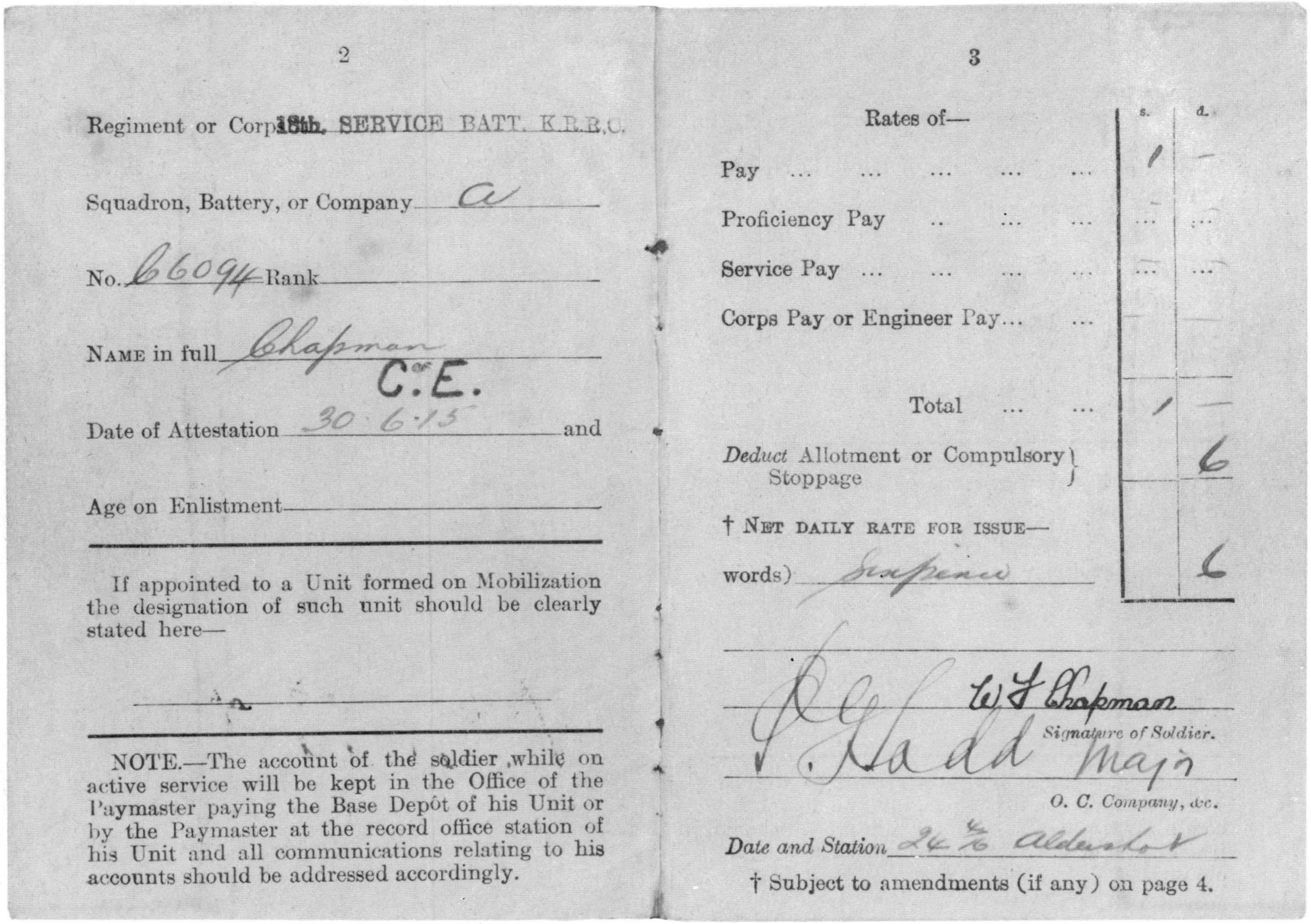

Page 2:

Regiment or Corps 18th SERVICE BATT. K.R.R.C.

Squadron, Battery, or Company *a*

No. 6609 Rank

NAME in full *Chapman C. E.*

Date of Attestation *30.6.15* and

Age on Enlistment

If appointed to a Unit formed on Mobilization the designation of such unit should be clearly stated here—

NOTE.—The account of the soldier, while on active service will be kept in the Office of the Paymaster paying the Base Depôt of his Unit or by the Paymaster at the record office station of his Unit and all communications relating to his accounts should be addressed accordingly.

Page 3:

	Rates of—		s.	d.
Pay	... ...	...	1	
Proficiency Pay	...	...	...	...
Service Pay	... ...	...	...	...
Corps Pay or Engineer Pay	...	...	1	6
	Total ...	...		
Deduct Allotment or Compulsory} Stoppage				
† NET DAILY RATE FOR ISSUE—				
words) *Sixpence*				

Alfd. W. F. Chapman
Signature of Soldier.

J. Sadd Major
O. C. Company, &c.

Date and Station *26.6 Aldershot*

† Subject to amendments (if any) on page 4.

A Soldier's Pay. 'Net daily rate . . . 6d.' Major Sadd, whose signature appears above, was killed later on the Somme.
[Contributed by Mr W. F. Chapman]

180

Above:
Pilckem Ridge. A British soldier kneels in the posture of death as a large shell bursts in the background during the Battle of Langemarck, 18th August 1917. [IWM]

Above right:
Pilckem Ridge, 3rd August 1917. Pack horses carry 18-pounder shells past a party working on a new road up the ridge. Railway sleepers form a 'corduroy' section over a muddy patch.

Right:
Enemies brought together by suffering. British and German soldiers conversing during the Battle of Pilckem Ridge 1917. [IWM]

181

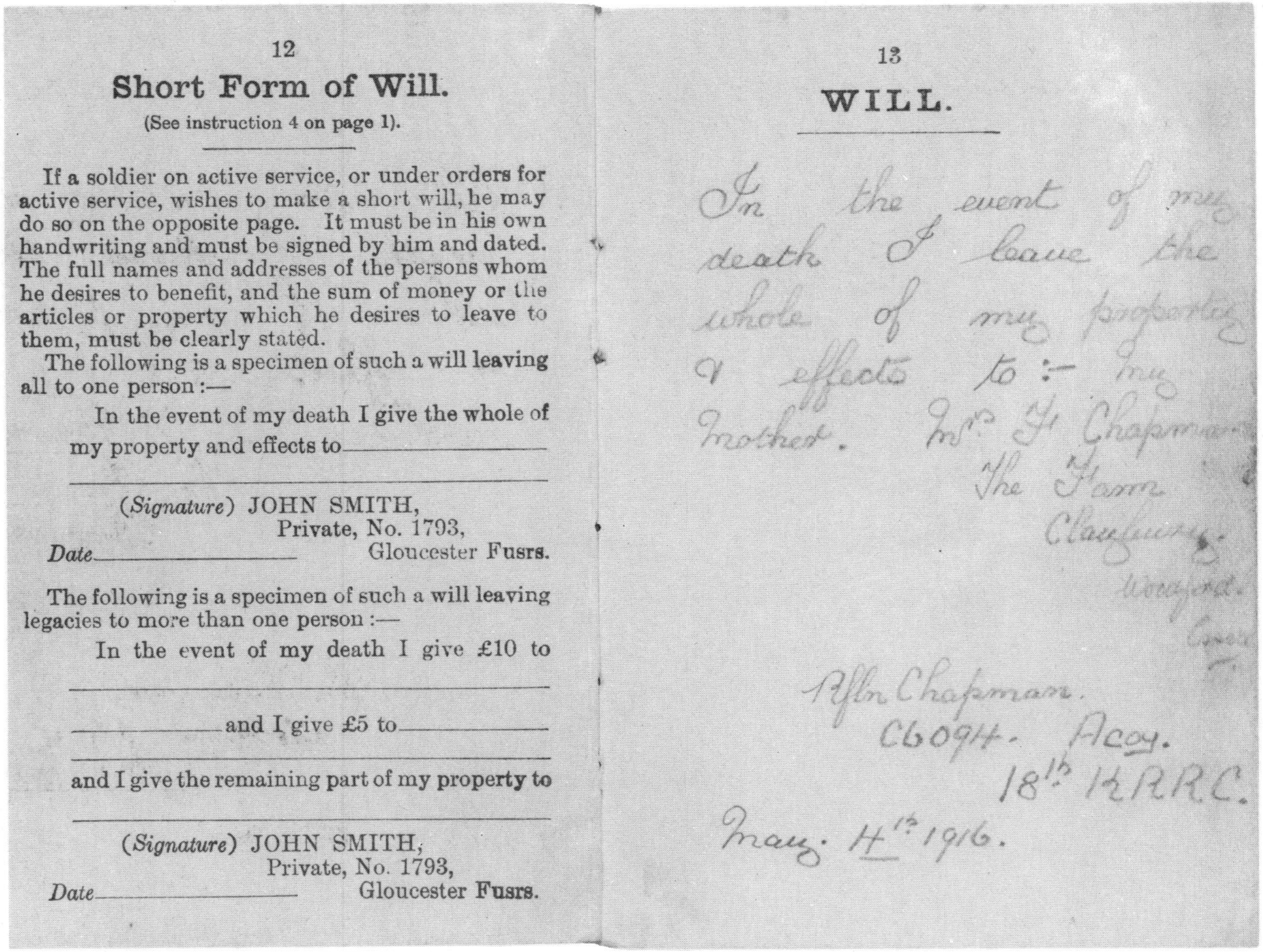

12

Short Form of Will.

(See instruction 4 on page 1).

If a soldier on active service, or under orders for active service, wishes to make a short will, he may do so on the opposite page. It must be in his own handwriting and must be signed by him and dated. The full names and addresses of the persons whom he desires to benefit, and the sum of money or the articles or property which he desires to leave to them, must be clearly stated.

The following is a specimen of such a will leaving all to one person:—

In the event of my death I give the whole of my property and effects to ————

(*Signature*) JOHN SMITH,
Private, No. 1793,
Gloucester Fusrs.

Date ————

The following is a specimen of such a will leaving legacies to more than one person:—

In the event of my death I give £10 to ————

———— and I give £5 to ————

and I give the remaining part of my property to ————

(*Signature*) JOHN SMITH,
Private, No. 1793,
Gloucester Fusrs.

Date ————

13

WILL.

On the event of my death I leave the whole of my property & effects to :- my mother Mrs G. Chapman. The Yews Charfield

A.H. Chapman.
C6094. Acy.
18th 12 R.R.C.

May. 4th 1916.

A Soldier's Will. An entry in Army Book 64.
[Contributed by Mr W. F. Chapman]

Pilckem Ridge. Pack horses heaving forward through the mud. A Crosley tender slides along the road in the background. 1st August 1917. [IWM]

Pilckem Village. British stretcher bearers in the ruins of Pilckem, 31st July 1917. [IWM]

Pilckem Ridge. The Pilckem–Bixschoote Road bisected by the Ypres–Staden railway as in the photograph above.

Pilckem Village lies approximately three miles north of Ypres. It was captured on 31st July 1917 by the 38th (Welsh) Division during the initial phase of Third Ypres known as the Battle of Pilckem Ridge. It was during this action that the famous German 'Cockchafers' were routed by the Welshmen.

LANGEMARCK

This village is approximately four and a half miles north-east of Ypres and was first lost during the spring of 1915 at the time of the Second Battle of Ypres. On 16th August 1917 it was captured by the 20th 'Light' Division after heavy fighting when a large number of prisoners were taken.

The ground was quite reasonable on the top of Pilckem Ridge but by Langemarck it was terrible — just a mass of shell-holes. The church was just a heap of rubble with not one brick upon another. . . . We just hauled off dead mules from the duckboard track and shoved the bodies into shell-holes. It needed 200-men working parties to clear up the mess.

[WF Chapman]

Near Langemarck, 22nd August 1917. German shells searching newly captured ground. [IWM]

Near Langemarck, 1968. The ground over which our troops advanced in the face of the murderous artillery and machine-gun fire during Third Ypres. Langemarck Church is in the centre.

German trenches in a wood near Langemarck after the British bombardment, 11th June 1917. [IWM]

Dappled Sunlight. The German Military Cemetery at Langemarck is stark in comparison with its British counterparts but has a sombre beauty of its own. This cemetery also has a mass grave containing the remains of 24,000 German soldiers.

POELCAPPELLE

Dreadful struggles under appalling conditions took place around this destroyed village lying about six miles north-east of Ypres on the Westroosebeke Road. This severe fighting was part of the third phase of Third Ypres during which tanks assisted the 11th and 14th Divisions to capture the western part of the village on 4th October 1917 against fierce enemy resistance. After much bitter fighting — particularly around the shattered brewery — the remainder of the village fell to our forces on 9th October with further advances being made later in the month. Poelcappelle again passed into enemy hands during the German push of April 1918 but was finally recaptured by the Belgians in September of that year.

Poelcappelle. The main road into the village from Langemarck, 13th September 1917. The photographer took this shot under observation from alert Germans in the pill-box to the left-centre along the horizon. [IWM]

'Their name liveth for evermore.' The grave of Brigadier General Frank Maxwell, VC, CSI, DSO. A winner of the Victoria Cross in the Boer War found his final resting place in the bloody soil of the Western Front on 21st September 1917.

*'An ideal soldier and
a very perfect gentleman,
beloved by all his men.'*

Poelcappelle. The village cross-roads at the end of 1918. A ruined Mark IV used as an observation post or forward HQ. Note the telephone wires leading into the hull.

[Photo: Antony of Ypres, by kind permission of Miss Gabrielle Antony]

187

A day's harvest. First-Sergeant Deneve of the Belgian Army Westroosebeke Bomb Disposal Unit, standing by a collection of World War I explosives dug up during road improvements, house building, and drainage works throughout the old Salient. Daily this dangerous 'old iron' is blown up in the heart of Houthulst Forest.

During January–August 1969 the unit collected 380 tons of ordinary shells and about thirty-two tons of gas shells. The total each year averages 350 tons. Seventeen men have been killed from the Houthulst squad (the latest in 1955) and thirty-one from a coastal sector squad. Their names are inscribed on a special 'Roll of Honour' in the mess.

I can quite vividly remember the long winding duckboard track across the wilderness of shell-holes from Pilckem towards Houthulst Forest. In the Houthulst area we had no trenches, just a breast-work of faggots and earth and we dare not show ourselves in daylight. To get to my posts I had to crawl in the mud along to a ditch which afforded some cover. I saw a '5.9' land in the middle of the track one night . . .

[WF Chapman]

Sudden Death. Some of the explosive ordnance to be destroyed by the Disposal Unit. A pile of Mills bombs is in the right foreground. A star shell leans against the bank and behind it, looking like bundles of string, are the cordite charges for an unidentified large gun. The enormous drums on the left were probably the propellant charges of German *minnenwerfers*.

Left: Battle of Poelcappelle, October 1917. German blockhouse captured by the Coldstream Guards on the outskirts of Houthulst Forest. In a different campaign far in the past, another British general, Marlborough, said, 'He who holds Houthulst commands Flanders.' During 1914-1918 its dark depths were held by the Germans and only limited parts were penetrated by the Allies. [IWM]

Below left: One of the fortunate ones. A wounded German, who escaped with his life from the maelstrom of Langemarck, in the prisoner cage, September 1917. [IWM]

Below: Houthulst Forest today.

Metal tablet on the wall of the rebuilt Zonnebeke Church.

The 2nd Worcestershires, the 9th HLI, and the 1st Queen's were lined out in readiness for the assault. I found the headquarters of the Worcestershires in a captured pill-box and handed over the weakest section, already without officers, to the Commander. Almost as I left the headquarters an enormous shell burst directly upon it.

My Company Commander reeled against me. I threw an arm around him. My hand found a great rent in his back, the blood streaming from it. I called for stretcher bearers. No reply. The candlelight of the pill-box was extinguished. I laid my companion upon the ground and ran to the pill-box. The Adjutant had been killed, together with the stretcher bearers. A candle was again lighted. The unbreakable reinforced concrete of the stronghold had bent and cracked beneath the impact. Corpses lay huddled in the doorway.

I carried a bottle of spirit to my junior. He was conscious; a big man, heavily built, and of great strength. I raised and supported him to the pill-box. The candlelight showed a gaping wound gushing blood. The shoulder-blade was pulp, and field-glasses and case were embedded in the mess. There was no medical aid. We dared not remove them but plugged the hole with fat shell dressings, great wads of antiseptic gauze.

'I'll go down the line now, sir,' said my subordinate. 'I'm a nuisance here.' He rose to his feet and staggered out into the black hurricane.

['Warrior']

ZONNEBEKE

Zonnebeke is about four miles east-north-east of Ypres. Most of the ground in this area was captured on 26th September 1917 during the phase of Third Ypres named the Battle of Polygon Wood.

Zonnebeke is situated below the Broodseinde Ridge which the Australians captured on 4th October. Many Germans were killed in this area when they were caught in the open by a British bombardment preliminary to an attack. Coincidentally, they had been forming up for an attack of their own which was timed to start ten minutes after ours.

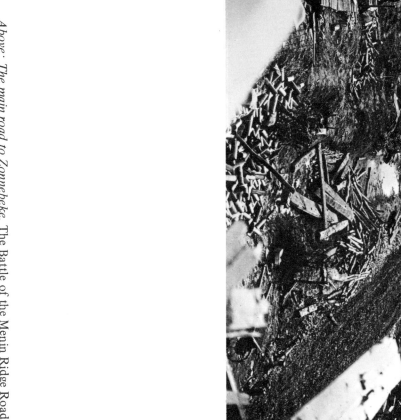

Above: The main road to Zonnebeke. The Battle of the Menin Ridge Road. A shell bursting on newly captured ground, 20th September 1917: [IWM]

Top right: Ruins of Zonnebeke, which was captured on 26th September 1917. Photograph taken on 5th October 1917. [IWM]

Right: The main road to Zonnebeke. A smooth strip of concrete through the green countryside. As in the photograph above, Zonnebeke itself lies about a mile beyond the bend in the road.

Zonnebeke. Dead Germans lying outside a blockhouse, September 1917. [IWM]

About eleven o'clock we set out on patrol, but had to take refuge in a deserted pill-box in No-Man's-Land because the enemy had sighted us. This pill-box had been used at one time as a charnel-house; it smelt strongly of one and the floor was deep with human bones. From there we watched the Very lights flickering outside, and, casting a weird light through the doorway, the red flash of bursting shells. Occasionally a direct hit shook us to the very soul. While sitting there, the odour overcame me and I fainted. Waking up an hour afterwards, I found myself alone, without the faintest idea of my whereabouts, uncertain where the enemy's lines were or my own. Some authors practise the description of fear, but nothing they could do could even faintly realise my state. It went beyond fear, beyond consciousness, a grovelling of the soul itself. For half an hour I stood inside, wondering whether to venture out or stay in at eminent risk of daylight coming to dis-close me to the enemy. At last, bravery returned, and I went out only to stumble over a derelict wire a hundred yards farther on, and find my hands clutching at a dead man's face.

[HQ]

192

Zonnebeke. The shell-pocked ground surrounding the ruins of Zonnebeke and its church. This type of desolation was common during Third Ypres. The Ypres—Broodseinde Road can be traced in the mud to the left of the ruined church. In front (i.e. left) of the church commenced the St Julian—Zonnebeke Road and in the right foreground is what remained of the Zonnebeke—Westhoek road. [IWM]

Zonnebeke. Smooth, well cultivated fields which were once a nightmare of mud and shell holes. The spire of the rebuilt church still rises above the village. In the mid-ground is a German blockhouse.

POLYGON WOOD AND BROODSEINDE

We of the 8th Battalion, 1st Australian Division, were in great form. We had reason to be. Since we were relieved at the right of the Bullecourt sector on 9th May, 1917, we had had a marvellous time. No screeching shells, chattering machine-guns of whining bullets for us. For the time being we were comparative strangers to the long days when we were supposed to sleep in the trenches, and to the nightly activity of putting out barbed wire in No-Man's Land, heaving duckboards around, carrying on our backs heavy monstrosities containing stew and tea and feeling the liquid penetrating beneath our jackets and running down our backs, transporting boxes of Mills bombs from dumps to the trenches, shivering on listening posts and, when on observation duty, gazing intently at shattered tree-stumps which appeared to move about like men if you looked at them long enough, and other tasks ingeniously thought out by the higher command when reclining in their beds.

We were enjoying our role of 'six-bob-a-day tourists', with pleasant memories of over four months as reserve troops in various parts of France. Apart from drill and other instruction, we played cricket and football and participated in athletic events, had many swimming parades, and when finances permitted, visited the *estaminets* in order to consume eggs and chips, drink weak beer and the wine concoction known to us as 'vin blanc' which had a vicious kick, and around the piano howl out our versions of 'Mademoiselle from Armentieres', 'Tipperary', 'Take Me Back to Dear Old Blighty', and other favourites.

In one cricket match, playing on a dirt pitch, I managed to obtain the ridiculous figures of 7 wickets for 8 runs. Our captain, Sergeant Collins, a pennant player in Melbourne for the St Kilda club, reckoned that I should also be able to bat. This I belied, however, by registering an inglorious duck!

At that greatest of all games – Australian Rules Football – playing on a forward flank for 15 Platoon against 13 Platoon, I kicked four goals in good style, and was very pleased with myself until 'Dobba' Dwyer, six feet of bone and muscle, flattened me properly. I was not much good after that.

In athletics our battalion had a champion runner – but today I am unable to recall his name with certainty. It might have been Cummings. He specialised in distance races and, to our great glee, at the sports meeting he left for dead the stars from other units.

POLYGON WOOD

Then, on 19th September, 1917, we found ourselves in bivouacs at Dickebusch, thoroughly equipped as assault troops, ready to take part in an attack east of Ypres which, if successful, would bring us to the edge of Polygon Wood, scene of many past battles. We were full of information. We had

studied a plan model of the area of the projected attack and had received instruction from a chap wearing a natty looking Sam Browne belt.

Just before dusk we assembled our equipment in readiness to move off. A lone German flyer, emerging suddenly from behind a cloud, fired machine-gun bursts among us and made a safe get-away. There were some casualties, including our famous runner 'Cummings', who received a bullet through an ankle, of all places.

At 6 p.m. we left for the trek to Zillebeke Lake. Rain commenced, and it rained and rained. Covering ourselves with our waterproof sheets we were able to get some protection, but what-ho from the thighs down. We were not half so perky now as we had been after downing our fourth glass of vin blanc at Caestre or Doulieu, or at the *estaminet* which proudly displayed the sign, 'English spoken. Australian understood.'

Arriving at quarters at Zillebeke Lake, we found protection from the rain. Since a soldier's life was a combination of fighting and waiting but mostly waiting, we waited. In fact we waited for two and a half hours. We then resumed our journey, following a tape which had been laid to direct us to our jumping-off position. After much foot slogging, some genius discovered that we were following the wrong tape which took us two miles off course. Just before our destination was finally reached we were caught in an enemy barrage and, in the resulting confusion, sought what cover we could, suffering only a few casualties. We reached the jumping off tapes just before our own artillery barrage opened with a tremendous roar, at 5.40 am on 20th September.

We followed the creeping barrage, endeavouring to keep our pace down so that we would not be caught in it. This was a difficult matter. Before long a man about twenty-five yards in front of me fell, and as I reached him he asked for a cigarette. I obliged, and recognised him as Arch Sneddon, who had resided about half-a-mile from my home in Ballarat. He had been hit by shell fragments in the back. He was cheerful enough, notwithstanding, but I was dismayed to hear later that he had died at the dressing station.

It had not been possible to bring the battalion up to strength after the previous attack. We complained vigorously, and why not? There was not much else to talk about, and this move enabled us to let off steam.

After dusk we of 15 platoon set out for Anzac Ridge together with the other platoons of the 8th Battalion. Proceeding in Indian file, we found the ground firm beneath our feet but slippery on the surface. After an hour or so I began to feel tired and dropped to the rear of the column. Why, I thought, am I only 5 feet 6 inches in height and 20 years of age, while almost everybody around me is taller, stronger and older? Take the two Richards brothers from Raymond Terrace, in New South Wales. Guesses on our part as to their height ranged from 6 feet 2 inches to 6 feet 6 inches. Thus because of their long legs they always maintained positions at the head of the column. However, although last in line I kept contact and plugged along. Our guide must have been a wizard as, believe it or not, he led us to our correct destination — a thing which had not happened often to us.

The trench assigned to us for the time being had funk holes in the sides, in which protection from the weather could be obtained. However, there were not sufficient of them, and a few of us at the rear missed out. It commenced to drizzle, necessitating our having to struggle to unpack our waterproof sheets.

About 2.30 a.m. on 4th October we crept forward to shell-holes to await our opening barrage, which was to be the signal for us to move ahead in an endeavour to capture, by front assault, our allotted section of Broodseinde Ridge.

Time dragged. Stray shells and intermittent machine-gun bursts were exchanged, mostly at some distance from our position. Otherwise it was quiet. About 5.30 am, all along our immediate front, the Germans began shelling our rear positions and raking with machine-gun fire. This increased in intensity and the din was tremendous. Our side did not reply, as it was not yet time for the artillery to open. On the principle that, on such occasions, the nearer the attacking lines are to the enemy the safer they are, we were not unduly worried in our position; but we realised that numerous casualties must be occurring in our support and reserve lines.

However, as the German bombardment continued unabated and without any retaliation by our side, we became anxious and restive, wondering how much longer this would go on. Eventually, at 6 am, with a terrific roar, our barrage came down on the enemy positions. This was a great relief, as it is much better for infantry men to take some positive action than cower in shell-holes.

We took it. Scrambling to our feet, we advanced over the wet ground. Visibility was bad, as a mist hung over the battlefield. After going some distance we made out dark, shadowy figures coming towards us. At close quarters we fired at them and passed on, not really knowing what damage we had caused.

I became hot and bothered, feeling that we were not getting far enough under the enemy fire. Pressing on hurriedly, I arrived at a hedge which had been broken in parts by shell-fire. I went through one of the gaps and, after a glance, took a frantic jump into a large, deep shell-hole and felt icy water soaking through my boots. The reason for my panic was a German pillbox

not more than ten yards in front and a little to my right. Through an aperture near the top a machine-gun was firing.

With difficulty, I commenced to aim my rifle at the gap, but before I could press the trigger, the machine-gun ceased fire and was withdrawn. While I was hesitating, a German left the pillbox and began walking in my direction, obviously without seeing me. I felt that my blood was turning to ice. Deflecting my rifle barrel, I aimed point-blank at his stomach and pressed the trigger. Down he went, on his right knee, and covered his face with his hands.

I gazed at him, wondering why he did not fall over. However, I was not given much time to ponder upon this, as another German emerged from the pillbox and started running, not towards me or back to his own lines, but across my front. I fired, and he fell to the ground; and the process was repeated when a third German followed in his wake.

Gefallen für Deutschland. A very young German soldier who died manning his machine-gun somewhere in the Broodseinde area. Passchendaele is off the picture to the right. [IWM]

I endeavoured to take stock of my position. The racket continued from both sides. Looking over my shoulder into the mist and drizzling rain I could see no sign of Australians. In my desire to get under the enemy curtain I had apparently outstripped my mates. I felt that I should take one of my Mills bombs from my pocket, rush round the pillbox and throw it down the stairs – but I was not game enough to do so.

With others I continued to follow the barrage. Nothing much happened on our immediate line of advance. The occupants of pillboxes dotted round our flanks did not seem to be putting up much resistance, and casualties from shell and machine-gun fire apparently were not high. Glancing to my right, where a British battalion was advancing on lower ground, I saw them surround and capture a pillbox. The Germans filed out with their arms raised. One prisoner appeared to go berserk and began jostling and pushing some of his captors, two of whom, becoming exasperated in the height of the battle, plunged their bayonets into his body.

After some time we arrived at a position overlooking the ground ahead. In the distance was a wood that seemed to have partly survived three cyclones and two tornadoes. As no officers or NCO's were around, a half-dozen or so of us conferred and decided that this must be our objective. We therefore marked out a line for a trench and started digging furiously with the spades we had brought along with us. Suddenly up bounces Corporal 'Bruiser' Rigby, 5 feet 8 inches of Wonthaggi belligerency.

'What's wrong with you so-and-sos?' he bawled. 'You are about seventy yards too far forward.'

We mopped our brows and gazed at him discontentedly. However, there was nothing to do but gather our belongings and retire to the place Rigby indicated. There we laboured mightily. In the end, we had constructed a suitable trench with much earth thrown up in front to form a parapet. In addition, our master-stroke was a sort of ledge at the bottom of the trench upon which we sat facing towards the enemy. The corporal posted a man at the right flank of the trench to keep a look-out.

We did not rest for long. Suddenly there was a deafening noise and a weight pressed upon me. Staggering to my feet, I gouged earth from my eyes and ears and found the others doing the same thing. Our carefully prepared parapet had been struck by a small shell. Next to me, on the left of the row, was a Digger named Malone, maybe 35 or 36 years of age, who had not long been with us and had not been very happy since he joined the company. In the arrogance of my 20 years, I had considered him too old for this sort of thing. As we sorted ourselves out, I noticed he was fumbling, and I asked him whether he had been hit. He said that he could not see. We gathered round him and one chap passed his hand to and fro in front of Malone's open eyes,

but he did not blink. A closer examination disclosed a tiny hole near his left temple. Apparently a piece of shell or a small stone had penetrated the flesh. The corporal decided that he would have to be taken to the dressing station and told me to escort him.

With me leading him by the hand, we left the trench for the rear. The shelling and machine-gun fire had died down considerably, and the ground was reasonably firm. As we threaded our way round shell-holes I saw men strewn over the battlefield. Doubtless, I thought, many of them belonged to our company, but this was no time to have a closer look. The stretcher-bearers would be doing their best to cope with the situation.

After going some distance I saw a small knot of soldiers slightly to the right. Out of curiosity I led Malone in their direction. Paddy Morgan, from Richmond, Victoria, one of our company stretcher-bearers, was there with a stretcher on which lay a wounded Australian. Three German prisoners were standing docilely by the stretcher, while a fourth German stood a little apart from them. It transpired that he could speak English and Paddy was pleading with him, cajoling him, threatening him to take hold of the fourth arm of the stretcher – all to no avail. The German, standing at attention and drawing himself up to his full height, stated that as an officer he would not help to carry the stretcher. This went on for a while until Paddy, losing patience, took a few paces forward and, drawing a revolver (which he had no right to be carrying), shot the German officer.

Still leading Malone, I moved on to the dressing station and handed him over. My task completed, I returned to our post to find the garrison still repairing the broken parapet and strengthening the trench generally. Months afterwards we heard that Malone had regained his sight.

BROODSEINDE RIDGE

After the attack at Polygon Wood on 20th September (officially known as the Battle of the Menin Road), the 1st Division was relieved and went back into 'rest', the 8th Battalion going first to the Steenvoorde area and later to Chateau Segard area. Within two weeks we were ordered into the line again, this time for the Battle Broodseinde.

In the midst of my muddled thinking I saw men of the battalion at last appearing in numbers behind me. Glad to get to my feet out of the icy water I scrambled from the shell-hole, and we rushed the pillbox from both sides. Someone threw a Mills bomb down the entrance. Yells were heard below and the Germans appeared with their hands in the air.

I now thought of my own little war and noticed that the first German I had hit was still on one knee, with his hands covering his face. The moppers-up would attend to him. Crossing to one of the others, lying spread-eagled and

Above: The mud covered corduroy track enables the men to pass over the Zonnebeke marshes, 15th September 1917. [IWM]

Above right: Zonnebeke–Broodseinde Road. Not a gun, but the wreck of a lorry — probably an AEC. [IWM]

Right: The same spot today.

apparently dead, I saw that he was tall, slim and blonde and not more than 17 or 18 years of age. The third man could have been his twin. I found the sight very depressing.

As the situation at the pillbox was now under control, I pushed on with the others. We skirted masses of barbed wire, and I temporarily got into difficulties in some mud. Beginning the ascent to Broodseinde Ridge, I came to a large shell-hole almost full of water in which was a man of the 8th. He had been shot in the neck but was still alive. Only his head was above the water. Although it was against orders for me, a fit soldier, to assist him — if every infantryman tarried to help another in trouble there might be nobody left to take the objective — I simply could not leave him like that. Taking him by the shoulders, I endeavoured to pull him out of the water, but he was a big man and I found to my great annoyance that I could not move him. To my relief another Digger appeared, and together we pulled the poor devil clear.

Continuing up the slope, we came into contact with enemy grenades thrown from the top of the ridge. One burst in the face of a man nearby and sliced off his left cheek. Farther on, I saw ahead a chap in a shell-hole, the upper half of his body above the rim. He was working at his rifle — possibly the bolt had become clogged with mud. A German grenade, thrown from the top, fell three feet in front of him, yet he did not notice it. I yelled to him as loudly as I could, but in the pandemonium caused by the roar of shells overhead, the rattling of machine-guns and the whine of bullets, he did not hear me. Seconds later the grenade exploded, and he had fought his last fight.

Our objective was the near side of Broodseinde Ridge, and it was there that we were to entrench. On arrival, it was obvious to me that our troops who had got there a little earlier had bunched together, whereas well over to the right and left were empty gaps. However, not holding any rank I could do nothing about this, so I dug a section of trench in which I ensconced myself. Next to me I found an experienced soldier of my platoon, Lance-Corporal Harry Glover, an Englishman.

While we were resting from our labours, Sergeant Stanley of our company appeared behind the trench. He had been wounded at Gallipoli and invalided to Australia, and after numerous attempts had re-enlisted. This was his first time in action in France. He stood on the parados and, noticing that the trench was rather crowded, seemed undecided what to do. At that moment a shell burst on the parapet showering us with earth and killing Stanley instantly.

When darkness fell, Harry Glover and I left the trench and found his body. After removing his identification disc and papers, we dug a grace and buried him, marking the spot with a discarded rifle that we plunged into the ground by the bayonet. Later in the night Harry and I crept over the ridge to deliver some bombs to one of the outposts, and on our return we found a great yawning hole where the grave had been.

The night passed with little incident. As the top of the ridge gave some protection to our trench, we were able to move round freely, to carry out the fatigue jobs that were our lot and also strengthen and extend the trench. After stand-to next morning, with its usual hymn of hate, we kept under such cover as we had. The rain let up and the day was reasonably fine. At dusk the 11th Battalion (W.Aust) took over our position.

Before the attack we had received instructions to the effect that on being relieved all survivors who were fit enough were to bring out as much scrap metal as possible. Harry Glover and I found a heavy German machine-gun which had been damaged by shrapnel. With some others we were allowed to leave for the back area at 3 pm. As the ground was muddy and very slippery in places we had to walk gingerly around the rims of recent shell-holes and take care not to step into old waterlogged ones. We tried carrying the gun together but this proved unsatisfactory, as frequently Harry slid one way and I the other at the same time. So we took it in turns separately to carry the weighty thing in short spells.

On reaching a field dressing station, situated in the protection of a pillbox, I became rather upset at the spectacle of so many soldiers lying on stretchers and numbers of walking wounded sitting and standing about, awaiting attention, and this despite the valiant efforts of doctors and men of the medical corps. By then I was no stranger to the sight of dead and wounded, but in the line one saw but a small area in his immediate vicinity. This was the first time I had seen casualties in such numbers.

A little farther on, while we were negotiating a very slippery piece of ground, Harry, who was then carrying the gun, slid into a shell-hole up to his waist in water. Grabbing the gun and placing it on the ground, I pulled and strained in effort to help out of the slimy mud. Soon we arrived at an old pillbox at which the scrap metal had to be dumped, and then, glad to have rid ourselves of the gun, we proceeded to our destination — a sunken road known as 'China Wall', containing a series of dugouts near our big guns.

Reprinted from an article by W. J. Bradby in Stand To: the Journal of the Australian Capital Territory Branch of the Returned Services League, by permission of the editors and through the courtesy of W. R. Lancaster Esq., Director of the Australian War Memorial .

Above: Objective Passchendaele. A destroyed tank bogged down in a sea of mud and shell-holes. Our troops attacked forward over this appalling ground during Third Ypres. [IWM]

Above right: Railway cutting, Broodseinde Ridge. The dead, the exhausted, the shell-shocked, the nerve-shattered, huddled together. October 1917. [IWM]

Right: The Ypres–Roulers Railway cutting in 1968. It is a warm sunny day. Bees hum over the disused railway and birds have built nests in the leafy bushes overgrowing the old cutting.

o

199

Tyne Cot Military Cemetery in former years. A blockhouse and wooden crosses. [CWGC]

Tyne Cot today. Time and the soft hand of nature have mellowed the concrete monstrosity into an ivy-clad keep.

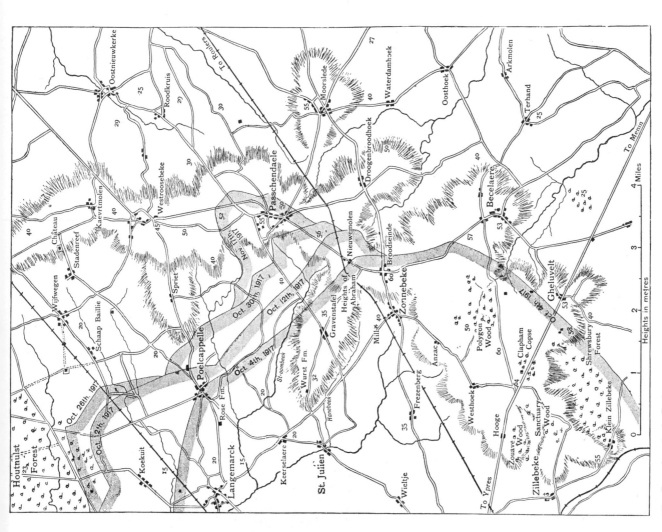

The Passchendaele Ridge.
Map from *Nelson's History of the War* (John Buchan) by permission of Thomas Nelson & Sons Ltd.

Tyne Cot today. These were fathers, sons, and brothers. Looking down from the steps of the Cross of Sacrifice towards the ground which was won at the cost of so many lives.

The purchase of the stones and the upkeep of the cemetery has been borne by the Commonwealth War Graves Commission.

The Cross of Sacrifice, Tyne Cot Cemetery. Ugliness transformed into serenity. The wall of the German pill-box can be seen in the square in the centre of the monument. The pill-box was captured by the Australians on 4th October 1917. [CWGC]

TYNE COT MILITARY CEMETERY NEAR PASSCHENDAELE

This is the largest British cemetery in the Salient and contains nearly 12,000 graves.

The names of over 34,000 men who were missing in the Salient between mid-August 1917 and the Armistice are engraved on stonework. Two German pillboxes are incorporated within the cemetery and another forms the base of the Cross of Sacrifice.

201

The eeriness of the bleeding landscape haunted me. Seemingly endless miles of rotting lifeless life, lying crazily in seemingly endless stagnant pools. Danger, deadly danger was always present, dogging the footsteps, and ahead. On either side death lurked tugging at the fingers, beckoning. And death shrieked suddenly from on high, breathing fire and gas and molten metal, and roared his laughter in great gusts as man ran and ducked and swayed and bobbed, eluding laughter, mocking the vale of tears.

I could stumble and glissade for hours across those trackless wastes, always finding something surprising, each day choosing a different path between my scattered posts. Duty, bravado, the desire to snap my fingers again and again in Death's face, contemptuously to kick the sweeping scythe aside, send me daily on my giddy tramp across the Salient.

Dodging the wheels of swaying limbers, evading plunging mules and horses as I plodded the road scuppers through Potijze to Zonnebeke. Then turning aside I went north-east, following the sleeper track which led to the battery positions behind Tyne Cot pill-box on its eminence. The great baulks of timber squelched and heaved upon the morass beneath. Some like the headstones in a graveyard stood on end mocking and marking the deathbed of a mule and his hapless driver. The night would yet be dark. Then feet, long accustomed to stealthy movement after dusk, instinctively groped, finding each firm step, discarding the place of treachery. I walked quickly. The night air was chilled, and it was hot with bursting cordite. I hurried for both reasons.

At Tyne Cot I would dive through the soaking heavy blanket and descend to flickering light bound by solid concrete. Great shadows fluttered on the roof and walls. The air was stuffy with coke fumes, soggy clothing, and unwashed humanity. It smote me unpleasantly as I came from the freshness of the night air, albeit tainted with the fumes of gas and rotting corpses.

There were bunks of wire netting stretched on timber upon which lay figures breathing heavily, one snoring. Before a rude table,

casting shadows, sat two officers, a map before them. They would look up warily, smiling wanly. A week, maybe a few days more or less, of that waste made men heavy-eyed. They slept little and intermittently. The eyes were seared with blood, dim and discoloured with mustard gas. They were unshaven, haggard, greyfaced, grimy; clothing stained, encrusted with drying yellow mud.

Thus was the portrait of the Passchendaele soldier. He lived unbelievably as it were upon the outer crust of a honeycomb, its honey putrid water. Each death pool was separated from its neighbour by a foot or two of muddy cone. To the sides of the greasy slithering edge, huddled above the stinking water, with bodies bowed beneath the crest, men lived out their days and nights, swept by shell and machine-gun fire, soaked in gas. When stormed by phosgene, its sickly, pear-perfumed stench dulling the senses, almost men ignored its delayed horrors. Then as maniacs, gripped by poison, they would hurry to the posts of battle civilisation, the Canteen and the Aid Post. There they would stagger, as the quickened blood defused the phosgene poisons through the system; and sink down, a stick of chocolate or a cigarette between the lips, coughing, retching. Dying. Gassed.

And there beyond barbarity men clung to their posts. What purposeless futility!

['Warrior']

202

Above: A track through the mud, between Broodseinde and Passchendaele, 11th January 1918. [IWM]

Above right: The dug-out of some Garrison Gunners and a war grave, Waterloo Farm, near Broodseinde, 11th January 1918. [IWM]

Right: Waterloo Farm in full working trim and showing no signs of the horror of former times.

It must be obvious that since there were many men of the highest intelligence gathered from out of civil occupations in which they had won the respect of their fellows, serving in the lower commands and ranks of a citizen army, a capacity for logical and hard thinking remained. As a Commander of one thousand men or more I found it frequently embarrassing when in chance conversation with a subaltern or sergeant to be asked to give reasons why. For example, 'Why do we always make our attacks in winter when any fool who knows anything about the front can see that they're bound to be a failure?' . . . 'What's the object of attacking Passchendaele? It only makes our position worse for the subsequent winter, and the position of the Germans better. Behind us there will be miles of land quite impassable except over tracks laid on sleepers which will be shelled to blazes day and night. . . . Surely the experience of October and November on the Somme has taught GHQ that it's sheer waste of life and material to attempt a break-through this season?' . . . 'Are we really short of man-power? If not, why are so many men being combed out of the transport services, and boys and Derby men being called up at home?' . . . 'Why don't we sit tight while the fresh reserves are being inured to these conditions?' . . . 'Why don't they give us a decent chance in the spring?' . . . 'Why do we always read in the newspapers that immense numbers of German dead have fallen to our arms, when as a matter of fact we all know that in these attacks our losses are usually about twenty to one? For one German corpse in 'No-Man's-Land' there are dozens of British. When we take a trench there are only a few pounded bodies in the debris, and we are blown to hell.'

Intelligent questions have to be answered with intelligence. I had friends on various staffs; and whenever an opportunity presented itself I used to look for them at a Corps, or Army Headquarters. Then, after the usual 'Cheerio' and a drink I would gently press my questions. I did so in fact in respect of the battle of the Menin Road. The answer, somewhat vague, was that our offensive before Ypres was intended to relieve the French in the south from German pressure. Several corps of the French, so I was informed,

had mutinied: very hush, hush of course; but the truth. If the British did not continue to keep the enemy fully preoccupied there was a grave danger of a weakened French front being pierced and the flank of the Allied Army being turned. For me this was a satisfactory answer, although it turned out to be an incorrect relation of facts based on reason. High strategy, even statecraft, was involved.

['Warrior']

German officers, captured in a dug-out at Passchendaele, in a Canadian Corps Cage, 9th November 1917. [IWM]

Panoramic view of Polygon Wood from Passchendaele Ridge. The 2nd Canadian Division area, 14th November 1917. [IWM]

The Slough of Despond: Marsh Bottom. In Third Ypres this was a churned up morass through which our troops struggled against massed machine-gun fire from the surrounding heights, particularly from the Bellvue Spur.

From the Bellvue Spur. A pleasant view over the Ravebeek Valley toward Passchendaele Church. The spot from which this photograph was taken was once the scene of dreadful carnage.

From Tyne Cot I would wander towards Broodseinde Ridge, and thence north as dawn broke along the front of my posts, so difficult to discover. I liked to see my men at daybreak and give them some word of good cheer. And they liked to see me.

Sometimes a sniper would pot at my wandering figure. I would amble quickly then over the maze of the cone, and drop from view beside a hole, worm my bellied way to another point, rise and shake my fist at the Boche, and pay another call. I ended my journey along the frontal posts usually at Passchendaele church.

In the stillness of dawn I could sink with fatigue in reverie, even as one may doze over a log fire, to be recalled by the crack of a bullet, just as a pine log spits and brings the dreamer to reality. The church had been razed to the ground. My post lay among its gathered bricks rebuilt above a vault, which served as sanctuary for the troops holding the eastern apex of the Salient.

They always gave me a cup of tea at the church, thus expressing the benevolence of Christianity. Men drank anything hot with gratitude. Even water, heavily chlorinated to its purification, so maddening to the palate, if hot sufficed. The flavour of tea and sugar imparted qualities in that hour which priceless Pekoe never yet possessed. Given by friends, Worcestershires.

Then, covered from direct fire, I would tour my other posts, disposed in depth to rake the valleys with fire lest the German High Command be seized with madness, and should seek to recover the cemetery of hope.

Even in December, for what purpose no god can know, we were ordered to carry out strong assaults across ground physically impassable against concrete machine-guns posts, fortressed islands rising above the quagmire.

I recall the mood and how curious were my sensations and feelings in one such effort eastwards.

I go on through the darkness. My eyes have learned to penetrate its blinding blackness.

Shapes and forms appear and disappear. I heed them not. Some are tree stumps and holes, corpses and carcasses. They are still. I realise their attitude and manner.

Others move, figures like myself, hurrying, groping, stumbling, slipping. Going on. Some lurch against me if we pass. Of what use a greeting or a curse? It must be shouted to be heard, and then either becomes absurd. We go our way, deafened, yet the ear pierced always with the chant of 'No-Man's-Land': 'Stretcher bearer! . . . Give me water.'

The legs carry the body mechanically; the brain knows the body's destination. On. If no metal strikes me I shall blunder on. The mind wanders. What dreariness, what boredom, even when the ground heaves suddenly before the eyes leaving a yawning hole to trap the unwary foot and drag the body, and the earth shrieks and belches above the tempest.

Time and reason — both have ceased. They are insignificant, inexplicable. Only the earth shudders and hate justifies itself in staggering noise. Little lights soar into the air, tremulously, like children's fireworks. They do not break the blackness, illumine only themselves as with a holo. All days are the same, all nights. But each night is for itself distinct.

The earth, the heavens, the body, the living-dead-thing which goes on and on and on. It perspires: the beads of sweat grow cold in chill wind. I am neither hot nor cold. I am nothing.

['Warrior']

Passchendaele. A stretcher carrying party of the 2nd Canadian Division bringing in wounded from the battle; a smashed German concrete emplacement can be seen. 6th October 1917. [IWM]

The Canadian Memorial at Crest Farm. This area was captured by the Canadians on 30th October 1917 and held against numerous counter-attacks. On the Memorial the words are 'The Canadian Corps in Oct.–Nov. 1917 advanced across this valley — then a treacherous morass — captured and held the Passchendaele Ridge.'

Passchendaele. Canadian stretcher bearers bring a wounded man over a duckboard track, 14th November 1917.. [IWM]

By the roadside. Two shells and a grenade awaiting the attention of the bomb disposal unit from Houthulst. Picture taken on the Bellvue Spur not far from Waterloo Farm.

['Warrior']

Public opinion in France was seeking for some new Commander upon whom to hang their hopes. The disaster of the Chemin-des-Dames had caused the French nation to lose all faith. Foch had been banished to obscurity. Joffre still sought to defend a vanishing reputation. Nivelle had been eclipsed. Marshal Lyautey, who had been brought to Paris from Morocco as Minister of War to exercise his autocracy, had resigned. Only Petain, perhaps less known, retained his reputation. So, while the French found a new Commander-in-Chief for their Armies, as I was given to understand at the time, the British Army was called upon to bear the burden of this new attack.

The cold analysis of history has since taught us that such was not the fact. On the Somme, in October and November 1916, by the obvious misuse of the weapon of surprise, the tank, too few in numbers and too late in season, with tired troops, Haig had believed that his Army could break through to Bapaume and beyond, when those familiar with the ground knew that even without enemy opposition it was well-nigh impassable. Again, in the Third Battle of Ypres, GHQ seems to have been possessed of an almost childish faith in chalk lines and arrows drawn on a map, while those to whom the attack plans were issued were assured from past experience that the objectives could not be won, even by the most redoubtable troops in the world. As to such troops the Divisions which made the assaults along the Menin Road were incomparable.

It is small wonder, therefore, that a feeling of exasperation grew in the minds of fighting troops against the Staffs. Red tabs on the facings of those with whom lesser commanders and soldiers were in daily contact, the staffs of Brigades and Divisions, had become the insignia for incompetence. The slander was ill-deserved, for, as history has recorded in a hundred fights, the Generals and Staffs of Divisions and Brigades did not flinch from incurring the heat of battle with the troops entrusted to their charge. Nevertheless, their military wisdom was daily impugned because those who fought the battles were asked to carry out tasks beyond human and military possibility, and which to intelligent men were often fantastic and absurd.

208

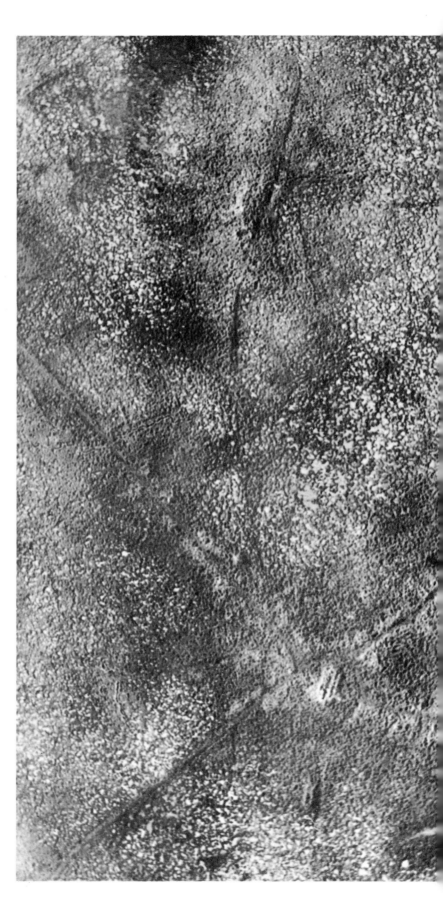

In this men lived, fought, and died. Aerial photograph showing the site of Passchendaele Village at the end of 1917, and the thousands upon thousands of overlapping, water-filled shell holes through which our troops struggled forward.

The site of the destroyed church is noticeable at the junction of the roads on the right of the photograph. The 'road' at the top right leads to Westroosebeke and the one at the lower right leads to Moorslede. The Broodseinde road runs toward the bottom centre and the curved road above it is that which now passes the Crest Farm Memorial.

Passchendaele, 1968. The hallowed ground over which the Canadians attacked on 6th November 1917 and captured the 'brick-coloured stain' which was all that remained of Passchendaele.

This photograph was taken close to the Canadian memorial at Crest Farm.

PASSCHENDAELE — Verdict of one who fought there

At this distance from the events recorded, with the evidence of history, and all the diaries and apologues of generals and statesmen available, it is with pain that I record the futile heroism of Third Ypres and Passchendaele. A boisterous publicity informed those who were sent into these muddy wastes that the need of the offensive was urgent in order to withdraw German pressure from the French.

True it is that earlier in the year France had lost 120,000 men in the twinkling of an eye in Nivelle's fantastic attack at the Chemin-des-Dames, and the French Armies had mutinied. But both Petain and Foch had exerted themselves to dissuade Sir Douglas Haig and Sir William Robertson from their purpose before Ypres. 'What is the use,' they had asked in effect, 'of a duck swim through the inundations?' Surely a warning. And it is recorded that an officer from GHQ, who persistently had urged Haig's offensive, in November, for the first time since its opening visited the front, and wept, crying: 'To think that we asked men to fight in that!'

And Foch had remarked: 'Boche is bad and boue is bad. But Boche and boue together . . . ah!' The French, indeed, had desired that Haig should extend the British front, until the French Army had been reorganised under a new command. But Haig had persisted in the Passchendaele pursuit.

Twice sacrificed within six months were the British Armies, thrown away at Passchendaele, overwhelmed in March 1918. There can be little room for doubt that the tardiness of Foch in coming to British aid in the Battle of the Lys was because Haig had defied the wishes of French GHQ six months before.

It is certain that the menace of the German submarine campaign persuaded Haig and Robertson in the attempt to outflank Zeebrugge and Ostend, by piercing the German line at Passchendaele, thereby throwing back the enemy's right flank to the line of the River Scheldt. But the Prime Minister, charged first with the

responsibility for statecraft, holding the people's pulse, strenuously opposed the Passchendaele offensive. Yet Haig persisted.

History is presented, therefore, with the spectacle of its greatest maritime power flinging its last military reserves into a death struggle with the world's greatest military power, while the under-sea naval force of that power tightened its grip on the throat of the adversary.

Plainly, statecraft and strategy dictated the waiting game. British troops would have been refreshed and reinforced by March 1918. The French Armies would have been reorganised, and inspired again under the leadership of new national heroes. America, having declared war in April, would have available its unblooded troops, with unlimited reserves, ready in cooperation with the Allies, as the counter-stroke, to throw back the cohorts of Ludendorff.

Though Third Ypres, with its ghastly aftermath of Passchendaele, remains a monument to the tenacity of British arms and the courage of the Warrior, history condemns the High Command. We were ever willing to forgive a fault. In war, as von Clausewitz has written: 'foolhardiness, even that is not to be despised.' But the propaganda of trumpeted excuses have galled us, where frankness, as in Napoleon's armies, would have won our sympathy. 'Qui s'excuse s'accuse.'

Raids, even more formidable attacks, carried out along a Corps' front opposite Passchendaele are lost and confused in a terrain, as a manoeuvre area beyond cohesive plan, topographically absurd, pock-marked by shell-holes, each one interlacing its neighbour, so that from the air the battlefield resembled a honeycomb.

We attacked the 'gasometers', and a variety of German strongholds, set in concrete, held by a score of men armed with machine-guns and flame-throwers. These concrete fortresses, rising above the mud and slime, squat like the old defences of Portsmouth set in the Solent, were well-nigh impregnable. Though British military policy exposed large numbers of men to shell-fire, gas, and the incredibly horrible weather conditions of the front defences of Passchendaele, the men being strung out, devoid of shelter in

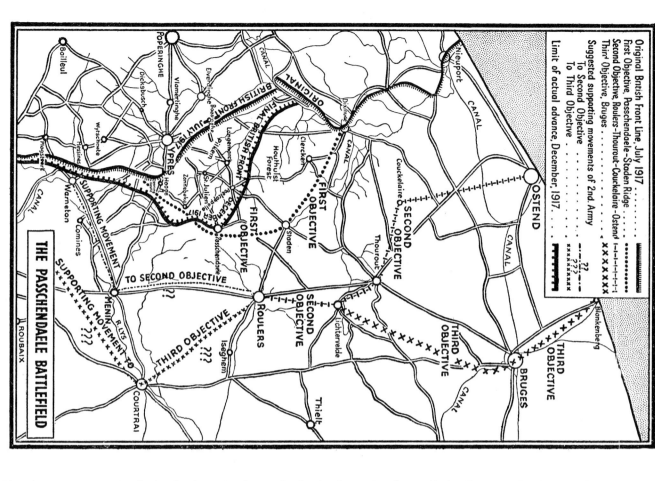

THE PASSCHENDAELE BATTLEFIELD

Original British Front Line July 1917 ....
First Objective, Passchendaele-Staden Ridge ....
Second Objective, Roulers-Thourout-Couckelaire-Ostend ....
Third Objective, Bruges ....
Suggested supporting movements of 2nd Army
To Second Objective
To Third Objective
Limit of actual advance, December, 1917 ....

water-logged shell-holes crudely linked by the spade, the German defences were but thinly held, and consisted of concrete 'pill-boxes' held by machine-guns, the main body of the troops being retained in reserve, well housed and rationed, considerably behind the battle front.

A knowledge of the ground made it plain that no major attack could develop over it without ample signs of preparation, and that any advance over ground of the character described must be very slow. An attack, either by British or by Germans, by day or by night, could be held for some hours by machine-guns placed in depth, fired from strongholds, indestructible, except by the rare possibility of direct hit by a shell of the largest calibre, or by a surprise assault by troops possessed of extraordinary hardihood, ingenuity, and courage, armed with bombs or flamethrowers.

The massing of British troops in and around Passchendaele was sheer waste of life and man-power, and wholly destructive of morale. Attacks sent forward were almost inevitably doomed to failure at high cost, and even if successful achieved nothing of tactical value. It is true that several Divisions occupying this front during the winter of 1917-18 achieved local successes by the capture of German 'pill-boxes'. But the aftermath of horror beggars description. Wounded men, lost in the trackless indulations of No-Man's-Land, cried bitterly by day and night from the shell-holes into which they had fallen, or into whose depths they had rolled for safety from machine-gun fire, until death stifled their cries, as weakened they subsided deeper into the slime or were drowned in the stagnant, gas-drenched water-holes. By day, owing to the vigilance of the enemy, it was impossible to search the ground; and, by night, the difficulty of maintaining direction, due to the straggle of our forward posts, and the confusion caused by light rockets appearing from every angle, made it impossible to

The Objectives. What should have been. Sketch map of the plan as envisaged by the generals. The ordinary soldiers saw it in a different light. Map from *War Memoirs of David Lloyd George* by kind permission of Beaverbrook Newspapers Ltd.

succour the men left out in No-Man's-Land. In and around out-posts, indeed, throughout the Passchendaele Salient, there were scarcely ten square yards from out of the waters of whose shell-holes there did not protrude an arm, a leg, or a helmeted head, some German, but mostly British. As loss of blood and faintness from wounds weakened and sapped their strength, and the intense cold cramped their limbs, the mud sides of the shell-holes declared how these men had slowly sunk lower and lower, until death surrendered them to a slimy grave. Such death, sketched on every hand, indeed, was the real horror of Passchendaele. The cry of lost, helpless souls in No-Man's-Land was the bitterest experience which fell to the Warrior's ears. It chilled his heart, froze the marrow in his bones.

I had heard those cries in the narrow stretch which lay between our lines at La Bassee, where it was suicide to attempt to bring the wounded in. And at Les Boeufs and in Third Ypres I had heard them, too. But the wanton futility of Passchendaele gave to those cries an added bitterness.

I never permitted a man to move at Passchendaele alone. And though Passchendaele held a strange fascination for me I was so fearful of being struck down and left to cry alone in that wilder-ness, that on my perambulations I always took with me some stout heart, in case one or both were stricken. Then, at least in comradeship we might die, if aid did not come. But so treacherous was the earth's surface, so binding to the feet and legs, that one man alone, however great his strength, was incapable of carrying a wounded comrade. If he left him, while seeking aid, it was a miracle if in the holes of that honeycomb he found his way back again to the place where his comrade had been left.

History must write of Passchendaele that it remains a military crime, a complete misunderstanding of ground, a misinterpre-tation of the quality of troops, and a misreading of the intentions of the enemy. No possible excuse, no extenuating circumstance, political, strategic, tactical, exists for the futilities of Passchendaele.

['Warrior']

212

The only thing our so-called admirers at home praised in the Passchendaele campaign was the heroism of the soldier; they might go a little further now and curse those men who led us into this ghastly shambles. What use was it for us to add a little more flesh and bone to that sewage-heap! The Passchendaele battle had absolutely nothing to recommend it — military, strategic, political, moral: every one felt when he was picking a gluey way over noisome shell-holes, beside poor broken relics of humanity, among bursting shells, that he was picking a way to death, certainly not to a glory of victory. The dull ache kept us in that silent misery which cannot be relieved by curses: with it was the feeling that we were paying rather dearly for this firework pageant, not so much with life as with self-respect.

There was no morale in the Flanders offensive, no infective enthusiasm, the mind must have something definite before it, some real purpose: but the Flanders offensive was a ghastly mistake and we knew it. Our friends at home expanded chests at the thought of heroism at Passchendaele; but was it heroism that should ever have been demanded from the Army? Was it not rather a disgraceful trifling with the most sacred instincts of life, when the soldier was asked to perform deeds of bleak horror, unrelieved by purpose or even success?

[HQ]

PASSCHENDAELE: A COSTLY VICTORY

Passchendaele was by far the hardest battle fought by Canadians in World War I — far harder than Vimy. Even now, 50 years later, the name is synonymous with knee-deep mud, the sickening smell of rotting bodies, and fierce fighting against a stubborn enemy.

Three operations during the First World War aroused great controversy — Gallipoli, the Somme and Passchendaele — and of these none so much as Passchendaele.

Even before the Nivelle offensive early in 1917, Sir Douglas Haig, the British commander-in-chief, had planned a northern thrust and at that time an offensive seemed justified. The Admiralty were desperately anxious for the capture of Ostend and Zeebrugge from which German U-boats and destroyers emerged to sink shipping in the Channel. And as the months progressed, the situation grew more critical. In February 470,000 tons of Allied ships were sunk; in April the figure had risen to 837,000. Sir John Jellicoe, the First Sea Lord, predicted a British collapse if the sinkings continued at their current rate.

The Nivelle offensive, despite the successful preliminaries at Arras and Vimy Ridge, failed and the over-optimistic French generalissimo lost his job to Petain. By the end of May, 1917, the French armies, disgusted with 'grand offensives', were in open mutiny and Haig turned to his Flanders plan for which he now had an additional pressing reason — to divert German attention from the French. He opened the Battles of Ypres, 1917, with an attack on 7th June by Plumer's Second Army against Messines Ridge which was brilliantly successful. Plumer pressed Haig strongly for permission to exploit his success in the direction of the high ground at Passchendaele before German reserves arrived and, in the light of what happened later, it is a pity that he was not given his head. But Haig restrained him. General Gough, whose Fifth Army would carry out the next phase planned for July, preferred to include Passchendaele in his own tasks. The propitious moment passed.

The main Flanders offensive would start on 31st July and meanwhile, further south, Haig maintained the pressure north and south of Arras to keep the Germans occupied. Currie's assault with his Canadians on Hill 70 was part of the plan 'to hold the enemy to his ground and prevent his moving troops elsewhere', and this took place in August.

LLOYD GEORGE'S OPPOSITION

In England, Lloyd George — who after the Somme had not had much time for Haig — thought the best course for the British would be to remain on the defensive and await the build-up of troops from the United States which had

Passchendaele Church and main street. It was here that on 6th November 1917, the Canadians bayonetted the few surviving Germans, before the village at last fell into our hands after three long months of blood and sacrifice.

213

now entered the war. He feared that Haig's northern offensive would exhaust the British Army before the winter without bringing much result. Artillery units, he suggested, might be sent from France to stiffen Italy.

Haig presented his case in London on 19th June. He demonstrated that an advance of only twenty-five miles would be necessary to free Ostend and Zeebrugge by the end of the year or accept defeat. But such were Lloyd George's trepidations that it was not before 21st July that he grudgingly allowed the offensive to go forward.

A 'DUCK'S MARCH'

But Haig persisted. Lloyd George was pressing for the transfer of troops to Italy. So long as the policy of the offensive prevailed, the War Cabinet could hardly reduce his strength. There were no longer valid strategic aims in Flanders, so the purpose of a resumed offensive could only be attrition, and a better site than Flanders might have been found for that. The axis of advance swung towards the coast, away from the enemy's main communications, so that there was no profitable basis for wearing down the German strength; the security of the Germany's position in France would not be endangered by Haig's advance. And, as Haig must have known from his experience there in 1915, the surface water in Flanders was so high that parapets had to take the place of trenches. He would be undertaking, as Foch cynically put it, a 'duck's march' through the Flanders mud.

Haig's offensive, officially known as the Battles of Ypres, 1917, but better known as Passchendaele, divides itself into three phases: first the opening assault from 31st July to 2nd August by Gough's Fifth Army; second, the limited advances made on 20th September, 26th September and 4th October by Plumer's Second Army; and third, the closing phase, culminating in the capture of Passchendaele village on 6th November by the Canadian Corps and the high ground beyond four days later.

As a preliminary to the first phase a bombardment of four million shells hurtled down on reclaimed bogland to destroy the drainage patterns and create in front of the British Army a self-made obstacle that doomed the offensive before it was even launched. Though the villages of Bixschoote and St Julien and also the Pilckem Ridge were taken, hard counter-attacks robbed the right wing of any results. Half the tanks bogged down and were lost in this first battle, and the casualty list showed the grim total of 31,850. Gough tried again on August 16 and was even less successful. Haig shifted the responsibility for resuming the offensive onto Plumer's shoulders and the careful Plumer paused to plan for limited objectives.

Haig might well have called the offensive off after Gough had failed. His reasons for it, valid before, no longer applied. The French Army had by now recovered. On 20th August it attacked brilliantly at Verdun to take 10,000 prisoners, and Haig, in recording this result, admitted that the French had had the quiet time Pétain had hoped for to effect recovery. Also, the peak of the submarine crisis had been reached and passed; the newly-introduced convoy system had cut down shipping losses far more sharply than could have been achieved by the capture of the Flanders ports. And in any case it must have been obvious to Haig that a deep penetration of 25 miles was no longer possible after early failure had sacrificed surprise.

In late September and early October, Plumer carried the line forward by means of heavy barrages and strongly-pressed infantry attacks on narrow frontages. Three battles – Menin Road Ridge, Polygon Wood and Broodseinde – though costly, were successful. A footing was obtained on Passchendaele Ridge, but Plumer's men were played out. Then the rains set in.

By the first week in September, according to Haig's Chief of Intelligence, letters from London revealed a 'marked weakening of trust' in Sir Douglas Haig. Against the advice of both Gough and Plumer, however, Haig was determined to have the ridge at Passchendaele for his winter line. His troops obviously could not winter in the swamp below the ridge and so Haig had two alternatives: to pull back to better ground, or to fight forward onto higher ground. Haig's reputation, less strong than formerly, would never survive the voluntary relinquishment of ground which had cost so much blood. The stubborn Scot, then, would go on.

HAIG SELECTS CANADIANS

On 5th October, the day following Broodseinde, Haig decided to employ the Canadian Corps which had given him Vimy in April and Hill 70 in August. He now counted on Currie to give him the ridge. The Canadians would go to Gough's Fifth Army, but Currie objected strongly; he had worked under Gough at the Somme and still remembered Regina Trench. Orders on the 9th directed Currie to Plumer's Second Army where the Corps relieved the 2nd ANZAC in the line on a front which was just forward of that which the 1st Canadian Division had held before the gas attack in 1915.

The artillery was the frame work on which Currie planned his battles and, when the warning order for the move north came in, he despatched two gunner officers – Major-General E. W. B. Morrison and Lieutenant-Colonel A. G. L. McNaughton – from Lens to take a look at the future battlefield. They found that opposite the sector to which the Corps would be assigned was a valley, the Ravebeek Valley, carrying what had been the Ravebeek stream from the opposite ridge into the Canadian line. The villages of

214

Passchendaele (right) and Mosselmarkt (left) were high on the ridge at either side of the stream and about a thousand yards apart. In fact the Ravebeek Valley cut the Canadian sector into two. To the north of the valley, on the Corp's left, a high spur (the Bellevue Spur), extending southeastward from the main ridge, carried the Gravenstafel road forward to Mosselmarkt. South of the valley the low Gravenstafel Ridge climbed higher to join the main ridge south of Passchendaele village. From there the Zonnebeke road followed the crest of the ridge to Passchendaele and on to Mosselmarkt.

The Passchendaele ridge, in this sector, can best be described as a big-nosed, crescent moon with its lower horn (the Gravenstafel Ridge) hooking into Canadian territory. The Bellevue Spur, on the Corps left, formed the nose which, with Mosselmarkt at its base, pointed towards the Canadian line. The upper horn hooked towards the British on the Canadians' left. The ground at both sides of the jutting 'nose' was so deeply flooded that the only practical approaches to the main ridge were up the lower horn (by the Zonnebeke road) to Passchendaele, and up the nose (by the Gravenstafel road) to Mosselmarkt.

Morrison looked at the situation along one road; McNaughton the other. What they saw appalled them. They had both fought at Second Ypres but could hardly recognize this ground. It seemed that a roaring cataract had poured over the countryside, scouring the earth and snapping off the trees; and then, after drowning the landscape for a long time, it was as though the high water had receded, leaving deep slime and stagnant pools, the crumbling fragments of buildings, the litter of rusting jetsam and rotting bodies. There was the pungency of marsh gas and the sweet smell of death. As for the guns the Canadians were to take over, these were not effectively deployed. They were sited in badly-bunched clusters either on or near the two roads; and where they were off the road they were tilted grotesquely and axle-deep in mud. McNaughton said that had he been the Counter-Battery Officer on the German side he would have relished the job of dealing with them. There would have to be more roads and firm platforms if the Canadians were to get any value out of artillery fire.

CURRIE'S PROTEST

Currie, who saw the battlefield on 17th October, agreed — *if* the Canadians were to fight at all. 'Battlefield looks bad,' he wrote in his diary, 'no salvaging has been done, and very few of the dead buried.' What he saw of the conditions convinced him that his Corps should not be committed to this attack. The operation was impossible, except at great cost, and futile. He protested to both Plumer and Haig so strongly that he was convinced that had he been a British officer, he would have been sent home. But he was ordered to go and make the attack which, he warned, would cost sixteen thousand casualties.

They turned out to be only 346 short of that. Currie had protested and been overruled. He could do no more than try to make the attempt less costly by careful planning.

Currie planned to seize the ridge in three phases, each of which would carry the Corps nearest to the final objectives. The guns would be the key to success. We have noted that these were bunched in clusters; but worse, out of 250 'heavies', 89 were out of action while 23 could not be found; and a similar situation existed with the 306 field guns the Canadians were supposed to get. Currie saw to it that he received the full complement of working guns and he then ordered the construction of firm platforms, sited at various positions forward, and plank roads so that the guns could be moved from one position to another. Continuous fire, it was hoped — though this was never fully realised — could thus be provided without the guns sinking and having to be relaid after every round.

Between Ypres and the forward troops lay six miles of shell-churned ground. Even duck-boards sank feet deep and to step off them meant drowning or being buried in the mud. Currie ordered roads — new plank roads or road repairs — over the six-mile distance to bring up reinforcements, munitions and supplies and to evacuate the wounded. Canadian sappers and the 2nd, 107th, 123d and 124th Pioneer Battalions joined the engineers of Second Army in all these tasks. Shelter was impossible. There were three thousand casualties before they were through.

The Germans had adopted a flexible system of defence. This called for a lightly-held 'forefield' of outposts (in craters or concrete pillboxes above the ground) with, farther back, strong defensive lines in depth. Farther back still, they held fresh troops ready for immediate counter attack. The method proved effective. A preliminary bombardment against scattered outposts would do little good. The Canadian artillerymen, therefore, planned harassing fire over the whole front, concentrations against known wire and pillboxes, and slow barrages moving as close as possible in front of the advancing infantry during the attack.

CANADIANS ATTACK

Currie, with his preparations completed, was ready to carry out phase one on 26th October. It would be a two-pronged attack on the only feasible approaches, right and left of the drowned out Ravebeek Valley. The 4th Division on the right — tackling the 'horn' where the Ravebeek Valley joined the main ridge in the vicinity of the Zonnebeke road — had a very restricted frontage. Only one battalion, the 46th of the 10th Brigade, could be employed. On the left, the 3rd Division, advancing across low ground towards the tip of the Bellevue 'nose', has a wider front. Here, from right to left, the 58th and the 43rd Battalions of the 9th Brigade and the 4th CMR of the 8th would carry out the divisional attack.

The attack went in at 5.40 am in a grey mist that turned into the steady rain of Flanders later in the day. The barrage, especially on the left, was very slow to match the pace of the infantry who were hampered by the mud. The 46th Battalion, on higher ground, moved astride the road and made good progress. It carried all its objectives successfully, including the stumps of what had been Decline Copse, and with that had advanced the line by 600 yards. The copse, however, was the common objective of both the Canadians and the Australians advancing on the flank; and, through a misunderstanding of boundaries, it was relinquished. The 44th Battalion, on the night of the 27th, recaptured it, and on the 28th two Canadian battalions — the 44th and 35th — held it firmly against a strong enemy counter-attack. The 4th Division, through these operations, had widened its grip on the main ridge.

On the Bellevue Spur, however, the 3rd Division did not get on as well as had been expected because of the German method of defence. Once the pillboxes around Bellevue had been lost, the enemy brought down heavy artillery fire on his 'forefield' defences which he had carefully registered, forcing the Canadians back to their start line. The 43rd Battalion, in the centre, managed to retain a grip on the spur however, through the bravery of Lieutenant Robert Shankland whose platoon held captured pillboxes and shell-holes just north of the Mosselmarkt road. This gave the 9th Brigade the opportunity of a further attack. By noon the 52nd Battalion closed the gap between Shankland's party and the main body and fanned out to capture the villages of Bellevue and Laamekeek. Though short of the final objective for this phase of the attack, by night-fall the centre of the 3rd Division was well-established on the higher and drier ground of the Bellevue Spur. Three members of the 3rd Division won VC's that day: Shankland, whose action had turned what must have been failure into success; Captain C. P. J. O'Kelly of the 52nd Battalion, whose company captured six pillboxes and 100 prisoners; and Private T. W. Holmes of the 4th CMR who himself accounted for two machine guns, one pillbox and 19 prisoners. The fighting for the 3 days, 26–28th October, cost Canada 2,481 casualties. Currie ordered a pause for the construction of new tracks, one to each brigade sector. These were ready in time for a second blow to be struck on 30th October by the same two assaulting divisions.

On the right the 4th Division now had a wider frontage. Three battalions — the 85th, 78th and 72nd of the 12th Brigade moved forward at dawn in cold and windy weather. Again, in this sector, it was a successful if costly day. The 85th Battalion, on the right, lost half it strength but overran every strongpoint in its path. In the centre, the 78th Battalion moved steadily forward to its final line beyond the Passchendaele road. The 72nd Battalion, on the left, cleared Crest Farm and briefly put patrols into Passchendaele village itself. By 8.30 am the 4th Division could report full success in this second phase.

The 3rd Division, as we have seen, had won part of the Bellevue Spur, but the frontage here was narrow. To gain a wider frontage on the right the PPCLI had attacked from Laamkeek during the night before the main attack. They struggled forward through the mire to take out Snipe Hall, a troublesome pillbox, at the edge of the Ravebeek swamp. From there they were to advance over equally low and sloppy ground on another pillbox, Duck Lodge, as part of the divisional attack. From Duck Lodge, on the spur itself, they would find the going better. The 49th Battalion, in the centre on the spur, had the best ground but faced grim defences, while on the left the 5th CMR must attack on the low ground between the Bellevue 'nose' and the northern swamp.

The attack went well. The PPCLI took Duck Lodge and kept going despite heavy fire from farther up the valley which thinned their ranks. The battalion encountered strongly fortified positions at Meetcheele, the main village on the spur, and at Graf House, deep inside the Ravebeek Valley. They cleared the first, largely through the heroism of two men — Lieutenant Hugh MacKenzie (a Patricia officer who was serving with the 7th Machine Gun Company) and Sergeant G. H. Mullin — who silenced a machine gun in a pillbox near the Meetcheele road. Mackenzie, who drew the Germans' fire while Mullin stormed the position, was killed. Both won the Victoria Cross. The Germans continued to hold out at Graf House.

In the centre the 49th Battalion kept level with the Patricias to capture Furst Farm, just off the northern edge of the Spur. This battalion, though it had better ground, was even harder hit than the PPCLI.

To the north of the Bellevue spur the 5th CMR despite atrocious ground, made good progress and ended the day in possession of Source and Vapour Farms, along the Corps boundary with the British. These farms were at the edge of the Northern swamp and were almost impossible to reinforce. Nevertheless, Major G. R. Pearkes, whose company seized them, successfully held them against a series of counter-attacks and they remained in Canadian possession in readiness for the third and final phase of the overall operation Pearkes won the Victoria Cross for his gallant exploit.

The fighting on the 30th had been expensive — 2,321 casualties; only a little more than a hundred short of the figure for the first, and longer, phase.

STEP-BY-STEP ADVANCE

The assault so far had been a step-by-step advance — all that was possible under the terrible ground conditions. Nevertheless the first two phases had carried the Corps forward from between 1000 and 1500 yards. The Canadians were now within striking distance of the crest of the main ridge. Currie, when drawing up the initial plan for the battle, had insisted on a seven-day pause between phases two and three, and he remained firm; he would not risk the final thrust with exhausted troops. The 1st and 2nd Divisions would relieve the 3rd and 4th for this, and Currie split the final phase into two stages: the capture of Passchendaele and Mosselmarkt villages, and, four days later, the seizure of the defensible main ridge beyond these villages to the east. He brought the fresh divisions in early to give them a chance to recover after the grim march forward from ruined Ypres. The reliefs were not completed until the morning of 5th November, and that night the incoming units moved into jumping off positions ready to advance at first light on the 6th.

The story of the attack can be briefly told. The 2nd Division, on the right, had Passchendaele as its main objective; the 1st, Mosselmarkt. The 2nd Division employed the 27th, 31st and 28th Battalions of the 6th Brigade, with the 26th Battalion guarding the right flank, while on the left the 1st Division used the 1st and 2nd Battalions on either side of the road to Mosselmarkt, with the 3rd Battalion, on the left, striking in from flooded Vapour Farm to take the village of Goudberg and a strongpoint named Vine Cottages.

Most of the front which faced the Corps was high, on the main ridge or the spur, and the troops had better going. At 6 am they sprang forward behind a powerful barrage, moving more rapidly than before so that the German answering fire mostly fell behind them. In the 2nd Division's sector the 28th Battalion, struggling out of the knee-deep, often waist-deep slush at the end of the Ravebeek Valley, had the toughest time, but, like the other battalions, it reached its final line. Passchendaele itself fell to the 27th Battalion, one of whose members, Private J. P. Robertson, won a posthumous Victoria Cross for disposing of an enemy post in the path of his platoon.

The 1st Division was equally successful. As with the 2nd, it was the unit on the left which found the going worst. There the 3rd Battalion climbed out of the swamp around Vapour Farm to seize Goudberg and to tackle the defenders of Vine Cottages who proved stubborn. Corporal C. F. Barron of the 3rd Battalion received the Victoria Cross for his work in taking out three enemy machine-gun posts in this locality. Elsewhere, however, the 1st Division swept on to seize Mosselmarkt and clear enemy garrisons from camouflaged shell-holes. By 8 am every objective had been taken. Canadian losses in both divisions numbered 2,238.

The second stage of this final phase began on 10th November to gain the remaining high ground. This the 20th, the 7th and the 8th Battalions successfully accomplished at a cost of 1,094 casualties in heavy rain. Vicious German retaliatory fire lashed the narrow salient. In all, the counter-battery fire of five German corps sullenly pounded the newly-won ground, but Passchendaele Ridge had been brought too dearly to be given up. The Canadians hung on.

COSTLY VICTORY

The capture of Passchendaele relieved Haig's anxiety, for the whole offensive had by now become associated with Passchendaele in the public mind. With Passchendaele captured, the operations could be painted as a victory and Haig could hold his own against the politicians. It was, he recorded, 'a very important success'. Certainly, it was a great Canadian achievement, solidly based on fighting spirit and adequate preparations before the battle. But the question must be posed. Was Haig's offensive justified? It served no useful strategic ends and, from the point of view of tactics, to drive a salient into a ridge four miles forward of the old line is of doubtful value. Was it worthwhile, then, on the grounds of sheer attrition? The answer to that is simple — Britain and her Dominions suffered the greater losses.

Reprinted with the kind permission of the author, Mr John Swettenham, Historian, Canadian War Museum, and Mr Lorne Manchester, Managing Editor of Legion, the national magazine of the Royal Canadian Legion.

THE BATTLE OF THE LYS (FOURTH YPRES)

The Battle of the Lys, also known as Fourth Ypres, was fought in April 1918 and the Germans, at last, nearly succeeded in capturing the famous town which had defied them for so long. It was also one of the series of battles which had commenced on 21st March and which constituted the last desperate attempts of the Germans to win the war.

On 21st March 1918 at 0440 hours and in thick mist, forty-three enemy divisions burst upon the forty-two mile long, weakly held, Fifth Army front on the Somme. Another nineteen divisions were hurled against the Third Army on the Fifth Army's left. Prior to the attack the defenders had undergone a shattering bombardment by nearly 6,000 guns of all calibres during which smoke and gas shells were mixed liberally with high explosives. Headed by well trained storm troops the Germans quickly overwhelmed the forward defences of General Gough's Army. Fog and smoke blotted out aerial observation and blinded our troops. Units were surrounded and in many cases annihilated almost before they realised what was happening. Companies, battalions, and even divisions were decimated and some virtually ceased to exist as fighting formations. Communications broke down completely and, due to a serious lack of reserves, little could be done to alleviate the worsening situation. In spite of heroic defences by small groups of men the German tidal wave rolled on; within three days the British Fifth Army had been routed and the line of the Somme smashed.

Fortunately on the twenty-eight mile front of General Byng's Third Army things were not as grievous for the fog was less thick and the defenders more numerous (sixteen divisions, as compared to Gough's fourteen plus the cavalry). Additionally they had better defensive positions and inflicted deadly execution on the attackers. By the 26th March the enemy had been thoroughly exhausted by his concentrated efforts and the offensive had practically ground to a halt although one final blow was directed at the Third Army two days later – without success and at the cost of more heavy losses to the attackers. Large numbers of French reserves were now

being massed following strong representations by Field-Marshal Haig and General Foch, the recently appointed Commander-in-Chief of the Allied Armies on the Western Front. (Shortly after he was given the title of Generalissimo and created a Marshal of France).

The Fifth Army had meantime been broken into fragments but was still fighting. Gough was dismissed – unfairly it is said – by Haig. The Third Army had been driven back but was still mainly intact. By the end of March the enemy was just nine miles short of Amiens and Albert had fallen. But Ludendorff recognised that his offensive had proved to be a costly failure and decided to try his hand elsewhere. His original plan to divide the British and French Armies at their juncture on the Somme and then to concentrate his full weight on each in turn had not proved successful and it is no exaggeration to say that this was due mainly to the incredible tenacity of the ordinary British fighting man – a quality fully appreciated by German Staff Officers even before the offensive began.

Sadly though, the savage fighting cost the British more than 100,000 casualties in just over two weeks whilst the French lost about 77,000. The Germans lost at least as many as the combined total of the Allies.

The emphasis of the offensive then shifted to the north. Ludendorff's first plan was to strike towards Hazebrouck, a vital railway centre on the plain of the Lys behind the British lines but, due to an initial success in the Lys offensive, St Omer (and eventually the Channel Ports) became his ultimate goal. So, on 9th April, after an intense artillery bombardment and with eight German divisions involved, the blow fell. The main thrust was directed at Portuguese troops holding a sector of the British front. Again mist aided the attackers and they smashed through the Portuguese lines against little resistance. Assaults were also made against British troops on either side of the Portuguese and with the breaking of the line a retirement became inevitable. On the right flank, however, our troops holding Givenchy threw back the attacking Germans and inflicted heavy casualties. This stout resistance by the 55th West Lancashire Division (General Jeudwine) played a major part in the failure of the German offensive.

In spite of this set-back, Ludendorff's troops exploited their break-through and rapidly pushed forward. Apprehension grew at British GHQ and a plea was made for French reinforcements. Foch refused to be rushed. He was convinced that the offensive would stagger to a halt in the mud of the boggy Lys plain. Subsequent events justified his viewpoint.

Nevertheless, the German Army continued to press strongly and in the three next week such well known places as Armentieres, Bailleul, Estaires, Merville and Neuve Chapelle fell within its grasp. After a short respite, the Germans renewed the offensive with fresh divisions from the south and again they met with success.

At this stage General Plumer was put in command of the defences from La Basse to the coast and one of his first moves — albeit reluctantly — was to give up Passchendaele and withdraw his lines at the apex of the Salient almost to the walls of Ypres. This was a terrible decision to have to make but since it shortened the line it automatically provided reserves for the fighting further south. As the Germans had already planned to attack the Salient with the object of destroying or capturing the many troops within its boundaries, the withdrawal was of considerable strategic value. Even so, it must have been a bitter blow to the British after the terrible struggles to capture this very same ground a few months earlier. The wasteland of mud was accordingly relinquished to the enemy and it then became his turn to undergo the rigours of surviving in those freadful acres in which so much blood had already been split.

Messines fell; then Wytschaete. The enemy brought up more divisions, some from Russia and some from France. Slowly but surely the British were pushed back towards Hazebrouck with the Germans making powerful efforts to extend the flanks of their advance. The situation was critical and again a plea was made to Foch to supply French reinforcements but it was not until 19th April that he allowed a limited number of French troops to become involved in Flanders. As it was, the French who took over Kemmel Hill from the exhausted British lost that vital pivot on 25th April. The enemy then fought his way beyond the hill to the small village of Locre where a combined force of French and British checked his advance and forced him to retire.

By the end of April, and after Haig had issued his famous 'Backs to the Wall' message, the Germans realised that their great thrust to the sea had not succeeded and they once more turned their attention to other places in the south. Fearing that a fresh attempt would be made by the enemy in the north the Allies discussed the possible evacuation of the whole area including the ports. (Fortunately it did not come to this and it was not until the Second World War that this particular nightmare became a reality.)

On the same day that Kemmel was lost, a limited but historical battle took place at Villers Bretonneux near Amiens. Six tanks were involved (three British against three German) in the first tank versus tank battle in history. The British won the battle but the village was lost until its recapture next day by the Australians on what, by a coincidence, was the third anniversary of Anzac Day.

Losses in the Battle of Fourth Ypres were staggering. Nearly 240,000 British casualties were incurred in six weeks whilst the total for the Germans was over 348,000.

Ludendorff blundered badly for although he had been warned of the ground conditions he still insisted on committing his fine divisions which rapidly became exhausted in the morass and lacked supplies and proper artillery support. He should have been forewarned by the disastrous British campaign of 1917 but like Haig he had been lured by the high ground and what lay beyond. In consequence he was unable to withstand the battering ram that hit him a few months later.

In spite of these set-backs Ludendorff still had plans for another offensive in Flanders but first he decided to strike again at the French in the Champagne area. This and subsequent attacks elsewhere on the French front in May, June, and July all failed to obtain the desired results (although once again Paris was seriously threatened). By then, however, the Americans had come into the fight, even if only to a limited degree, and their involvement raised Allied morale. Some American infantry divisions had been formed before Fourth Ypres but this situation changed in September 1918 when the Americans went into action for the first time as an actual Army. The slow build-up of American forces after the USA's declaration of war in April 1917 was a bone of contention to some, and even today many people retain the incorrect impression that it was America who won that war with masses of her troops. Had the war lasted until 1919 there is no doubt that America would have shouldered a considerable share of the fighting, but this was certainly not the case in 1918. Additionally in the heavy fighting which occurred as the Allies fought their way forward, it was British troops (with Canadians, Australians, New Zealanders, and South Africans) who bore the brunt of the action. This does not detract from the splendid work of the Americans for they played a most important role towards ending the conflict and the very fact that they *were* there, and that hundreds of thousands would be following, sealed Germany's fate — as it did again twenty years later.

Fourth Ypres ended without Ludendorff achieving his planned objective of a final thrust through Flanders against the British. Before his plans could be put into effect Foch struck back and the Germans slowly gave way during what was known as the Second Battle of the Marne. Then on 8th August (the Black Day of the German Army, according to Ludendorff) Haig commenced the operations which paved the way to final victory.

Nowhere had the Germans been completely successful during the previous few months but on several occasions it had been a near thing. Ludendorff had inflicted heavy blows in a number of directions but there was little to show in compensation for his enormous casualty list (totalling nearly 'one million men) from the overall operations which began on 21st March.

Along the Menin Road on our right flank we could see our Brigadier riding with his staff. We now got orders to close on the road, as no enemy were in sight. We formed up and moved off in fours towards Gheluvelt. As we marched we heard that the Messines Ridge had been captured by our troops. We passed a few Boche transport waggons complete with horses; there were quickly annexed by our people for rations. Abandoned guns, also left at the last moment with smashed sights, were ditched along the roadside. Several shells burst over us without doing any damage, and the column of fours was not broken. There were some large heaps of broken stones piled on the side of the road, and in some places the road had been freshly mended. The enemy evidently had very optimistic plans for holding Ypres for another years at least! On the western outskirts of the Gheluvelt shambles at exactly 11.30 the Battalion halted and fell out. Immediately out came the mess-tins, and 'drumming up the char' commenced.

Several of C Company used an old 'pill-box' close at hand for the sun, which had at last come out. I took off my equipment, jacket and shirt, and wrung the latter out. It was absolutely sodden.

[FCH]

THE END OF THE SALIENT – THE ATTACK

28TH SEPTEMBER 1918

The order of battle for the Great Flanders Offensive: General Plumer's Second Army, comprising the II, X, XV and XIX Corps, were to advance from Ypres in co-operation with the Belgian Army, and a French division under the supreme command of the King of the Belgians. The Second Army was lent to King Albert for the Flanders offensive. At dawn the Second Army was to advance from the jumping-off trenches around the Salient, pivoting on the XIX Corps, which was on the right flank at St Eloi. The left flank would rest on the Ypres–Potijze road in touch with the Belgian Army, whose front extended up to the sea. The actual frontage allotted to the 29th Division lay astride the Menin Road.

The 86th Brigade was to capture the first objective, the Hooge Ridge. Here it would be leap-frogged by the 88th Brigade, whose objective was Gheluvelt. The 87th Brigade was in reserve.

The cursed rain was now coming down as it always did for all the British operations in the Ypres Salient. Having had a short spell of fine weather, we were all in hopes of a fine day for the attack, as rain had such a terrible effect on the sodden and churned-up Ypres terrain. However, it was not to be. Boche retaliation was slight, a few shells exploded near us, still our bombardment went on. Soon the barrage was lifting for zero for the Boche line, and we knew that the 4th Worcesters had left their jumping-off position.

The going was now very bad indeed, the south side of the Menin Road being caked with mud and pitted everywhere with slate-coloured shell craters full of water. It was raining steadily in our faces as we moved up the rise of that desolate and shell-ravaged region, not even the rank grass was to be seen on that denuded ridge — just mud, brown, clinging mud, and shell-holes overlapping themselves in the water-logged area. C Company's advance lay through Zouave Wood — just stumps of trees and their fallen shell-splintered trunks.

Some of the men took shelter in an old derelict tank, and Farrell, myself, and the CSM occupied a very dilapidated dug-out, and studied our maps under head-cover. * News came of the capture of Gheluvelt. This objective had been reserved for the 4th Worcesters 2nd Battalion during the 1st Battle of Ypres, 31st October, '14.

We formed up as a battalion in mass, just east of Hooge, on the north side of the Menin Road. All hostile shelling had now ceased. From our vantage-point we had a good look round the desolate area. Nothing was left of Hooge; only the colour of the ground was slightly red from the bricks. Not one of the old landmarks was left, and the Salient from this ridge looked as featureless as the Sahara. It was impossible to make out the Bellewaarde Lake, or where Chateau Wood had been; even the mine crater had disappeared. The earth had been so churned up that the small water-courses had been altered. The only thing that could be seen was the long straight road stretching away behind us towards Ypres Ridge and the four solitary tanks spread along the ridge. They had been ditched and knocked out in the 3rd Battle of Ypres, 31st July, 1917.

The tank near Railway Wood had been bogged in a crater and looked grotesque rearing up on its stern. Although the country was so terribly altered from the time I saw it last, I had the satisfaction of looking back on it at my ease, and more or less in safety, remembering the days I had hugged the very same ground from the bottom of a trench in mortal terror. Hooge commanded a huge stretch of country, and I could well understand the importance the enemy attached to holding it. We could see men of the 9th Scottish Division advancing on our left towards Zonnebeke, and we watched over 400 Boche prisoners being marched back over the Bellewaarde Ridge. There was a continual rumbling of guns going on in the Belgian theatre of operations, and we wondered if the Forest of Houthulst had been captured. The

---

*   We were in the exact locality which was held by our 1st Battalion in the 2nd Battle of Ypres, and close to the spot where Major Conyers, Captains Gould-Adams, Bates, Goodbody, and Lieuts Westmacott and Blatchy had been killed.

Germans had fully realised its strategic importance and had turned it into an impregnable fortress of redoubts. The Forest of Houthulst had been held throughout the War by the enemy; the allies had never penetrated its fortifications, though they had reached its edges in the bitter fighting of the 3rd Battle on 26th October, '17. During the wars of the Spanish Succession, the Duke of Marlborough declared that 'He who holds the Houthulst Forest dominates Flanders.'

A torrential rain was now driving in our faces, and we got soaked to the skin as we moved off from Hooge, C Company leading, with platoons on a wide frontage, in snake formation, on the north side and parallel with the Menin Road. FitzSimon was detailed to guide the Battalion's right flank with a compass. The going was very heavy over the bleached rank grass. There were numerous shell craters and disused telephone lines mixed up with the rusty strands of old wire entanglements.

The whole area was intersected with trenches of every description, which had to be negotiated; consequently the advance was tedious. The Lewis gunners had a hard task carrying the weighty Lewis guns. Earlier in the day I had helped one of the crew to carry his spare magazines. Here and there we passed an old derelict field-gun, or a recently abandoned one in its muddy pit.

Where the edge of Inverness Copse had been, we passed British graves of 1914, and I particularly noted 2nd Worcestershire Regiment and 2nd Battalion Connaught Rangers printed on the wooden crosses. They were all dated October and November, 1914.

[FCH]

Rations and rum came up, and were issued out. I supervised the rum issue. Pte Coughlan drank my health. At midnight we advanced; it was very dark. Platoons advanced in snake formation, my platoon being on the left flank of the Company. We had to swing in to our right, owing to the saturated state of the ground near the Menin Road. There were also some patches of barbed wire. Expecting to find the enemy holding the rise, we moved cautiously. After advancing some 300 yards over broken and marshy ground, I was suddenly pulled up by direct machine-gun fire at short range. We all lay down or jumped into the nearest shell-holes, but L/Corpl Richards and that great old 'tough', Pte Coughlan, who had delighted all with his songs at the Hazebrouck concert, were killed when returning fire with their Lewis gun. In getting into a shell-hole just behind me, I felt a thud in my back, which knocked me sprawling on my face. I wasn't hit, but narrowly missed being so. FitzSimon's platoon, which was advancing on the right flank, ran into another machine-gun nest, and had several casualties, and one man missing. Advance was now out of the question, as we could not see more than six yards ahead owing to the darkness. On the rising ground, some 200 yards from the cross-roads, I split the platoon up into parties of four, and occupied a chain of shell craters stretching from the edge of the Menin Road to FitzSimon's platoon on the right. Old and new shell-holes were studded about in the long rank grass; filling the spare sandbags which all the men carried, we built up parapets and a battle position for our only Lewis gun. Throughout the night the Boche machine-guns kept up an endless chatter, and it was fortunate that we had built up cover.

[FCH]

29TH SEPTEMBER

The morning broke with a thick mist enveloping the country. In fact it was a typical raw Flanders morning. Dawn revealed the Company's position in the improvised rifle pits, which were just like grouse butts. Not having had the chance to dry our clothes properly after the drenching we got the day before, we were all very cold indeed. I took off my Burberry, which I had been wearing rolled strapped to the back of my web belt, and to my astonishment found it riddled to pieces; two bullets must have gone through it, so thoroughly was it cut about. My haversack had had a bullet right through it from end to end, and everything in it in the shape of shaving gear, etc, was smashed.

My luck had been decidedly in on the night 28/29th September, 1918.

[FCH]

Throughout the early hours of the morning, we were sprayed with enemy machine-guns, which traversed backwards and forwards. We watched B Company on our left, north of the Menin Road, trying to advance with a line of skirmishers out in front. They took advantage of all the folds in the rugged ground, but could make no headway against the enemy machine-guns which fired from a commanding ridge in their front.

As B Company's skirmishers stalked forward, I watched a company of the enemy forming up on the high ground, and in front of a small wood; they then disappeared. B Company had several casualties, and I saw a few of their men tumbling over like shot rabbits in the long grass, and stretcher-bearers running in their direction. At about 6 am we, C Company, advanced, and made good the small ridge in front unopposed. Coughlan was still lying there stretched, with L/Corpl Richards,* who was in a sitting attitude, right in front of what had been the Boche machine-gun nest.

[FCH]

* L/Corpl Richards had been wounded in my platoon at St Eloi on 5th November, 1915.

We now dug in on the new ridge, employing the same system as before, consolidating shell-holes; we were in a fine commanding position. At 10.30 am the 2nd Hampshires advanced through us, and later we watched them clearing a wood down in a hollow by a stream on our left front, where they had some casualties. Since we had passed Hooge we could have counted the shells we had seen on our fingers, but now the enemy started a systematic strafe, and it seemed as if he was firing off his ammunition before carrying out a further retirement.

Our artillery had so far not put in an appearance, and practically all day the enemy shelled away undisturbed. Our gunners could not get up, so impossible was the state of the Menin Road; across country was out of the question for heavy guns, owing to the water-logged state.

Ammunition was sent up by mules, and also the Brigade trench mortars under 2nd Lieut Woods, MC. The mules were placed under cover in a fold of the ground just in front of us. However, they suffered severely from shrapnel which burst over our area spasmodically all day, and a good few of them had to be put down. The cross-roads got heavily shelled with HE all morning, and all the wooden huts were turned into matchwood. SAA mules were caught at these roads coming up, and suffered severely. Their drivers had a rough time. A few direct hits put the coal waggons on fire; they blazed away all day and on into the night. The Hampshires utilised their prisoners as stretcher-bearers, and all day long they went up and down the road with the wounded. It looked strange seeing four figures clad in long field grey great-coats carrying a wounded khaki figure on their shoulders. They had to run the gauntlet of their own barrage at the cross-roads, but they behaved well indeed, and took their time with our wounded.

A battery of RFA, the first of our guns we had seen during the 'push' coming up, came in for a terrible mauling. Two teams were caught by direct hits, and we watched wheels and limbers being blown sky-high with great fountains of earth. The other two teams managed to canter out behind our right flank, and took up a position. This was a very thrilling sight.

[FCH]

We turned our shell-holes into cover for the night. Sergt Jenkins, MM, O'Leary, and I shared one water-logged crater; we passed a most miserable night in a torrential downpour of rain. I dozed a bit, as I was, like the rest, very tired, not having slept since the short night of the 27/28th September. All night long the cross-roads behind us were lit up by the coal waggons, which blazed furiously, being stoked up every now and then by another Boche crump. We, in my shell-hole, had alternate fits of dozing, shivering, and cursing; hungry, wet, and cold.

[FCH]

2ND OCTOBER

After a terrible night, in which I was actually doubled up with cramp and pains in my legs and feet, we tumbled out of our 'bivies' into a cold but fine morning. Rum was issued. Throughout the four days' fighting the Battalion had not suffered many casualties, but the hardships had been very severe. From the morning of the attack the weather had been of the vilest description, and we were all suffering from exposure and fatigue.

For its share in this great and successful offensive the Battalion added *Ypres, '18* to swell the list of honours on the colours.

[FCH]

The Second Army had everywhere gained its objectives, which included all the heights of Flanders; 4800 prisoners and 100 guns had been captured by General Plumer's Army, and another 4000 by the Franco-Belgian forces co-operating on our left. A big wedge had been driven into the Boche position. He had suffered heavy losses, and his morale had been decidedly shaken.

The 36th (Ulster) Division took the place of the 29th in the outpost line, and we watched them going up. Further advance was out of the question until a pukka line of communications had been built up across the devastated, waterlogged, but historic stretch of flats in front of Ypres. Company paraded for our billeting area in the Vlamertinghe Woods.

Although during our advance we had been but slightly shelled, yet our back areas, especially the Menin Road, had been heavily strafed. There was full evidence of this along the route, particularly at Hooge, where there were numerous transports, all put out of action, lying derelict on the side of the road, or thrown off it into the crater swamps below. Teams of dead artillery horses, transport animals, SAA mules, and 'heavy draughts', were heaped on top of each other in the ditches off the wooden track which made a detour of the Menin Road by the north from Hooge to Hell Fire Corner. The traffic here had been terribly congested, there being only the one road for the supply of rations and ammunition. When the enemy shelled the transport, they just had to remain where they were, as the muddy swamps on either side forbade deployment.

The last I saw of Hun Kultur in the Salient was the reflected glare in the sky at night from the burning houses around Menin, which the enemy was destroying in his wake.

[FCH]

Extract from a letter of an unknown German officer found in the mud of the battlefield, quoted in *Realities of War*, by Philip Gibbs.

I am the only one who withstood the maddening bombardment of three days and still survive. You cannot imagine the frightful mental torments I have undergone. . . . After crawling out through the smoke and debris, wandering and running in the midst of the raging gun-fire in search of a refuge, I am now awaiting death at any moment. *You do not know what Flanders means. Flanders means endless human endurance. Flanders means blood and scraps of human bodies. Flanders means heroic courage and faithfulness even unto death.*

Two unknown soldiers who died for Germany.

This was a soldier. Skull found in an old German trench, 1919. [IWM]

T/Sec. Lt. C. Mitchell att'd. Argyll & Sutherland Highlanders.

For conspicuous gallantry and devotion to duty under exceptionally dangerous conditions. During a hostile counter attack he took charge of a Lewis Gun of another unit when the man working it was killed and continued to fire it from its exposed position in front of the front line, regardless of enemy fire, until the attack was repulsed. Later when some of the men in front were retiring in confusion, owing to our own shells falling short, he went forward and rallied them, finally succeeding under heavy fire in restoring the situation. Again he showed the greatest gallantry in taking out a patrol both by day and again by night, returning after a long absence, having successfully gained his object. His gallantry and cheerfulness under adverse conditions set a fine example to his men.

The above are the words of a citation covering the award of the Military Cross to 2nd Lieut. C. Mitchell, father of Lt. Col. Colin Campbell Mitchell M.P., Former Commanding Officer of 1st. Bn. Argyll and Sutherland Highlanders (renowned for his famous action at Aden).

The incidents referred to in the citation took place at Frezenberg in the Ypres Salient during the Third Battle of Ypres, August 1917. 2nd Lieut. Mitchell was at that time still recovering from wounds obtained at Arras.

His widow, Mrs. Janet Gilmour-Mitchell, recently received a letter written by one of his former comrades, in which the latter said, "He was one of the most efficient and one of the bravest subalterns in the Argylls. He was also one of the nicest chaps and one of the straightest."

In Flanders fields the poppies blow
Between the crosses, row on row,
That mark our place; and in the sky
The larks still bravely singing fly
Scarce heard amid the guns below.

We are the dead. Short days ago
We lived, felt dawn, saw sunset glow,
Loved and were loved, and now we lie
    In Flanders fields.

Take up our quarrel with the foe;
To you from failing hands we throw
The torch; be yours to hold it high.
If ye break faith with us who die
We shall not sleep, though poppies grow
    In Flanders fields.

This famous poem was composed by Colonel John MacCrae, a medical officer with the Canadian Army. With the kind permission of the Secretary of The British Legion, Capt R. G. Tickner, MBE.

Lyssenhoek Military Cemetery. The grave of Lt-Colonel G.E. Beaty-Pownall, DSO, Commanding Officer of the First Battalion, King's Own Scottish Borderers, said to be the last British soldier killed by direct enemy action in the 1914—1918 Salient.
Beaty-Pownall became a casualty from a German shell fired at extreme range and died just prior to the Armistice. *[Photo: Miss R. Coombs]*

228

Flanders. Another time. Another war.

The gravestone reads:

A SOLDIER
OF THE
1939-1945
WAR
27TH MAY 1940

KNOWN UNTO GOD